Education for Ministry
50 Years of Engaging, Responding, and Reflecting

COLLECTED ESSAYS

EDITED BY
MAGGIE TALIAFERRO
MARY ANN PATTERSON
KEVIN M. GOODMAN

Copyright © 2025 Education for Ministry

All rights reserved. No part of this book may be reproduced, stored in a retrieval system, or transmitted in any form or by any means, electronic or mechanical, including photocopying, recording, or otherwise, without the written permission of the publisher.

Unless otherwise noted, the Scripture quotations are from New Revised Standard Version Bible, copyright © 1989 National Council of the Churches of Christ in the United States of America. Used by permission. All rights reserved worldwide.

"A History of the Education for Ministry Program: 1975-95," by Edward O. de Bary, is reprinted with the permission of the Sewanee Theological Review.

Church Publishing
19 East 34th Street
New York, NY 10016
www.churchpublishing.org

Cover design by Education for Ministry
Typeset by Nord Compo

ISBN 978-1-64065-819-6 (paperback)
ISBN 978-1-64065-820-2 (eBook)

Library of Congress Control Number: 2024947731

Contents

FOREWORD

The Story So Far
James F. Turrell vii

FINDING A PLACE WITHIN GOD'S STORY

The Importance of Stories and Storytelling
Melford E. Holland Jr. 1

Becoming an Adult with Education for Ministry
Richard E. Brewer 9

Sacredness of Spiritual Autobiography
Jenny Replogle 15

EfM'S FORMATION WITHIN GOD'S STORY

An Evolving Curriculum for Ministry in a Changing World
Karen M. Meridith 25

Four Sources and Four Movements: A History of EfM's Practice of Theological Reflection
John de Beer and Tricia de Beer 39

Reflection and Revisioning: The Reading and Reflection Guide
Angela Hock 47

Living TR: EfM's Theological Perspective Questions
Karen D. Byers 53

Room for the Spirit and the Need for Framework
Jim Papile 65

ADMINISTERING EfM WITHIN GOD'S STORY

The Story Through Numbers
Joshua D. Booher 71

The Evolution of Training Mentors and Trainers in EfM
Elsa S. Bakkum 77

Future Training Implications
Elizabeth Cavey 85

The Diocesan Coordinator: A Continual Calling of Volunteer Leaders
Cynthia C. Hargis 89

Education for Ministry in the Diocese of North Carolina: This Coordinator's Journey
Marcia Houck Moore 95

Waters Under the Bridge: A Time of Transition
Sissie Wile 103

Insights: Reflections from the EfM Staff
Bobbie Ashley, Dawn Baker, Donna Layne, Sara Limbaugh, Debbie Shrum, Mary Turner 107

Beyond the Mountain: EfM Partners Around the World
Marguerite Casparian, Tricia Carter, Annette Cowan, Greg Davies, Christopher Halliday, Yvonne Symmonett 111

PROCLAIMING GOD'S STORY

Realizing Then Reconciling a Multitude of God's Voices
Phoebe A. Roaf 127

Holy Ground in Cyberspace
Kay Flores 133

Send Them Out! EfM and the Ministry of Church Planting
Katie Nakamura Rengers 139

EfM in Prisons
    Anne Moats Williams 149

God Kept You Around for a Reason
    Termaine Hicks 157

EfM'S EMERGING VOICES

EfM and the Challenge of Gender: Past, Present, and Future
    Tara K. Soughers 165

Seeking Racial Diversity
    José R. Fernández 171

Seeking Political Diversity
    Gaines Campbell 177

Exploring the Challenges and Opportunities of EfM in Reaching Adults Across All Ages
    Hannah Graham 183

EPILOGUE

EfM: All the Pieces Matter
    Kevin M. Goodman 187

APPENDIX: STORYTELLING

EfM Stepping Stones
    Margaret Taliaferro 197

A History of the Education for Ministry Program: 1975–95
    Edward O. de Bary 201

The Beginnings of Theological Reflection in EfM
    Flower Ross 251

Contributing Authors 257

The Story So Far

James F. Turrell

EfM emerged from the imagination of Charlie Winters, a faculty member of the School of Theology at the University of the South. He believed that an educated laity could transform The Episcopal Church. Fifty years ago, Charlie's dream became a reality. Turrell, the School of Theology's current dean, invites us to remember that time and how we got to where we are today.

Education for Ministry (EfM) was born during a period of seismic change in The Episcopal Church and it continues to bear the marks of its revolutionary origins. In the 1970s, The Episcopal Church upended its understanding of the Church, of ministry, and of what it means to be a baptized Christian. Formerly, it held an ecclesiology in which the Church was defined by ordination, not baptism; ministry was something the clergy did; baptism itself was merely the first step in a two-step initiatory sequence (the other being confirmation). In the second half of the twentieth century, The Episcopal Church adopted a new theology based on baptism. This "baptismal ecclesiology" can be reasonably summed up in three propositions: baptism constitutes the Church; the Church is the whole people of God (clergy and laity alike); and baptism is a call to ministry. The birth and growth of EfM was both a response to, and fueled by, this baptismal revolution.

The story of the baptismal revolution in The Episcopal Church has been told in a variety of books, which admirably describe both the theological shift and the ways that it was manifested in the new prayer book of 1979.[1] To make a long story short, the baptismal rite itself incorporated elements that made it clear that baptism was a full, sacramental initiation into the Church. Confirmation and its cognate rites (reception and reaffirmation) were reinterpreted as pastoral rites rather than initiatory. The catechism explicitly stated that baptism constitutes the membership of the Church, and it outlines a specific ministry for the laity:

> The ministry of laypersons is to represent Christ and his Church; to bear witness to him wherever they may be, and according to the gifts given them, to carry on Christ's work of reconciliation in the world; and to take their place in the life, worship, and governance of the Church.[2]

The "new" prayer book of 1979, born out of a long process of revision, reflected a new understanding of the role of the baptized.

This new understanding saw baptism as the "common ground within which all ministries, both lay and ordained, take their source." In Louis Weil's view, there is no higher status than baptism; ordination exists to set aside individuals with particular function to serve the common good of the whole people of God, rather than as a distinction or benefit for the ordained."[3] That this has been received unevenly across the Church is readily apparent: we find ordination used sometimes as a synonym for ministry, as when one speaks of the laity as "ordained" in baptism (or—in an older era—in confirmation).[4] This shows, in its way, the pernicious hold of clericalism on our imaginations, in that even when we strive to make the point that ministry flows first

---

   1. In particular, the reader should seek out Ruth A. Meyers, *Continuing the Reformation: Revisioning Baptism in The Episcopal Church* (New York: Church Publishing, 1997) and Michael Moriarty, *The Liturgical Revolution: Prayer Book Revision and Associated Parishes: A Generation of Change in The Episcopal Church* (New York: Church Hymnal Corporation, 1996).
   2. Book of Common Prayer (Seabury Press, 1979), 855.
   3. Louis Weil, "Baptismal Ecclesiology: Uncovering a Paradigm," in Ronald L. Dowling and David Holeton, eds., *Equipping the Saints: Ordination in Anglicanism Today* (Dublin: Columba Press, 2006), 25.
   4. For example, Massey Shepherd, quoted in Meyers, *Continuing the Reformation*, 62–63.

from baptism, we can fall back on ordination to explain it. Yet at its root, all ministry is baptismal, and ordination is a means of setting aside persons with particular functions to serve the people of God and enable their (larger) ministries.[5] This is the teaching of the 1979 prayer book and the ecclesiology of The Episcopal Church.

The Episcopal Church was not unique in this recovery of the role of the baptized. Most notably, it was reflected in the documents of the Second Vatican Council, particularly *Lumen Gentium*, and in the liturgies of the Roman Catholic Church (particularly the Rite of Christian Initiation of Adults). But The Episcopal Church has, in its rhetoric and its practices, arguably been the most vigorous proponent of this view of baptism, not least in describing a ministry of the laity that springs from their baptism.[6]

It is against this theological background that Education for Ministry emerged. EfM was meant to give the laity the formation required to live fully into their baptismal callings. EfM was based on the premise that theological education is the birthright of the laity. To borrow from Anselm, the great eleventh-century theologian, theology is the work of "one who strives to lift his mind to the contemplation of God, and seeks to understand what he believes."[7] As such, it is not the specialized discipline of the clergy or of academics, but rather the province of anyone who wishes to examine their faith thoughtfully.

A further innovation of EfM was to make reflection upon experience a cornerstone of its approach. Doing first, and then reflecting upon the doing as a means of learning is, in some

---

5. Perhaps we might better use the language of being "commissioned" in baptism for ministry. One might also long for the day when ordination liturgies (and the sermons within them) highlight service and duty, and when baptisms have more ritual embellishment than the ordination of a priest.

6. Colin Podmore, "The Baptismal Revolution in the American Episcopal Church: Baptismal Ecclesiology and the Baptismal Covenant," *Ecclesiology* 6 (2010), 8–38.

7. Anselm, "Proslogium," preface, in *Basic Writings: Proslogium, Monologium, Cur Deus Homo, Gaunilo's In Behalf of the Fool*, trans. S.N. Deane 2nd. ed. (Chicago: Open Court Publishing, 1962), 48.

respects, a very old practice. We find it in the early church catechumenate, in which participants were not fully informed about Christian worship until its mystagogical catechesis—the post-baptismal instruction that explained everything the catechumens had just experienced. The educational philosopher, John Dewey, elevated experience in his approach to learning in the late nineteenth and early twentieth centuries.[8] But experiential learning as a pedagogical theory emerged in the 1970s, developed by David Kolb and others, out of its roots in training groups run by the National Training Laboratories and other experiments of human relations training. This model was a direct influence on Charles Winters and others who developed EfM.[9] EfM thus drew both on very old Christian models as well as on contemporary currents when it made reflection on experience a core element.

In doing so, EfM took seriously the experience of laity in their everyday lives. EfM uses four sources for theological reflection, as described in its "core practices": life experience, the culture, the individual's beliefs, and the Christian tradition.[10] Thus, the contemporaneous experience of participants became a coequal source for theological reflection. (While a historian would view the tradition itself as the accumulated experience and accumulated reflection of the generations of Christians who have gone before us, this is not always how Christians have used it.) By framing the four sources the way that it did, EfM made a clear statement: the life of the baptized became raw material for theology alongside the Christian tradition.

---

8. Joop W.A. Berding, "Towards a Flexible Curriculum: John Dewey's Theory of Experience and Learning," *Education and Culture* 14 (1997), 25–27.

9. Jayson Seaman, Mike Brown, and John Quay, "The Evolution of Experiential Learning: Tracing Lines of Research in the *JEE*," *Journal of Experiential Education* 40 (2017); Linda H. Lewis and Carol J. Williams, "Experiential Learning: Past and Present," 5–7. For an example of work from this period, see David A. Kolb and Ronald Fry, "Towards an Applied Theory of Experiential Learning," in C. Cooper, ed., *Theories of Group Processes* (New York: John Wiley and Sons, 1974), 33–57. For the particular influence on EfM's founders, see Edward O. de Bary, "A History of the Education for Ministry Program: 1975–1992," *Sewanee Theological Review* 37, no. 2 (1994), 228–29.

10. "Core Practices in Education for Ministry," https://theology.sewanee.edu/files/resources/core-practices-in-efm-handout-2018-1.pdf, accessed 15 September 2024.

Finally, EfM framed its theological formation explicitly as a means to empower lay ministry in the world. Every Christian is called to ministry through baptism, as the prayer book catechism notes. For most, that ministry is lived out as a layperson in the world in some particular vocation. EfM was designed from the beginning to equip laypersons, first to discern their calling and then to live it out.[11]

EfM's early growth can be attributed to its timeliness, both in relation to the baptismal ecclesiology then emerging in The Episcopal Church and in relation to currents in educational theory. Subsequent enrollment growth reflects the way that the program, at its core, addresses the basic needs of engaged laity by giving them the formation and tools to live out their baptismal callings.

Over subsequent decades, EfM has evolved considerably. The curriculum has been revised several times, online groups have emerged alongside those that meet in three dimensions, and new training models have been deployed. As we look to the future, new offerings will take their place alongside the classic, four-year program. Yet the basic commitment to empowering the baptismal ministry of all members of the Church remains. For this, we can give thanks.

---

11. Charles Winters's original proposal called out as "clericalism" the belief that the laity did not need theological education (de Bary, "History of the Education for Ministry Program," 235).

FINDING A PLACE
WITHIN GOD'S STORY

The Importance of Stories and Storytelling

Melford E. Holland Jr.

EfM believes that our experiences matter and say something about who we are and what we value. By connecting our individual experiences, captured in stories with God's story, we discover how God is active in our lives. Holland, priest and former mentor and trainer, shares that once we find our place in God's story, we can discern together what God wants us to do.

I was introduced to storytelling at a very young age. I lived in a small village in West Virginia and had many aunts, uncles, and cousins living there and nearby. We got together in various configurations and shared life's journeys. I sat in on these discussions and learned a lot about our weaknesses, struggles, hopes, and dreams. We gathered in small groups without being interrupted by TV, radio, or other distractions and learned that each of us had stories that were important to us. Collectively we shared stories that bound us together. Some of our stories took us back in time and others were very recent. It was a time when we gathered around our dining room tables as individual family units and in our living rooms with other family members. In retrospect, I see those times as priceless and the opportunity to listen and support as crucial to our living. Of course, several of our family members did not participate, and occasionally the time was a little boring to me as a youngster. Upon reflection, I realize how important those times were to my family and to me.

Stories are at the heart of what it is to be human and to be in community. Stories are the way we, as human beings, bring into our present moments our memories and the vehicles upon which we share our memories and experiences with others. Stories are also the ways we create community. It is in the sharing and receiving of stories that we realize the deep truth of Ubuntu: I am because you are. It is in the articulation of these stories that we seek to mine them, nestle them in our memories for use, and experience them to define who we are as people. Our articulation of stories is what makes each of us real to ourselves and to others. And stories multiply and amplify throughout our lifetimes.

Stories can be celebratory, edifying, complex, painful, hopeful, and horrific. They can span the whole range of human emotions and experiences. They can be a well of memory that brings into our consciousness the values and treasures that can help us weather the storm of our present or the storm that we anticipate. They can also be a well of memory that continues to tear at the heart of our sense of self-worth. Our personal stories are a key link to our capacity to live into the present and contemplate the future. Sometimes, our stories can become blocked due to dementia or by a very difficult past that is so painful that we have consciously or unconsciously blotted it out. But stories are to human experience and communication as fire is to burning.

In the sharing of stories in reading, art, music, hearing, in lived experiences, and a whole host of other ways, we communicate to others something of who we are, what we value, and what we sense is important to share. In the process of doing this, our stories can move from sharing to a place of transformation. In other words, our stories can be so powerful for us and for others that life becomes different for us and them and, in this process, we can all be changed.

There are times when people do not feel important or valued enough to share their stories. They may feel that their stories are insignificant or don't have enough content to contribute to the conversation. So at the heart of storytelling is the valuing of the person sharing their story. This value is at the center of what it means to be in a community of faith with one another. At other times, stories from other members of our community are not heard by the community itself because, inadvertently or perhaps by intention, other voices occupy all of the airtime. The church community does itself a great service when it provides opportunities to learn from the stories of all its members—from the strangers gracing their midst and from the broader stories of their communities.

At the center of our life as members of The Episcopal Church is our baptismal covenant. Within the covenant we are reminded of the story of God's continual love for us, God's sharing of life in the gift of Jesus of Nazareth, in the ongoing presence of the Holy Spirit, and in the invitation to each of us to be about the co-creation of life, forgiveness, healing, and love. Collectively, the story of God's creative and reconciling work fills countless books, papers, and histories of faith communities. This is old news but also present and future news. The covenant reminds us of ways to engage the story and to create new ones. Within the covenant we are reminded of several things: a) we are able to engage our lifelong commitments to God and one another only with God's help; b) there are powerful forces within us and around us with which we need to contend in order to be vessels of grace, truth, and love; c) we are inextricably connected to one another and marked as Christ's own forever; d) our journey needs forgiveness, work, study, and worship; e) we are called to see the face of Christ in the other and to respect the dignity and freedom of every human being; and f) all the rest of our life is interwoven, informed, nourished, prodded, and celebrated with the fabric and mosaic of the covenant.

The Bible is full of stories and the composition of the Bible was determined by choosing what stories to tell. Each of the Gospels has a point of view or intention in the telling of the Good News. The Episcopal Church has, at its heart, the invitation to hear stories related to scripture, tradition, and reason, as well as reflections from the community of faith. So, the decision of which stories to tell comes about through wrestling with the texts.

There are occasions for the use of story in the retelling of the stories of the Bible. A wonderful group, Biblical Storytellers, reminds us that the presentation of stories can often be shared in story form with accents, passion, and nuances, calling attention to the human drama and setting—all of which can invite the hearer into the setting and story itself in deeper ways. So, as is the case of sharing our stories and passing them along, the storytelling can be evocative, provocative, and compelling.

There are stories of congregations, families, communities, nations, cultures, and ethnic groups. All of these stories can, and do, impact each of us and our common life. To know one's community's stories is to know more about ourselves, our histories, our values, and our future direction. Knowing our communal stories also helps us celebrate our giftedness, recognize ways in which we might need to grow and change, and strengthen our ability to be about the work that is before us. Not knowing our stories can often trip us up when we try on something new or can cause us to miss the giftedness that is in our common tradition. Knowing other communities' stories provides important insights into their centeredness, challenges, values, perspectives, and contributions to life, all of which are crucial to understanding and appreciating their offerings to our collective human story. To value, learn from, and be affected by others who are different from us is one of our most critical journeys. Will we seek to live together despite our differences?

Sometimes stories need to be told even when others might not want to hear them. Stories can illuminate our thoughts and hearts and challenge our thinking and doing. Stories are reassuring at times, risk-taking at other times, and compelling most of the time.

Stories can challenge, edify, move us to new action, connect us with our own stories and journeys, lift our vision and imaginations to new heights, identify issues that need addressing, and awaken us to resources within us and around us. They are the lifeblood that nourishes our bodies. They collect waste that needs to be discarded, and by their need for refreshment of new thoughts, provide oxygen, food, and drink to remind us of our need for the same in our lives.

At the heart of Education for Ministry's (EfM) practices, there is a profound recognition of the importance of stories—individually within the people who gather and collectively as we engage tradition, history, experience, and personal positions. Each of our sessions includes time to share personal stories from our past week, reflect on stories in our readings, bring our stories into theological reflection, and ponder what stories our actions may be creating or will create in the weeks ahead. We share our spiritual autobiographies, which seek to relate our personal journeys and stories with the profound wondering and reflection about what God has been up to in our lives and what God might desire from each of us. We engage learning from a communal perspective while recognizing that our stories are meant to engage with others' stories and still others in the broader world. We gather in groups of six to twelve people plus mentors to demonstrate the importance of community learning. These groups are just the right size to ensure that each participant might benefit from others' perspectives and points of view and that there will be time to hear from everyone. EfM reminds us of the importance of hearing other stories from a broad diversity of human experience, which can inform us in our work and personally enrich us. To quote Elizabeth O'Connor, we are called to be a liberating community that has the following aspects: "To be a people of prayer and dialogue; to reflect on how our personal journeys and decisions can be examined in the light of God's work in the world; and to remain inextricably committed to the poorest, weakest, and most abused members of the human family."[1] So in EfM, we offer our stories to ourselves and others, explore our stories in relationship with the stories from tradition and the baptismal covenant, and

---

1. Elizabeth O'Connor, "Chapter 6. The Marks of the Liberating Community," in *The New Community* (The Potter's House, 1997), 100–117.

contemplate how our stories will emerge again in our broader communities. We are a people of contexts of life, a people of the gathering, a people of the table, and a people of the dismissal. All of these stations inform us about who and whose we are, what our vocation and work in life are, how we proceed, and how we know we are proceeding.

One of my favorite stories took place along a road in West Virginia. My Dad and I were hitching some miles from home when it was getting dark. I remember sharing with him that I was becoming afraid as it was getting dark. He assured me that we would get home and that he was with me. He said, "Buddy, you have to be somewhere. This is where you find yourself now. Let's look around and see what we can see." He pointed to a small stream of water coming down a cliff on the other side of the road and invited me to look at it. It appeared to me to be a waterfall. He then pointed to a purple flower by the railroad track and said, "Look at that flower. Isn't it a beautiful flower? All the coal trains coming down this track have not been able to squish that beautiful flower!" And for me, at that moment, the flower became a garden. I became aware of the resources all around me and welling up within me. This experience happened time and time again throughout my life. And we got home safely. What is welling up for you where you are? Who is accompanying you? What are your hopes? What resources are dwelling within you for your journeys?

I have long been buoyed by the following prayer from Thomas Merton:

> My Lord God, I have no idea where I am going. I do not see the road ahead of me. I cannot know for certain where it will end. Nor do I really know myself, and the fact that I think that I am following your will does not mean that I am actually doing so. But I believe that the desire to please you does in fact please you. And I hope I have that desire in all that I am doing. I hope that I will never do anything apart from that desire. And I know that if I do this you will lead me by the right road, though

I may know nothing about it. Therefore will I trust you always, though I may seem to be lost and in the shadow of death. I will not fear, for you are ever with me, and you will never leave me to face my perils alone.[2]

---

2. Thomas Merton, *Thoughts in Solitude, Part Two: The Love of Solitude*. (Farrar, Straus, and Giroux, 1999), 79.

Becoming an Adult with Education for Ministry

Richard E. Brewer

Education for Ministry believes that by creating lifelong learners, a seeker of God will have the tools necessary for a fulfilling journey of faith. Brewer started in EfM as a mentor with the original texts, the "yellow books," in 1976 and became a trainer in 1978. Since then, Brewer has played a major role in each revision of the EfM curriculum. In the first revision, he developed the Parallel Guides *and* Common Lessons. *Brewer, along with Angela Hock and Karen Meridith, shaped the 2012 revision of the EfM curriculum and wrote the* Reading and Reflection Guide *(RRG). He continues to contribute his wisdom, creativity, and humor to enhance ministry formation of EfM trainers, mentors, and participants.*

I first learned of a project called Theological Education by Extension (TEE) in 1974 when the associate rector, under whom I was serving in Stillwater, Oklahoma, came into my office and handed me a sheet of legal-sized paper. It contained a description of TEE. It was of interest to me because the commission on ministry in the Diocese of Oklahoma planned to establish a deacon formation program. Having a core curriculum of the Christian tradition available to people was attractive. Based on the strength of this handout and the interest in deacon formation, the commission on ministry sent me to the Diocese of the Rio Grande to meet with Charlie Winters. During his sabbatical in 1974, Charlie met with Church leaders around the country, presenting the vision of the program. He had a meeting scheduled in Albuquerque, where we were to meet. I got a look at the text material, which was only the first third of Year One, as the rest had not yet been produced. I returned home sensing that in some way or another, TEE would be a part of the deacon formation program.

My next involvement with TEE came in May of 1975. I took a prospective seminarian to the School of Theology in Sewanee, Tennessee, to meet with the dean of the seminary, the Very Rev. Urban T. Holmes III. While he was meeting with the dean, I scheduled a meeting with Charlie to talk more about the project. I remember sitting in a classroom as he spoke of his vision. He sketched a few things on the blackboard and then took me to lunch. We returned to the classroom and after about an hour he asked, "Are you interested in being a mentor?" I was indeed. I returned to Stillwater intending to establish a group; however, I decided to wait a year so that there would be a year's worth of material available. In the fall of 1976 I started my first group with nine students. We met weekly until December, breaking for Christmas. When we resumed in January, I had only one student. That experience told me that there needed to be a fuller training for mentors—at least for this mentor.

In January of 1977, I became the vicar of Saint Aidan's Mission in Tulsa, and that fall I started another group with parishioners from three different parishes in Tulsa. I began to increase my involvement with TEE by becoming the Diocese of Oklahoma's coordinator. We organized a mentor training event in the fall of 1977 where I met John de Beer, who recommended me as a trainer. In March 1978, I attended my first training of trainers event led by Flower Ross with a group of nine from across the country. We met together in March for three years in succession, working specifically to hone the intricacies of theological reflection—a profound experience of the power of theological reflection.

While in Sewanee during those March events, I had frequent opportunities for short conversations with Charlie Winters. One in particular involved my concern about students understanding the material. I remember asking Charlie, "How do you know that they get it right?" Much to my surprise, and even a little shock, he said, "I am not concerned with that. I don't care if someone is a Manichaean. I want them to know when their position is Manichaean." I have reflected often over the years on that conversation. Contained in that short exchange is a profound understanding of adult learning. The task of the teacher with adult learners is to provide material that is engaging, interesting, and relevant, and the learner's responsibility is to keep engaged in the learning process so that they can make a judgment as to when "they got it right."

Somewhere in the late 1970s or early 1980s, TEE became known as Education for Ministry (EfM) to make room for other offerings. Education for Ministry was more descriptive of what the program had become with emphasis on ministry, the purpose of this education.

During the training of trainer events from 1976 to 1980, Charlie would join us, taking a break from writing the materials. Two particular evenings taught me a great deal about experiential learning. There was a four-legged stool in the room that Charlie used as prop to illustrate a truth about experiential learning. The floor represented our basic experiences. If we moved up one of the legs of the stool and reached the top of the stool, that represented where we would have abstract discussions. I remember Charlie saying if you start from a particular place in experience (he tapped the floor) and move to an abstract discussion, you reach a point where you will want to ask, "What difference does this make?" You can always get back to experience. However, if you start from an abstract discussion and then along the way ask, "What difference does this make to our experience?" you cannot always find an answer. I have learned through EfM, whether it be through training events, seminar discussions, or in my individual reflection, that that principle rings true. I can identify an existential concern, then seek the wisdom of those who have gone before me and have a discussion that could seem abstract until I reach the point of wanting to know what difference it makes. When we start from experience, we can always find implications for one's experience.

Another evening, Charlie said, "We don't learn from experience, but only when we reflect on the experience." In an instant, I realized the centrality of reflection for learning. No reflection, no learning. That is true also for the experience of reading. I can read, but until I reflect on what I have read, I am not learning.

EfM started nearly two years ahead of the original plan, crafted to begin in 1977. The Episcopal Church Foundation published an announcement in their newsletter saying that two $20,000 grants had been awarded to the Saint Luke's Seminary (the previous name of the School of Theology) for the development of the core curriculum for laity. The response was immediate and overwhelming, so much so that Charlie decided to start the program immediately. When I asked him why he decided to do that, he said, "I felt I needed to start while the iron was hot."

The early response created two qualities in the culture of EfM. First, the people in the field are trusted to learn how to realize the vision of the program. Second, the vision of the program's realization grows organically out of the experience of people in the field. EfM became a learning organization before learning organization theory was developed.

The EfM curriculum has about a ten-year currency, meaning that once a decade the content of the material should be revised. The original texts began to be revised in the early 1980s. David Killen, the executive director of EfM, asked me to work within the revision process designing the "learning apparatus." The *Common Lessons* and *Parallel Guides* carried the learning processes. The original *Common Lessons* consisted of presentations of spiritual autobiography, theological reflection, and vocational discernment. Two optional essays were added to the first edition of the *Common Lessons*: "Life in Christ" and "Mapping Your Theology." The *Common Lessons* were a precursor to the unit essays in the *Reading and Reflection Guide*.

An example of how things grow organically out of seminar experiences is "Reflection In Motion." In the spring of 1989, while debriefing a seminar, Angela Hock, my co-mentor for several years, commented that EfM was exclusively conversational and sedentary. We sit around tables and talk, which may be a problem for some, especially kinesthetic learners. Her comment stimulated an image of a group standing in the middle of the four-source model. Using the image, we designed a way for people to move around while they were reflecting theologically. On each of the four walls of the room we had placed signs that marked that place as one of the four sources. We asked the group members to stand in the middle of the room, inviting the presenter of the theological reflection to go to the "Action" pole and present the incident for reflection. As the group unfolded the theological reflection process, they would move around the room to speak from the place in the room that was marked for the source from which they were drawing. In a short period of time, the room was filled with motion as participants moved about the room stopping at the appropriate source. The design was wildly successful and the light went on for a fourth-year participant who had never understood theological reflection. How wonderful if all of our new ideas could be that successful!

Over the decades, I have watched centers of creativity move through the EfM network, first centering on Charlie and Flower. After a few years it seemed to center on trainers. Unquestionably, the centers of creativity are now dispersed throughout the mentors and others in the program. Some mentors who have been involved with EfM for more than 30 years, along with others, have been responsive to the guidance of the Holy Spirit.

As the fiftieth anniversary of EfM approaches, several of us wondered when the culture source was added to create the four-source model. In the earliest years, we worked with a three-source model: tradition, belief, and experience. By 1980, culture had been added as the fourth source. I clearly remember a theological reflection in which one of the participants, during the connection phase of the process, quoted the psychiatrist Carl Jung. Immediately we saw that when content was offered sometimes it was from a source other than tradition, belief, or experience. That fourth source was culture.

Another person recalled that Flower Ross had named a fourth source culture, and was referring to the context out of which the person was speaking. Flower had trained in the Bahamas and Alaska among indigenous people and recognized that their culture profoundly influenced the reflection. These two memories of the development of the four-source model help explain the ambiguity sometimes found when we name the culture sources. Sometimes it's a quotation from literature. Other times it is an orientation of a particular kind of context, usually evident in the family in which the person is raised.

The culture source discussions have helped me understand more fully the discoveries found throughout the EfM network. The experiences that led to the naming of a fourth source were occurring simultaneously across the network as if God revealed new insights simultaneously among several groups. These corporate experiences invite further reflection so that we may more fully understand how God lives and moves among us. God's revelation is corporate as well as individual.

Many years ago I watched a film called *The Invention of the Adolescent*. The thesis of the film was that adolescence began with puberty and continued until approximately age 30. Since I became involved with EfM when I was 30, that would mean that my adult life has been shaped by the Education for Ministry process. Who I have become as an adult Christian is profoundly formed within the totality of the experiences manifested in EfM.

As I enter my eighth decade, I encounter many challenges—physical, psychological, social, and certainly spiritual. I cannot imagine facing these challenges without the resources, community, and wisdom that EfM has brought into my life. It is with profound gratitude that I thank God for the opportunity to be involved with the Education for Ministry program.

Sacredness of Spiritual Autobiography

Jenny Replogle

Writing, creating, and reflecting upon one's spiritual autobiography is how EfM seminar groups worldwide begin each year. For the majority of EfM's participants, it may be the first time they have been invited to consider the formation of their spiritual lives, reflecting upon how God was present, absent, or not even a part of the picture in their journey of faith. Replogle—EfM alumna, former mentor, and member of the Executive Directors Council of Advice—shares an experience of encountering her father's spiritual autobiography,

I grew up deeply aware that a great cloud of witnesses surrounds us on life's journey, known to me because of the stories I heard from my family, both given and chosen. I remember hearing stories through the years similar to what I understand most families have—stories of good, crazy, beautiful, broken people trying to get by, sometimes doing that well and sometimes not. Despite all of their differences and eccentricities, what they held in common, and what was most important, was that they were part of *our* story, and that we were all part of a larger story together. Somehow, although I don't remember it ever being explicitly articulated, we knew the stories conveyed the truth that all these people, even the ones I never met, were somehow fundamentally part of who we were. However, it wasn't until my Dad's death that I really became aware of how these stories, and the people whose lives they share, took such a fundamental role in making us who we are.

My Dad perhaps best illuminated this truth when he wrote his spiritual autobiography for Education for Ministry (EfM), that essential practice that makes up such a core piece of the program. Dad and I were very close. I had heard stories from him my entire life, so I did not expect to learn as much as I did from that autobiography. But what we never could have anticipated was that Dad would die in a car accident just two weeks after he shared his story. Having a written account of his spiritual autobiography became an incredible blessing, the immensity of which could never have been anticipated.

At the time, I was at the beginning of my year of Anglican studies at Virginia Theological Seminary. My parents had joined The Episcopal Church only a few months before, and when they learned about EfM, they decided to join the cohort that was beginning that fall. Each week they would update me about how the class was going, and in those first few weeks they mentioned that they were each preparing to share their spiritual autobiographies. I remember my Dad talking about preparing his. He had been told that he should keep it to fewer than twenty minutes. He told me one day, "I don't know what I'd talk about for twenty minutes!" Now, for some people, this may be understandable. But I always said that my Dad could talk to a brick wall if it would stand still long enough, and there was plenty of truth to that. He was an extreme extravert who could converse with anyone. In retrospect, after reading his autobiography, I realized that the issue for him was not in having a story to tell, but in *writing* something that would take twenty minutes to share. Dad was highly successful in the pharmaceutical industry—incredibly smart and good with people. But he was also severely dyslexic. I did not realize this until after his death when I read what he wrote for EfM. His account was short, as expected, and relatively simply written, but through the story of his life told in a way I had never heard before, I came to know my Dad in a new way. His spiritual autobiography became a gift that cannot be measured since this new knowledge came at a time when I could no longer continue our relationship in the way I had always known it before.

Coming to know my Dad in that new way, it was all the more profound that he did not begin the story of his spiritual life with his own remembered experience, or even with his birth. He began, "My spiritual life probably started with the death of my older brother at four years of age, ten years before I was born. Buddy had leukemia. It was in the middle of the depression and Daddy made about 10 or 12 dollars a week. Mother and Daddy, who were a happy young couple coming out of the Roaring 20s, found themselves with a death sentence for their little boy and they grew up really fast. Somewhere in that last year of Buddy's life, my uncle, who was the local doctor, reminded Daddy that he should try not to worry about how he was going to take care of Buddy and pay his medical bills. Uncle Andrew told him, 'God doesn't make a possum that he doesn't make enough persimmons to feed.'"

This was not the first time I had heard of Buddy. Every Christmas, as we laid out my Dad's toy train around our tree, we also laid out the toys Buddy received his last Christmas, which they celebrated a couple of weeks early so that the young family could have one last holiday together. They knew Buddy was unlikely to live until Christmas day. Just a few months before his own unexpected death, Dad showed me the scrapbook my grandmother kept of that time, which started as a normal baby book, then became a chronicle of an increasingly ill little boy. It included heart-wrenching letters to doctors, articles about possible treatments, receipts from selling land to pay the medical bills, the trip from Mississippi to Minneapolis for an experimental treatment, and pictures and letters from the friends they made there. At the end, there were obituaries for some of those same children, the final one for the boy for whom the baby book had begun.

What Dad wrote in his spiritual autobiography about Buddy revealed his understanding of how Buddy's death shaped him, and I came to know my father in a new way through it. Understanding how that heart-rending tragedy shaped the faith of his parents and created the environment of the home in which he was raised allowed me to know Dad in a new way, something I did not believe was possible in those days when his absence was so palpable.

Reading his autobiography for the first time, as I was reeling from my own unfathomable loss, I was fascinated that in Dad's simply written account of his own life, he communicated how his very soul was connected to a brother he only knew through stories. His parents' work to create a loving home for all of their children meant making it through each day of their own grief, which was the continuation of love for a son whose presence had become absent far too soon. I never heard him talk about it this way, and it reminded me that those who die before us, even those we may not know, are somehow part of us. They continue—not just as memories, but alive in us—even when their absence seems as real and physical as their presence once was.

After Dad's funeral, we invited everyone to our house. In so many ways, the time was wonderful: the people from so many parts of his life gathered in one place, the unending stream of stories told, the laughter and love shared. I learned about parts of Dad's life I had not known. I was learning how other people knew him and thus coming to know him in a new way myself. That new sweet knowledge, however, was bitter because it could not be separated from losing the way I had always known him. He was someone who was so full of life, and then suddenly he was not.

Shortly afterward I wrote, "The stories of my Dad have now joined the folklore of our family, stories of those of whom there will be no new stories to tell. There are many funny stories that still make me laugh so hard, but now the tears in my eyes are not tears of joy. The touching stories make me smile, but my heart breaks because no more will it be touched by him. I cannot stop listening and telling the stories because there is something healing in the repetition. But that does not change that each story is a reminder that there will be no more about him."

As hard as it was to hear those stories then, that time helped me to understand the power of storytelling in a new way. Although I'd grown up hearing stories of our family, the telling of them now took on an entirely new dimension for me. These weren't just stories told for entertainment and the laughter that inevitably came with them; those stories were a way we knew each other, a way we continued to know those we loved but could no longer see. They were a way that we knew ourselves and let ourselves be known to others.

Three weeks after Dad's death I met with a friend, the Rev. Sarah Kinney Gaventa. She articulated a truth that I encountered in Dad's autobiography and in all of the stories I was hearing during that time: that my relationship with Dad had changed incredibly, but that it was not over. Her explanation reminded me of one of my favorite prayers in our funeral liturgy: "For to your faithful people, O Lord, life is changed, not ended. . ."[1] When she said it, I could not imagine how it was possible through the still-thickening wall of numbness and shock. Yet I also knew deeply that it was true and this knowledge has helped me understand much of this journey of grief, which is the continued work of love for someone who has died. Our relationships go on, and like any relationship, they continue to evolve over time. Our stories provide a powerful path that we walk as we navigate that continuing, combined relationship of love and loss. Ultimately, our stories and memories form us, yet they are not static recitations, but changing, dynamic parts of who we are in this world.

In his memoir, *The Sacred Journey*, Frederick Buechner explains that even as people have died and are physically absent, the dynamic nature of memory means that even the death of others "can never put an end to our relationship with them. . . . Dead and gone though they may be, as we come to understand them in new ways, it is as though they come to understand us—and through them we come to understand ourselves—in new ways too. [T]hrough them something of the power and richness of life itself not only touched us once long ago, but continues to touch us."[2]

---

1. 1979 Book of Common Prayer, 382.
2. Frederick Buechner, *The Sacred Journey* (New York, NY: HarperCollins, 1991), 21–22.

Death is a mighty and powerful change in our lives and in our relationships. But the heart of our faith is that death is not the end of the story—not the end of the story that God is telling in our world, not the end of each of our stories. As humans, storytelling is one of the most powerful gifts we have and that is the reason we practice it in EfM. It is not separate from our study of scripture, church history, and theology, but rather our way of embodying our humanity as we learn.

Telling our stories can be painful, no doubt. We all have parts of our stories that we would rather not remember or share. We all carry in our bones the pain of things that happened to us, the trauma of the tragedies we and those who went before us have survived. Our stories also include the darker moments of our own hearts and the actions of our ancestors that we would prefer to forget. Especially for those of us in a majority white, colonial-settler Church, our stories often involve painful, shameful, guilt-ridden actions of ourselves and those who came before us. We cannot fully know ourselves and join the story of God in this world if we step away from the difficulty and discomfort that the fullness of our stories entail.

Dennis Covington, a journalist, wrote *Salvation on Sand Mountain* about his experience studying snake-handling congregations and, in the process, found himself reckoning with his own past and that of his ancestors as a white man born in the Deep South. Speaking of the horrors of white supremacy in his heritage, he says "What happened in Birmingham in 1963 not only redeemed the oppressed. It also redeemed my people, although we haven't been able to accept it yet. We haven't yet taken that particular snake out and lifted it aloft in the light—that dangerous, unloved thing about us: where we came from, what we did, who we are."[3] Parts of the past we carry within us may be shameful and dangerous, yet they are part of our story even when we desperately wish they were not. Those parts of our story also determine who

---

3. Dennis Covington, *Salvation on Sand Mountain: Snake Handling and Redemption in Southern Appalachia* (De Capo Press, 2009), 153.

we are just as much as the beautiful stories of those who went before us, and avoidance does not lessen the effect of those parts of our story. Rather, it prevents us from knowing the past—and thus ourselves—as redeemed. "That dangerous, unloved thing about us," the past of the people from whom we come, is deeply part of who each of us is, and it must be brought forth in order to open us to be fully loved, and to fully love others. This is also part of the work of telling and retelling our stories. We must know the fullness of who we are, who we have been, and where we come from. Hopefully, in so doing, we can join in the larger story that will go on beyond us.

The way we tell our stories changes as we come to understand ourselves and those in our lives differently, and this is why we share our spiritual autobiographies each year of EfM. These stories are no more static than we are. They change as we come to understand our lives differently and, hopefully, as we understand our stories more in the larger story of God's work in our world. Through story, we can integrate the gamut of our experiences into a larger understanding of ourselves, our whole lives, other people, and the larger creation. As we tell and retell stories, we add newer understandings of why others did what they did, why we acted the way we did, and consequently, we can begin to understand our own brokenness and healing, our own wounds and joys in the larger story of the reconciliation and redemption of the world that we are living into as the people of God.

In his book, *Free of Charge*, Miroslav Volf tells of the death of his brother and how his parents were able to forgive the man responsible for his death because of this embodied narrative of their community. He shares, "They prayed in that community; they listened to preaching about the love of enemies; they celebrated Christ's death for the ungodly as they partook of the Lord's Supper; they sang together about God's faithfulness and love... they celebrated the baptisms... and they mourned the dead in the hope of resurrection."[4] They grasped a narrative of

---

4. Miroslav Volf, *Free of Charge* (Grand Rapids, MI: Zondervan, 2005), 213.

God's creation, forgiveness, and work of reconciliation—a story that had plenty of room for their own misery and grief but was far larger than their pain. Like theirs, our own stories are also held in the story of our larger community and the movement of God throughout time. As our understanding of our place in those larger movements evolves, so does our story, and so the telling and retelling throughout our lives is essential to our work in finding our place in God's story, and through it, becoming the people God created us to be.

We find our place in this story through the many ways of telling. Through our liturgy and the sacraments, we join in this larger story as we are literally remembered into the story of the people of God. We join the great story of God as we are buried in the waters of baptism and raised to new life with Christ, in which we share with all those who already live the fullness of that life which does not end. Each week, we join in the story as we hear the Word of God shared, as we confess our brokenness and are reminded of God's infinite grace, and most of all, as we take Jesus's broken body and shed blood into ourselves and are made whole together along with that great cloud of witnesses that feasts with us.

When we tell the story, we become the story. We don't just assent that these things have happened in the past; we join them and claim them as our story now, and we know ourselves as part of it. Today we are dying and being raised to new and eternal life. Today we are forgiven for all the ways we have fallen short. Today we take in Christ's broken body and are made whole and today we are sent out to take part in God's work of healing this world. Tomorrow we will tell it again and become part of it and each other in new ways. This is the story of the communion made of saints who came before us, the saints with whom we live and move and have our being now, and the many saints who will come after us for whom we will join that great cloud to surround them on their journey. Through the telling of this story, through the living of this story, through the continued writing of this story, may we come to know ourselves, may we come to know those who have gone before us, may we come to know each other, and may we come to know with ever-increasing fullness the God who is continually enfolding us all together in the ultimate story of love.

EfM'S FORMATION WITHIN GOD'S STORY

An Evolving Curriculum for Ministry in a Changing World

Karen M. Meridith

Education for Ministry continues to be educational, formational, and vibrant because the program changes and evolves with the times. EfM looks toward our faith tradition in conversation with the voices of culture, in order to find deeper meaning in our experiences and beliefs. Meridith, former EfM executive director, updated the curriculum to incorporate academic texts and interlude books to bring more voices to the formation conversation. Meridith's major contribution was shepherding an updated curriculum that meets people where they are.

It is widely said that Education for Ministry (EfM) changes lives. A program that continues to do this for 50 years in a changing Church in a changing world does not do so by remaining static. From its inception, EfM was intended to meet the evolving needs of laypersons for building a substantive theological foundation that supports them in their call to ministry in everyday life. The curriculum has been regularly updated to keep the academic content current in the swiftly evolving world of theological scholarship. Likewise, as content has been updated, so have the experiential processes for connecting life with faith been refined, both as an individual and also as a member of a community gathered for intentional learning and spiritual practice. In fact, since its introduction in 1975, the EfM curriculum has launched major curricular revisions about every 12 years—in 1984, 1999, and 2012. Another revision is anticipated to be introduced in 2025.

Distance learning requires attention to delivery for local use, so even the physical format of the curricular content has been changed several times. From the typewriter-set, comb-bound "yellow books" of 1975 to the red three-ring binders of 1999 to the workbook format of 2012, each change was made through a real desire to render the materials easier for participants to access, work with, and transport. The move in 2012 to using standard theological textbooks allowed the readings to be replaced to reflect new findings and ideas more quickly than the labor-intensive revising and reprinting of the earlier self-published materials. Advances in electronic publishing made it possible and practical to lightly revise the individual *Reading and Reflection Guides* A–D in each of the three cycles of their use. Finally, with the newest EfM curriculum set to launch, the program is poised to move to a format that uses electronic resources on an online platform in addition to print books and e-books.

Shaping a Curriculum That Supports the Ministry of All

Charles Winters began his work on a program to support lay ministry in 1973–1974, a time when the belief that God calls all the baptized to ministry had become fundamental to the development of a new Book of Common Prayer for The Episcopal Church (eventually authorized in 1979). He envisioned a program that linked knowledge of the Christian tradition with thinking theologically about life and service to others. Winters believed that a laity called to ministry needed access to information about the depth and breadth of the Christian tradition. This was a course of study much like the seminary education offered to those preparing for ordained ministry, but one that provided laypersons with a comprehensive overview not typically found in parish Bible study. For this reason, EfM's earliest curricular materials focused on academic learning drawn from faculty lectures at the University of the South's School of Theology in Sewanee, Tennessee.

Using transcriptions of recorded lectures as well as syllabi, class notes, and outlines provided by seminary faculty, Winters produced the first curriculum for what would become Education for Ministry, a series of readings in thirty-six lessons per year for four years of study. Each lesson identified a learning objective and offered a few questions to consider, from which the seminar group could find a focus for discussion at a weekly meeting. Winters believed that these weekly discussions would encourage program participants to make connections between what they read and how they lived that would support their sense of call to ministry. He called it Theological Education by Extension: Education for Ministry, abbreviated to TEE.

The program, as originally conceived by Winters, would have relied on seminary faculty sent out to local areas as lecturers with parish priests leading the weekly discussion. Over the course of refining the program, TEE evolved into a seminar-based curriculum designed for a group of laypersons meeting with a discussion facilitator (eventually called the group mentor) who was unlikely to be a seminary-trained academic or priest. In a lay-facilitated program conducted far from seminary classrooms and theological libraries, the materials had to carry the freight of instruction as well as help the seminar participants consider how their readings about the Christian tradition related to their own lives.

Early on, Winters used an image of a two-rail fence to represent the academic study of the Christian tradition running parallel to a person's life experience, with the upright posts holding the fence together signifying seminar discussions that would enable participants to look for connections between learning and life. The question of sourcing the academic content was answered by adapting parts of the existing seminary curriculum. The harder question concerned formation for ministry: how to help seminar participants learn to make and examine the connections to their lives from a theological perspective, and then apply insights that arose from those connections to discern what God was calling them to do. In the seminary, this was done under the tutelage of professors of pastoral theology. The question was, how could this be done effectively in a nonseminary setting?

One solution was to help seminar participants begin the year making connections within the group by sharing their spiritual autobiographies, a basic tool of community building with a theological twist. Another grew out of processes developed to train group mentors to facilitate discussions framed in theological terms. Theological reflection (TR) became an explicit curricular process tool for helping EfM participants connect faith and life through considering four sources of meaning—putting the Christian tradition they were learning about into conversation with the whole of their lives, their life experience, their social and cultural context, and their cherished beliefs and values.

The first building blocks of the EfM curriculum, laid during Winters's time leading the program, from launching TEE in 1975 until his departure from Sewanee in 1980, have remained integral to the program through its revisions. These building blocks include the seminar as a community of adult learners; a deep and substantive dive into learning about the Christian tradition; and connecting lives with that tradition through reflection using a theological lens that helps identify implications for ministry in daily life.

Winters was adamant that the purpose of the learning was to promote spiritual development, thus the academic content of the curriculum was in service to the important work of identifying connections between the faith handed down and life experience. For him each was equally important, even though the process for learning to make those connections was more implicit than explicit in the earliest materials. It was the processes for training mentors developed by John de Beer and others that eventually gave a shape and model to the reflective work in the seminar. In fact, early mentor training focused on group process and the reflective method and gave less attention to the content of the readings. It was probably inevitable with Winters's departure, as Edward O. de Bary notes, that a tension developed in program leadership between those who wanted the curriculum to put the greatest weight on academic content and those who felt the processes for reflection and connection should have primacy.[1]

The genius of the EfM curriculum lies at the crossroads of content and process. Being grounded in the Christian story handed down through the Bible, church history, and the sweep of theological thought grounds a developing ability to reflect theologically. At the same time, standing at the intersection of life and faith takes on new meaning when a pattern for reflecting on that encounter through a theological lens becomes internalized. This push-pull between academic study and reflective process has continued to surface and inspire curricular revisions as the years have progressed. As movements ebb and flow in the Church and society, addressing the balance of content and process through revision becomes critical to the EfM curriculum's effectiveness in providing support for the ministry of the laity.

In ways, sometimes confusing to participants and mentors alike, the tension between content and process surfaced in the seminars. Participants grappled on their own with graduate-level academic readings on the Bible, church history, and theology for which parish Christian education had not prepared them. Many group members wanted to spend much of the seminar time discussing the new learnings they encountered in the readings, and because a classroom model was more familiar to them than a seminar, these discussions often devolved into "book reports," recitation of the main points of the reading assignment. Mentors, after intense training focused on facilitating experiential learning in reflection, often had internalized a message that the academic content was much less important than the process for connecting. In addition, the reflective method required a significant portion of limited seminar time, so mentors felt a need to move swiftly into a theological reflection, shutting down the discussion of the readings. Mentors also felt unprepared to manage pushback from the

---

1. "A History of EfM: 1975–1992," *Sewanee Theological Review* 37, no. 3 (Pentecost, 1994): 237.

group who sometimes struggled through a complicated reflection process, a process often abandoned as too challenging. Revisions over the years would introduce various ways of addressing this tension.

Vision and Revision

The first edition of the EfM curriculum started with the Year One materials published in 1975, with the materials for subsequent program years added one year at a time through 1980. Almost immediately the program needed to evolve to meet the needs of participants. Winters originally assumed that a seminar group would form to begin in Year One, staying together through to Year Four. This proved impractical in many places. Participants dropped out of groups for various reasons: job changes, family needs, all the realities of modern life. Some who left wanted to return to the program and resume their study when they could, even if in a different group or location. Since each year's readings were self-contained, the curriculum was flexible enough to accommodate participants studying different materials at the same time. The program adapted, allowing groups to function as one-room schoolhouses. Countless participants have found that working alongside others encountering different aspects of the Christian tradition has enriched their own learning, and that considering insights from study across the curriculum enriched the whole group's work in theological reflection.

The first major revision of the content was issued in 1984. By 1982 it had become clear that the reading materials needed updating to bring them in line with recent changes in The Episcopal Church's theology and practice, among them the ecumenical liturgical movement's influence on the 1979 Book of Common Prayer (with its centering of baptism as the call to ministry), women's ordination, and questions of inclusive language in worship, as well as significant changes in culture and society.

The content revision (this time done by a committee rather than by an individual faculty member) was fraught with problems, from significant editorial and spelling issues in the texts published in 1984 to the outright rejection by participants of the new Year Two materials.[2] In the midst of the revision, however, a curricular evolutionary leap occurred as Richard E. Brewer proposed and produced the addition of the *Parallel Guides* (study guides to enhance understanding of the readings) and *Common Lessons* (providing whole group reflective work on themes in a four-year cycle). This was a response to the needs of participants to find balance in the foundational tension between content and process across the curriculum.

Although there were some minor changes made to the 1984 curriculum going forward, the second major revision of the curriculum was launched in 1999 with the publication of a new Year One, and the remaining years' books followed in sequence. The most obvious change was the move to a format using red three-ring binders and a page numbering system akin to legal documents, the thought being that updated sections could be replaced as needed without having to reprint the whole book or alter its overall pagination. But many found the pagination confusing and had trouble replacing existing pages when new pages would arrive.

There was of course more to the new curriculum than just a change to the physical appearance of the books. The reading content for every year underwent extensive revision and reorganization to keep current with new theological scholarship, the march of ongoing church history, and rapidly changing global events. It was a daunting task, and as de Bary writes in his 2002 preface to Year Four, "I suspect that this portion of the EfM materials will be out of date very quickly as events on the global stage pit economic, political, and religious differences against one another." Despite this, the 1999 curriculum, with instances of minor revision, was used through the spring semester of 2012.

One of the significant changes in the 1999 curriculum was the expansion of the *Common Lessons and Supporting*

---

2. de Bary, "A History," 247.

Materials (CLSM). For the first time participants were given materials that had previously been given only to mentors. In addition to the cycle of *Common Lessons* themselves, the CLSM contained process flowcharts and detailed descriptions of processes for theological reflection. A section also contained information about learning theory, group process theory, and various aspects of forming and maintaining healthy community life.

The Turn to Practice

By the time de Bary retired in 2004, the 1999 curriculum was in urgent need of significant revision to incorporate more recent biblical and church history scholarship, and to better respond to the needs of laypersons seeking to articulate their faith in an increasingly pluralistic and interfaith world. The thirty-year-old program, with more than 20,000 graduates, also faced the dilemma of trying to recruit new participants in an Episcopal Church with fewer members than before the theological culture wars of the new century.

A time of some administrative turmoil in the program followed de Bary's retirement, and instead of the major revision it needed, some less extensive editing of the curricular content was undertaken to keep the venerable program going. In 2008, the Very Rev. William Stafford, dean of the School of Theology, convened a working group to develop a strategic plan for EfM. In it, some key areas of concern for the ongoing life of the program were identified. Most concerning was that the content and the format for delivery presented barriers to ongoing recruitment of new learners. The reading content in the curriculum became increasingly dated as each year passed and the materials were costly to rewrite and publish. In addition, participants found that following the very detailed process charts sometimes made a theological reflection proceed like a step-by-step exercise rather than a fluid, collaborative conversation. Finally, younger adults were skeptical of a program format that still relied on information delivered in hard copy in bulky three-ring binder notebooks.

The plan called for hiring a new executive director for the program who could design and produce a full revision of the curriculum and institute programmatic changes that would make the venerable program more appealing to younger and more diverse participants. After a churchwide search, I was offered the position, bringing to the table my experience as a Christian formation professional with doctoral studies in practical theology that focused on the ministry of the laity.

In the spring semester of 2010, I came to the work of curricular revision with three objectives: 1) to move away from the self-published reading content and take advantage of substantive yet accessible theological textbooks that could be more easily replaced as scholarship changed; 2) to reconfigure how the study guides, common lessons, and instruction in theological reflection could be arranged to work fluidly across the program year in an accessible format; and 3) to draw on scholarly work in the field of practical theology that emphasized reflective practice as foundational to lifelong spiritual formation. The goal was deceptively simple: to create a new EfM curriculum built on the foundation of what made EfM uniquely EfM, the intersection of content and process, learning, and practice.

My observation, drawn from my own experience as an EfM graduate and mentor, and from conversations with other graduates and mentors, was that the program had reached another tipping point where content and process needed rebalancing as well as reframing. Many EfM learners continued to have trouble understanding that the academic content was to be learned, not as an academic goal, but for integration through the discipline of theological reflection into their own lives in ways that could inspire them to ministerial action in a hurting world. My vision for the revision was to apply a theological prism to the curriculum, breaking out the layers in such a way that the formative framework would be just as explicit and just as integral as the educational content.

The revision work began in 2010 with listening to EfM constituencies (learners, mentors, trainers, diocesan coordinators, and alumni) who shared what worked well and what no longer worked in their seminar groups. It became clear that the formative aspects of four years in an EfM group were still deep in the curriculum, but perhaps just a little too deeply buried. The step-by-step explanations for group process in theological reflection, presented as resources to participants as well as mentors in the 1999 revision, were perceived to be complicated and not accessible, for some participants. In addition, it was not always evident that those who could work well at theological reflection in the group were effectively translating the process to individual reflection, thus missing the program's desired end of helping them view their own experience through a theological lens in daily life.

Respecting his long experience in EfM as a group mentor and a mentor trainer, and with his history with previous curricular changes that sought to bring the academic content more in balance with the reflective process, I invited Richard Brewer to partner with me in designing a curriculum for EfM that addressed the evolving needs of a theologically educated and reflective laity called to ministry in a changing world.

EfM's third major revision of the curriculum was launched in the fall semester of 2012. Accessible academic textbooks commonly used in undergraduate and graduate theology programs, as well as in Episcopal seminaries, were chosen for the readings in the Christian tradition. These covered the Hebrew Bible in Year One, the New Testament in Year Two, and the history of Christianity in Year Three, as had been the case for most of the curricula in the past. Year Four was reconfigured to cover systematic and practical theology, ethics from an Anglican viewpoint, and interfaith encounter.

The format for curricular delivery was changed to a four-year cycle of thematic and proprietary *Education for Ministry Reading and Reflection Guides* A–D that incorporated all four year-levels' assignments in a single volume. Each volume in the cycle centered a theme in the work toward a spiritual wholeness that undergirds ministry in and to the world: a) identifying and understanding a layperson's ministerial context; b) situating lay

Christian ministry in a global context; c) growing toward spiritual maturity as a Christian; and d) understanding ministry as a part of our journey with God. Each RRG was self-contained so that a learner could enter at any volume and complete the cycle in four years. Two additional texts were assigned each year for "Interludes," times when all group members, regardless of their year level in the program, read and reflected on a common book related to the theme of the RRG.

Five unit divisions within each volume in the RRG sequence were a reimagining of the earlier *Common Lessons*: story sharing and listening as fundamental ministerial skills for building relationships; theological reflection as a life skill; developing a sustaining spiritual life; integrating belief, behavior, and doctrine; and lifelong vocational discernment. Theological reflection also was reframed as a simplified path in four movements, and teaching about the spiritual reflection process was approached differently in each RRG volume to accommodate different learning styles while situating lifelong theological reflection within the volume's central theme. And finally, the curriculum was framed with an emphasis on Christian practice and a rule of life.

Core Practices

In addition to the fundamental tension between content and process, a recurring issue in EfM has long been how to describe what is essentially a unique program in adult Christian formation in The Episcopal Church. Drawing on analogy from the negative, it has most often been described as not a typical Bible study and not a typical academic theology course, leaving group mentors and diocesan coordinators grasping to articulate what EfM is.

At its heart, Education for Ministry is a practical theological endeavor, an encounter with faith on the ground examined through reflection in an intentional community pointed toward Christian service in the world. Fundamentally, it is the pursuit of spiritual development through experiential learning. And aspirationally, it is a course in ministry development.

Ministry, of course, is itself a loaded term in contemporary understanding, requiring even more nuanced explanation. Despite the popular understanding that ministry is a profession like law or medicine, and that a minister is one who is ordained to and trained for that profession, the doctrine of The Episcopal Church teaches that baptism is the sacramental marker of ministry and all baptized Christians are called to minister to others in their daily lives.

An EfM seminar then can be defined as a community of praxis—practice with a value-laden purpose. As an athlete practices to acquire greater skill in a sport, so the Christian practices living in a way patterned on the life of Jesus Christ and his followers. The goal is not to become simply a more skillful disciple but a more faithful one. Christian practices are embodied ways of acting out values embedded in the tradition of Christian discipleship so that over time those values become embedded in our own lives. Ongoing practice changes how we understand our lives as well as our relationship to the lives of those around us. This is why so many say that EfM changed their lives, although the concept of practice buried deep in the processes of the curriculum itself had mostly gone unexamined until the 2012 revision.

As Elaine L. Graham wrote, "Practice has the capacity to engender new realities as well as develop greater skill; and in turn, practice informed by new insights may transform subsequent experience."[3] In the regular practice of learning about the Christian tradition while reflecting on daily life in the context of that tradition, the EfM seminar group learns to make not only faithful connections with past life events but also to apply new perceptions to life going forward. EfM nurtures lifelong spiritual development through a core of ongoing value-laden practices from the Christian tradition that inform new learnings, transform understanding of experience (past, present, and

---

3. Elaine L. Graham, *Transforming Practice: Pastoral Theology in an Age of Uncertainty* (Eugene, OR: Wipf and Stock, 1996, 2002), 101.

future), and equip the reflective practitioner for ministry in daily life.

EfM's core practices identified in the 2012 curriculum form a rule of life during the group's four years together: living in community, regular prayer and worship, theological reflection, study of the Christian tradition, and vocational discernment. They are meant to be internalized as the seminar group works through the curriculum each year, inspiring lifelong ministerial practices for forming relationships through sharing and listening, developing a sustainable spiritual life that supports the sometimes hard work of serving others, identifying and drawing inspiration from the nexus of faith and daily living, learning from the great cloud of witnesses of the Christian tradition, and fostering an openness to the guidance of the Holy Spirit along with quiet confidence in the ability to respond to that call.

EfM's core practices lead participants to practical spiritual formation for discipleship in their everyday lives. While named explicitly for the first time in the 2012 revision, these core practices have been embedded in the EfM curriculum from its early days. It is no coincidence that they are congruent with the Baptismal Covenant in the Episcopal Book of Common Prayer 1979, promises made individually and corporately that point us to the practices of discipleship in the early church: fellowship and community, teaching and learning, worship and prayer, evangelism and service, and justice and respect for all. The EfM seminar group practices individual and corporate faithful living centered on the baptismal call to ministry.

The framework of EfM's core practices brings into balance the curriculum's foundational tension between content and process. They are practices of discipleship in community where knowledge of the grand sweep of the Christian story partners with bringing that story into conversation with the experiences of daily living. The core practices in EfM create a space where the conversation between faith and experience opens possibilities for life going forward so that new experiences can be examined through the lens of Christian witness for insight into how to live as reflective practitioners of the Way. They give the EfM curriculum the ability to evolve regularly to support a laity called to ministry in a changing Church in a changing world while remaining firmly grounded in the Christian tradition of discipleship.

Four Sources and Four Movements: A History of EfM's Practice of Theological Reflection

John de Beer and Tricia de Beer

Theological reflection, one of the core practices of EfM's seminar life, is a guided discussion that brings diverse sources of knowledge into conversation. It helps participants embody the interconnectedness of our faith, experience, culture, and context so that they live as whole people. The de Beers, who have provided leadership for EfM from the early days, are passionate about adult spiritual formation.

Education for Ministry (EfM) began in 1975 when The Episcopal Church was emphasizing the ministry of the baptized. The 1979 Book of Common Prayer describes lay ministry as follows:

> . . . *to represent Christ and his Church; to bear witness to him wherever they may be; and, according to the gifts given them, to carry on Christ's work of reconciliation in the world, and to take their place in the life, worship, and governance of the church.*

The intention of the founder of EfM, the Rev. Dr. Charles Winters, was that the program would provide laypeople a comprehensive exposure to the Christian tradition. He drew from the core curriculum of the master of divinity program at the School of Theology. The EfM seminar group was intended to help participants connect their increasing knowledge of the Christian tradition with their daily life and ministry. His vision was a quiet revolution in the making!

The original model of theological reflection (TR) had two sources—Christian tradition and human experience. There was little guidance as to how group participants would make the connections. Initially there was a model but not a clear method. The Very Rev. Urban T. Holmes, then dean of the School of Theology said, 'I have experienced a constant frustration in seminary teaching trying to help students 'do' theology... 'reflection' is a stumbling block for many students."[1]

In 1975, mentor training was a lunch meeting with Dr. Winters for him to share his vision of the seminar group with the prospective mentor, who was almost always an Episcopal priest. In less than ten years, the EfM program uncovered a way to help participants "do" theology in a process of theological reflection that was both structured and yet aware of the energy of the group.

EfM became a powerful engine for transforming the ministry of the laity. At a General Convention session, the moderator asked people who had been involved with EfM to stand and a large proportion of the Church's leadership represented at that convention rose from their seats. How did this happen?

In 1976, Flower Ross was recruited to become the manager of training and program. She drew on her expertise in experiential education and group process from the Association of Consultants and Trainers. She stayed in close touch with mentors, helping them learn from what happened in their groups as they connected "tradition" with "experience." As she accumulated an understanding of how to enrich theological reflection, she shared it with new mentors and trainers. Mentor training evolved from a lunch meeting to an eighteen-contact-hour training event. Long

---

1. Urban T. Holmes III, *To Speak of God: Theology for Beginners* (New York: Seabury Press, 1974).

before the term "learning organization" would be coined, Ross was creating one. A learning organization prioritizes personal and professional growth through knowledge transfer.[2] These organizations encourage learning as part of their fundamental culture and overall vision for long-term success. She trained trainers to learn the process and make it their own. It was not something they had to "get right." We believe that EfM's long-term success depends on decisions and practices that encourage a continuous loop of collaborative learning. I wrote:

> In December of 1977, I found myself sitting in a circle with six others in the conference room of the Bairnwick Center in Sewanee, preparing to become a mentor trainer. Bairnwick had served as a large family house. Now it was the headquarters of EfM. Guest rooms were upstairs, the living room downstairs had a fireplace and plenty of room for us to meet comfortably. Charlie and Flower had offices on the ground floor and in the basement; Cindy Sherrill was developing an administrative system to keep up with the expanding enrollment. As Charlie outlined his vision and Flower led us in sharing and reflecting on our human experience, I felt deeply at home among people who shared my vision of church and welcomed my gifts.

In 1980, Tricia graduated with a master of divinity degree, and we moved to Sewanee, Tennessee. I accepted a position as staff trainer for EfM. Shortly thereafter, I became director of education. It was an exciting time for EfM and for the residential seminary. Three of the seminary faculty—William Hethcock, Robert Hughes, and Patricia O'Connell Killen, were members of the EfM training community.

Tricia wrote:

> In 1980, teaching seminarians how to reflect theologically was so central for Dean Holmes that he required

---

2. Peter Senge, *The Fifth Dimension* (Doubleday, 1990).

every student to meet regularly in a facilitated group. In addition to traveling as a trainer, I was one of the group facilitators for a couple of years. After a short period in which I facilitated 11 theological reflections, I remember saying to myself that I needed a life on which to reflect! One of the struggles I witnessed was the difficulty in getting to the "heart of the matter." What we learned from doing TR with seminarians was also grist for the mill as we refined our understanding of theological reflection. The learning community was growing in strength and numbers.

At the time we were using three sources: Tradition, Belief (later called Positions), and Experience.

The stages of Identify, Explore, Connect, and Apply (what later became the Four Movements) were more of a pedagogical framework than a central focus. We learned the importance of finding a metaphor or image that unified our various experiences into a shared experience. Then, we would enter the world of the image from the inside and use the four theological perspective questions related to creation, sin, judgment, and redemption to explore that world. We then moved to another source and asked the same theological perspective questions to explore the other sources. We focused on the relationship between the different sources, and attention was given to identifying insights and concrete implications for action.

The above understanding of theological reflection allowed the newly certified trainers to share the load of mentor training and, as a result, EfM expanded rapidly. We were then thirty-five in all. This community of trainers had a profound impact on all of us. Attention was given to the personal and the professional development of the trainer. As we experimented with TR in the training of trainer events, we made ourselves vulnerable to one another and to the Spirit that moved through the reflections. It is with gratitude that we remember many individual moments in which some deep shifts in understanding ourselves, the tradition, or our world came into view. For example, with the support of colleagues, Tricia worked through her response to ordained mentors resistant to the idea of having to be certified by the program, and especially by a young laywoman.

This community shaped the learning environment in the seminar groups as we invited mentors into a similar trust in the mentor training events. Being willing to be transformed by God is not for the faint of heart and is much more likely to happen in a group where the mentor models love, trust, and respect.

Learning to lead a group in theological reflection requires a complex set of skills: an understanding of the sources, the Four Movements, the perspective questions, and attention to "the flow"—a more intuitive ability to read the energy in the group and open up the questions and issues that are alive for the participants. At its best, TR is a balance of structure and flow.

At some point along the way, those who thought more sequentially than intuitively asked for a description of the concrete steps of the Microscope Method. A ten-step process was created to provide clear guidance. Later, two more steps were added. Some mentors found this rigid and unhelpful and rebelled. Many mentors learned to use the steps lightly, balancing structure with intuition as they paid attention to the energy of the group and the Spirit's leading.

Another example of the dynamism of the learning community was a training of trainers in 1982 in which culture was added as a fourth source. One participant, who had an extensive background in Jungian psychology, was working with that—the culture that had impacted his perspectives. We experimented with diagrams and pipe cleaners. Rick Brewer built a 3D cardboard model and the "Four Source Mode" became the framework of theological reflection in EfM. It also became widely used in religious education programs and seminary education throughout the United States.

The additional source brought clarity to the process and helped participants become more thoughtful about how our culture has shaped us. If four perspective questions were asked of four sources, however, the reflection easily bogged down. Reducing the number of perspective questions and the number of sources used in reflection and allowing at least ten minutes for the "Apply" stage, regardless of how far along the reflection had progressed, helped address these problems but did not resolve them.

The EfM system was focused too much on structure. Angela Hock and Rick Brewer addressed that issue with the language of the first RRG in 2013, reminding us that the Four Movements are the main components of TR. Together, they are the core method. Tricia remembers teaching people that the four-source model was equivalent to the map, but the Four Movements were like a GPS, enabling us to start from any source. It was a refreshing reminder that theological reflection needed to retain a sense of organic dialogue in which there is deep listening, and that simply listing answers to ten questions was not going to create the kind of transformation we were seeking.

Along the way, additional sets of perspective questions were added and new methods identified. In addition to the need to highlight flow rather than steps, there have been other changes in describing TR that have made the process more organic. Although the original theological categories of creation, sin, judgment, and redemption have not been eliminated, additional theological categories have become acceptable. The deliberate expansion of possible perspective questions during TR has made the process more flexible. The gift of the wide range of theological perspective questions, however, depends on the mentor's ability to listen to the conversation. The greater openness works well with more experienced or skilled mentors.

In 2024, from our limited data point as trainers, we see two challenges that may need to be addressed.

First, doing theological reflection in a group on Zoom makes it harder to provide enough visual structure to compare and contrast the sources while at the same time maintaining the natural flow of energy in the conversation. This is always a challenge, but using the computer screen to illustrate the contrasting perspectives means that participants lose visual contact with one another. In the training sessions, we see an increase in TR as a largely unstructured conversation that does not lead to deep insight or a change in behavior. We wonder if, for some, the pendulum has swung too far toward attention to the "flow." Second, the increasing polarization in our society has put some topics off-limits for many groups. Attention to strengthening our life together in a fractious world seems important. In our resilient learning community, no doubt these challenges will be met in ways we cannot now imagine.

Fifty years after its founding, EfM has discovered a comprehensive way of helping people learn to reflect theologically. In our four-plus decades with EfM, we have met thousands of mentors who are deeply thoughtful, inspiring, and committed leaders. The quiet revolution continues. The signature characteristic of EfM is that mentors, participants, and trainers are participating in a continuous process of teaching one another and forming one another for ministry.

Tricia and I were blessed to find EfM early in our ministries. Learning along with others in the EfM community shaped us profoundly and gave us a way to allow the Spirit to empower the ministry of the laity in each of the congregations and communities we have served. Our congregation's EfM groups were fertile ground, giving birth to ministries in Haiti, in homeless shelters, in healing ministries, and in the formation of groups that brought Jews, Muslims, and Christians together. It enriched every part of our life together. We are deeply grateful.

Thanks be to God.

Reflection and Revisioning: The Reading and Reflection Guide

Angela Hock

EfM texts have evolved from spiraled yellow books to bound books to binders, which gave way to the creation of the Reading and Reflection Guide. *Affectionately known as the RRG, this invaluable resource provides the program's syllabus. Hock and Richard Brewer became partners through marriage as well as co-authors working with Karen Meridith to produce the EfM* Reading and Reflection Guides. *As a mentor, trainer, and author, Hock shows participants that theological reflection is a natural conversation that can become a habitual way of discerning one's ministry.*

In 2011, Karen Meridith invited Richard (Rick) Brewer and me to toss around ideas for a revised Education for Ministry (EfM) curriculum. All three of us were interested in shifting to published texts for each year's primary study source. Our thinking was that such a move could make it possible to stay current in the theological studies field. We also wanted to honor and incorporate previous aspects of the EfM program, particularly the *Common Lessons* and the *Parallel Guides*.

Gradually, we envisioned a single volume that would include the reading assignments for all four program levels. We knew that we would need four separate *Reading and Reflection Guides* so that anyone going through all four program years would encounter different perspectives with which to view their study.

A centering theme carried through each volume. We also wanted to convey the ongoing nature of Christian life that seeks to be faithful to the teachings of faith in terms of engagement with our external and internal worlds. Those considerations led to themes of "Living Faithfully in a Multicultural World," "Living Faithfully in Our World," "Living as Spiritually Mature Christians," and "Living into the Journey with God." We hoped to create a sense of progression through the volumes.

Because the EfM structure allows new people to join an ongoing group at any point during the movement through the themes, however, that sense of progression couldn't be fully realized. One of the major shifts that occurred with the RRG was to focus on experiencing education itself as both educational as well as formational and to provide support for a person's own theological and spiritual formation. That intention drove us to keep spiritual practices present throughout the entire RRG and not only in what became Unit Three—Spirituality.

Previously in EfM, each program year had its own volume that contained weekly lessons. Those volumes used a *parallel guide* to make the weekly reading assignment, provide vocabulary, and offer a prompt under "Deepening Your Understanding," that invited connection to one's life, the weekly study, and the contemporary world. We wanted to continue that unifying sense by creating one question that all levels of participants could engage for seminar conversation each week. We developed an RRG that would be a single volume each year, containing weekly reading assignments for all four program levels along with a focusing possibility for each level—a question that all levels could respond to—and a theological reflection outline to use at home. Each week's sequence developed into "Read," "Focus," "Respond," and "Reflect." In addition, focusing, responding, and reflecting regularly helped bring the volume's theme into a conversation. My major contribution was creating the weekly Respond and Reflect pieces, working to keep the volume theme and unit topic in focus.

The *Common Lessons* of previous EfM materials contained essays to engage and support group members and mentors in their Christian formation. There were separate essays in each of five units—Spiritual Autobiography, Theological Reflection, Spirituality, Personal Theology, and Vocation—plus a great deal of information on conducting seminars and supporting group life. We planned the RRG to have five similar units of those titles (Personal Theology was changed to Belief and Behavior), introduced by an essay that fleshed out ideas that united and wove those ideas into the theme for each volume. We added an opening "Getting Started" and a closing "Farewell" week, which gave us thirty-two weeks of curriculum. Karen incorporated quite a bit of the *Common Lessons* group life material into the resources section of the RRG.

The unit essays for the new RRGs considered the original ones written for the *Common Lessons* by Rick Brewer, John de Beer, Carolyn Lankford, Tricia de Beer, and Elizabeth Lang. Rick wrote some of the new ones for the RRG and Rick and Karen identified other authors, such as Steven Charleston, Diana Butler Bass, and Sarah Coakley, who had written essays that would be pertinent to the unit and volume for which we considered them. Steven was especially chosen for Volume B, the multicultural year, because of the ethnic diversity in his writings. In general, Rick chose all essay authors because they wrote around a unit's theme and offered a particular voice. We attempted throughout the volumes to access voices that represented a diversity of gender, race, ethnicity, and faith traditions. In Volume D, "Living into the Journey with God," which explores the subject of *theosis*, Rick stepped away from the practice of including such a variety and made Robert Davis Hughes III's voice and his book, *Beloved Dust*, the spine of that volume. The attempt to find or write essays relevant to a given theme and at the same time pertinent to the unit it introduced was the biggest, most frustrating, and yet most exciting challenge.

The Week Two essays of each RRG volume combined an exploration of the year's theme with beginning work on spiritual autobiography and listening. These essays laid the foundation for the year, encouraging participants and mentors to delve into dynamics of the volume's theme and how that theme might have played out in their personal lives. The RRG carried those considerations throughout the year, bringing them into the conversation, sometimes in focusing questions, other times in group response questions or in their theological reflections. We tried to keep the volume's theme and the program study level engaged with people's lives. To do that, listening was essential—listening within oneself to inner promptings; to the voices of scripture and history and theology; to the prayers and yearnings of others; to those in the EfM group; in our lives and in our study; and to the voice of God mediated through any of those avenues.

The interlude books provided an occasional common point of study in the group and helped keep the program's offerings current, since changing the textbooks would have necessitated major changes in the RRG each time, which was prohibitive. The RRG had to change every year without primary text changes. With the interludes, we could give readers entrée into current topics (sometimes referred to as "hot topics") from a theological/spiritual perspective. Karen Meridith selected the interlude books with the help of professors at the School of Theology and in consultation with others whom she respected. We did not want to be driven only by "currency," as though writings now considered classics couldn't be included. We wanted representation from both and did not want to shy away from topics that could challenge people; both with their currency and with their coming from another age. We believed that just because something was written in another century didn't mean it couldn't say something relevant to us now. Classics will do that; they are timeless because of their insight though sometimes dated in language.

Above all, we designed the *Reading and Reflection Guides* for home use: a guide for a participant's home study and reflection between seminar sessions. Our delight abounds as we have discovered that mentors do use the Respond and Reflect prompts as grist for the seminars. As John de Beer was known to have said in the 1980s, "In extension education, you design what you know will work and then you send it out there and wait to see how else it can work." That wisdom has sustained us often over these twelve years as we've experienced creative work with the *Reading and Reflection Guides* that speaks to the strengths of our trainers, mentors, and participants.

Thanks to the heroic efforts of Karen Meridith in editing and co-authoring the work, and to Sharon Ely Pearson and the team at Church Publishing Company, *Reading and Reflection Guide,* Volume A arrived in the world in September 2012. I am so grateful to be part of this amazing effort that has relied on the numerous gifts and perspectives of many others. To have a chance to at least view the promised land from the peak of Mount Pathwright is a breathtaking gift. Thank you, Kevin Goodman, for inviting me to continue on this journey.

Living TR: EfM's Theological Perspective Questions

Karen D. Byers

Within EfM, carefully constructed questions are essential for small group facilitation. Exploration of an image, metaphor, or statement through the theological perspective questions about creation, sin, judgment, repentance, and redemption has been part of EfM from the beginning. In recent years, mentors and trainers have introduced new patterns of perspective questions. Byers explores various ways of looking at the focus of the reflection and what those different patterns say about our understanding of God.

How do we think about God? How do we come to have a glimpse of the all-knowingness, all beingness, eternal, transcendence, and immanence of God? We are told in Genesis 1:1 that creation begins with light and wind, reverberates through the days with fish and plants and bugs, and reaches its apotheosis on the sixth day with human beings and on the seventh with rest. It is good. Always good. And, as the biblical story unfolds, we learn that creation brings its own kind of chaos. Down the ages, that chaos of creation has not abated.

We too, in 2024, face the chaos of creation. We wonder how the claims of Christianity are relevant to us. Many of us, like St. Thomas, are skeptical. In a world infused with artificial intelligence, unending wars, political division, and climate catastrophe, we wonder about the relevance of God. And yet, we, like Thomas, find evidence of people encountering God in the stories of others, in the histories and the gospels, the Hebrew Scriptures, and the Christian revelation. We meet God in our experiences of seeing faith in action and in our own prayer of following the Creator.

Education for Ministry (EfM) is one way of making an intentional search for God. We engage in the regular experience of theological reflection in the weekly seminar. The exploration of a metaphor through perspective questions is a very specific tool for the journey. These questions arise in the second movement of the reflection, the "Explore" movement. The following is about my engagement with those perspective questions.

From the start, fifty years ago, all the elements of theological reflection we know today were in the program, including exploration of an image or metaphor through the theological perspective questions. As a program in practical theology, the question right from the beginning was how to link Christian teachings and practice with our ordinary lives. How can we help spiritual seekers feed their hunger to know more and their desire to do more?

The theological reflection process was designed for this. When we begin a theological reflection, we start in a "wisdom source"—a passage from the Bible, a slice of someone's experience, a cultural moment, or a personal belief—and we generate an image or a metaphor about that bit of wisdom.

And then we explore.

We explore using theological perspective questions. We ask a specific set of questions. We interrogate the answers. And we let new questions arise. It has been my experience that gently and slowly, week in and week out, this process of asking questions about an image or a metaphor leads to clearer insight, deeper understanding, and greater appreciation. Questions are raised, questions are answered, doubts are assailed, and new actions are taken.

When we explore theologically, we are not asking a series of random or disconnected questions. Rather, we are asking questions intended to open up the nature of our world, the nature of

God, and the relationship of God to the world and to ourselves. We are trying to unpack our own feelings and experiences of God. We want to understand mercy, grace, hope, and forgiveness. I like to speak of "theological perspective frameworks," because the questions comprising these groupings have a theological, historical, aesthetic, or ethical continuity. They are a system, or tool, that provides us with a structure to focus on God.

When I started in EfM in the late 1990s, there were seven methods of theological reflection, each of them with eight to twelve steps. The perspective questions were embedded in the steps.[1] All but one of these used the "systematic theology" categories, as follows.[2]

> **Systematic Theology**
> **Creation.** What is life like in the world of the metaphor?
> **Sin.** What would count as negative, or a failure? What is a distortion or a darkness in the world of the metaphor?
> **Judgment.** What brings you up short, surprises you, or takes your breath away?
> **Repentance.** What prompts a change of heart?
> **Redemption.** Where is there celebration? A new creation?

I think of this as our foundational form of exploration—a root or default. To this day, it remains a powerful and durable set of questions relevant for many situations inside and outside of EfM. It is also, for me, the starting place of the evolution of the perspective frameworks that we have seen in the last couple of decades.

In this framework we follow the pattern of redemption which describes—as against the creation—our fallen and redeemed

---

1. Microscope, TR beginning with scripture, TR beginning with a text from culture or tradition, wide angle lens, issue, personal position and reflection in motion (a variation of the microscope).
2. The "issue" or "dilemma" method used cost and promise, which emerges from moral theology—the weighing of one set of options or constraints against another. Cost and promise: this is a framework of assessing value and risk. It is no less theological; indeed, the cost of crossing the desert is the promise of arrival at the promised land.

nature. We always begin with what is given, what is presented to us. This is what we need to "see." What we need to see is the focus, image, or metaphor that we have arrived at in the prior movement, the "identify" movement. In group theological reflection, in "identify," we must first agree on what our metaphor will be. Then, this set of perspective questions (and others) starts off by asking us, "What is given here?," "What does God present to us (in this metaphor)?," and "What is the goodness of THIS creation?" Moreover, and powerfully so, in group theological reflection, we need to agree on what is given. In effect, we need to "see together." Once we "see together" what the creation is, we can move on to the next questions, which take us on the journey of sin, judgment, repentance, and redemption.

Remember, we are always one or two or three removes from God, so we are in that sense, looking through a glass darkly (1 Cor 13:12) and hoping thereby to catch a glimpse of God. Our "seeing" can be impeded by the standpoints of certitude and self-assurance,[3] which block our ability to see. This is why theological reflection in a group is so important. We begin to understand (and, we hope, become a bit humble) when we encounter others who may be within their own standpoints of certitude and self-assurance, but whose standpoints are different from ours. Thus, it might be fair to say that in a group we can have more clarity about what the thing is, what we see, because we bring to bear the "looking" of all participants in the room.

When we ask the questions, "What is the creation?" or "What do we see?," this begs the question of whether there is indeed an objective reality out there, or at least a reality upon which we can agree. That is another matter outside the scope of this essay, but it does suggest that if you look carefully and closely, you will come to see the thing at which you are looking. After that, having seen as clearly as you can, the interpretation can come. I think there is something to be said about looking as clearly, calmly, and as

---

3. P. Killen and J. de Beer, *The Art of Theological Reflection* (New York: Crossroads Publishing, 2009), chap. 1.

objectively as possible before you begin the process of interpretation, which is to say before you ascribe value judgments, for example, that something is sinful.

The other thing worth noting about this process is that it has a cyclical, or spiral, pattern. We begin with creation, what is given to us, and we explore to understand more deeply our actions and attitudes about that creation: to see the ways in which we might be redeemed. This redemption is, in fact, a new creation. So, our exploration of an image or a metaphor takes us into the well and we climb back out again, only to find that something has changed and has given us a new creation to explore. How exciting! For me, the perspective questions are not random, disconnected questions; they are leading me somewhere. When we come out of the perspective questions, we have a deeper resonance with the metaphor or image, perhaps even a changed understanding, and this informs how we connect with the other sources. It opens up our thinking as we move on to the next movement in the reflection.

The Perspective Question Options Multiply

Some new patterns of questions began to enter the EfM lexicon and they bear some similarities to the systematic questions. The Ubuntu I and II approaches come out of an African perspective of human interconnectedness: "I am what I am because of who we are."

> **Ubuntu Theology I**
> **Wholeness/Goodness.** What is whole or good in the world of the image?
> **Brokenness/Separation from God.** What threatens wholeness?
> **Recognition.** What makes you see that threat or see it differently?
> **Reorientation.** How might you return to God?
> **Restoration.** What does the new wholeness look like?

Ubuntu Theology II
Goodness. Where is cooperation, freedom, or gift?
Failure. Where is there estrangement or isolation?
Choice. Where is power? What are rights? Where am I challenged? Where do we meet God?
Call. What prayer does God pray? Who or what is called?
Love. How is all made well? Where is interdependence? What is reassembled?

The slow-looking framework comes from art appreciation. It is a meditative approach to viewing an image such as a painting. Imagine here after each question, a long pause to accommodate your attention and focus.

Slow-Looking Questions
What do you see in the image?
Where are the rocks that could be a threat?
What stands out or draws your attention?
What shines light on the matter?
What is the source of the light?

In Volume D of the *Reading and Reflection Guide* series, we are introduced to the Eastern Orthodox concepts of theosis (participation of the human person in the life of God) and scotosis (darkness on the journey).[4] These concepts, joined with the work of theologian Robert Hughes, gave rise to a set of questions with a slightly altered framing.

Eastern Orthodox Theology
Theosis. What is good? What flows? Where is fulfillment? How are the particles assembled?
Scotosis. What obscures? What resists? What is forgotten? What prevents clarity from emerging or being present?

---

4. *Reading and Reflection Guide*, vol. D (2016–2017), 9–18.

Conversion. What causes a crisis? What calls for confession? What calls for courage? What do you turn from? Turn to? What are you turned by? What risks must be confronted?
Transfiguration. Where do you see the illumination of God? What needs to die for something else to live?
Glory. Where is grace? Hope? Forgiveness? God within?

The questions emerging from theologian Alan Jones's work come from the tradition of the desert fathers. They offer a concise and succinct version of this same pattern.[5]

Desert Father Questions
Look! What do we see without interpretation?
Weep! What are the "gifts of tears" that separate us from God and others?
Live! Joy is the fruit of desert patience. What restores wholeness and brings us back into the action of life?

The Perspective Questions Evolve: New Frameworks

Of particular interest to me in the last decade or so of mentoring and training in EfM has been not just about an expansion of the ways in which we explore, but what the exploration frameworks say about God and theology. The systematic theology framework brings with it a set of assumptions about God and human beings. Other frameworks bring a different set of assumptions.

For some, God is accessed through intellect, for others through prayer. For some it is through emotion or beauty, and for others it is community. What the different frameworks do is facilitate different ways of getting to God.

---

5. From Alan Jones's *Soul Making: The Desert Way of Spirituality* (San Francisco, 1989), as captured and summarized by the Rev. Dr. Brooks Ramsey, "Soul Making: Journeying to the Desert with Alan Jones," exploringfaith.org, accessed January 28, 2025, http://www.exploringfaith.org/steppingstones_soulmaking.html.

The following two generalist frameworks are more open-ended. These do not presume sin or redemption. They do assume that there is a God, but then, we are a Christian program!

Trinity Questions
Where is God in the world of the image?
What actions would Jesus take in this world?
How is the Holy Spirit active in this world?

God/Human Relationship
What does the image say about God?
What does it say about humans?
What does it say about the relationship between God and humans?

Steve Isham (mentor and trainer) and I, finding ourselves of common mind about this, sat down one day and wrote a document that had twenty different ways of approaching the Explore questions, many of which are captured in this essay. Some had been circulating on bits of paper. Some came up from our own readings or engagement with material inside and outside of EfM, and some we extracted from the *Reading and Reflection Guides*.[6]

New frameworks provide new ways of looking at things and new ideas. This expands our awareness and offers different ways to approach the divine. A framework that works for one metaphor or for some people may not work for other metaphors or other people. And as we mentors grow in experience, we are able to become more discerning about this as we are facilitating a reflection.

The eucharistic exploration questions offer me a very visceral mode of exploration. Coming, as they do, out of our corporate

---

6. For this, we owe a debt of gratitude to Rick Brewer, Angela Hock-Brewer, and Karen Meridith, who developed and nurtured this era of the EfM curriculum that spanned 12 years, from 2013–2025.

faith-life and liturgy, I feel these questions and answers more in my body than I do in my head. Whenever we use these questions, I can see myself taking communion and it feels like a holy moment.

EUCHARISTIC QUESTIONS (Henri Nouwen, *With Burning Hearts: A Meditation on the Eucharistic Life*)
What is offered (in the image or metaphor)?
What is blessed (in the image or metaphor)?
What is broken (in the image or metaphor)?
What is fed (in us as we respond to these questions)?

OR
What is taken (from the image or metaphor)?
What is broken (in the image or metaphor)?
What is blessed (in the image or metaphor)?
What is given (back to us from this exploration)?

In 2011, EfM entered a collaborative relationship with the Kaleidoscope Institute. Eric Law's work brought us a new and very powerful set of perspective questions.[7] These questions speak to me as a feminist and as a person who finds considerable connection with liberation theologies. They are rooted in the Gospel and they are not easy questions to answer. They can be provocative to people, so in my experience it is helpful to pave the way with your group before tackling them. Consider doing some work on power dynamics ahead of time. Also, ensure that the group members trust one another and that a good covenant is in place.

Eric Law's Cycle Of Gospel Living
Powerful. Who has power? What is powerful?

---

7. This material was introduced into the curriculum in the Reading and Reflection Guide, Year B, issued for the 2014–2015 academic year. It has been incorporated into the *RRGs* since then, most recently in *RRG*, vol. D (2024–2025), 326.

Powerlessness. How is power yielded? What sacrifices are made?
Empowerment. What causes a shift in the power dynamic? How is power transformed or transmitted?
Resurrection Power. What is left behind? What is the hope of new power?

Probably my favorite of all the perspective question frameworks comes from the work of Cambridge theologian, David Ford, introduced to EfM in 2015.[8] He advocates doing theology beyond the dominant voices that issue affirmations of "right belief" and directives of "right action."[9] (I learned this in Sunday School: You will believe this, and you will do that!) What I love about Ford's approach is that desires, doubts, and exploration have a prominent role. It is respectful of me as a whole person and it offers hospitality for my views and my experience as valid elements for understanding God.

David Ford's Questions
Desires. What do you long for?
Questions. What do you wonder or doubt?
Explorations. What possibilities do you want to explore or test?
Affirmations. What are you coming to believe or affirm?
Imperatives. What action(s) are you moved to take?

In 2019, Angela Hock (mentor and trainer) and I developed the group theological reflection training manual we called "The Heart of the Matter." We thought that the theological reflection material in the *Reading and Reflection Guide* could be augmented with specific help for mentors on facilitating theological reflection in a group. We included the list of perspective questions that Steve Isham and I had developed earlier, and we began using the

---

8. *Reading and Reflection Guide*, vol. C (2015–2016), 17–18.
9. Ibid., 17.

material in our training sessions and sharing it with other trainers in the network for their use.

Over time it has become clear to me that, unlike the original systematic theology questions, not all perspective frameworks work with all metaphors. This does not make their theological relevance any less potent: some sets are not as fruitful with some metaphors as others. As I and others have developed facilities with these frameworks, it becomes easier to find a productive set of questions. But we always have the default systematic theology questions to fall back on. They are everlasting and, in their own way, a testament to the wisdom of the early developers of EfM.

Once you notice that these are patterns, and that the patterns actually express a set of values or a way of getting to meaning, you might begin to notice them everywhere. Find a new pattern. Come up with some questions to facilitate a discussion and try it on!

In conclusion, think of the EfM experience as a telescope. We come into the seminar bringing all of our hunger for spirit, longings, questions, and doubts. We discuss the material we have read, bringing some of the material into focus. We transition into a theological reflection, identify a metaphor or focal point, turning our telescope for even more clarity. We direct our sharply focused gaze on the object of our reflection and explore it deeply using perspective questions. Then, as the reflection continues and we shift into connecting our focus with other sources of wisdom, our telescope begins to pull back and we see more and more, perhaps with more clarity, perhaps with more connections, until we reach the movement to apply what we have learned in the reflection to our lives.

Verna Dozier says that we need to hold what we know lightly, and for now.[10] If we think of the process of doing theological reflection over and over, asking these exploration questions again

---

10. Verna J. Dozier, *The Dream of God* (New York: Church Publishing, 2006). See, for example, top of page 112.

and holding our conclusions lightly, we will find that, over time, we come into a sense of ourselves and our relationship with God.

As EfM embarks upon its next fifty years, I look forward to learning new ways and new patterns for exploring the metaphors we generate to understand God.

Room for the Spirit and the Need for Framework

Jim Papile

Education for Ministry strives to create seminars that provide brave space for reflection and formation. Some participants need a structured approach to learning, while others need to follow where the Spirit leads. Are these two mutually exclusive or can they be embraced simultaneously? Papile, a mentor and trainer, explores these approaches and the potential of using both.

Charles Winters, professor of theology at the University of the South's School of Theology, had an idea after a sabbatical to travel to First Nations communities in the West and Alaska. He embarked on this mission with a question—with a lack of theologically, biblically trained clergy, how can you grow the Church? His answer was to educate the laity. Returning to Sewanee, he began to enlist the help of colleagues to design a program that could do just that.

Once he had an outline for a program, he needed to introduce it to the greater Church. Being an Episcopal priest, he had a built-in mechanism—the dioceses of the Church. Convincing diocesan leadership of the efficacy of the program was the next step. On one of his trips to the Diocese of Louisiana, he met Lilian Flower Ross. Flower had been trained in the Human Potential Movement and she convinced Charlie that while he had an excellent program to expose participants to the academic side of the material—Bible, church history, and theology—what was lacking was a way for the participants to reflect on the process of their learning. Having a keen knowledge of small-group organizational development, Flower had much to contribute as to how to round out what a semblance of a seminary education would look like for the Church's laity.

Theological reflection (TR), as it came to be called in the program's parlance, was born. I remember being taught as a new trainer the anagram "Identify, Analyze, Generalize, Organize" (IAGO), a process of exploring ideas and experiences distilled from an organizational structure called Bloom's Taxonomy. This became the foundation upon which a group process of discussion was formed. Practitioners experienced in adult education began to work with the process and develop it for our purposes. John de Beer and Patricia O'Connell Killen wrote *The Art of Theological Reflection*, with contributors Rick Brewer, Tricia De Beer, Angela Hock, and others adding their expertise.

When I started in the program as a participant/student, there was only one method of doing theological reflection—the Microscope Method. In those days it followed a strictly defined process, at least that was the way it was taught to me. It started with a personal experience from a presenter, had a series of defined necessary steps, and involved finding a metaphor in the middle that was emblematic of the experience. This became a powerfully enriching process for me. Each reflection helped me define, in a "slow-cooker" fashion, a different way of looking at my own experience and the world around me. I remember once in my third year sitting in my car at an intersection perplexed by an issue at work. Suddenly I realized I was using the TR process to examine my problem.

My group was in the early days of using the program then called Theological Education by Extension (TEE). The Rev. Bill Dols was the mentor of that group. He was a very strong proponent of laity education, with five EfM groups going at one time. We used homely yellow books with plastic bindings and everyone was in the same year. During a conversation at the time of graduation, one member of the group, an engineer, stated that he had never been comfortable with the TR process, having no notion of how to come up with a metaphor. Finding metaphors is not so much a learned skill, I realized, but a way of thinking, maybe a left brain/right brain kind of thing. The training network—those who regularly train mentors—is the most intellectually creative group of people I have ever been around. They began to develop other methods for TR. Soon the Dilemma Method was created, which directly addressed the problem of using metaphors. Using a chart, much like a financial ledger, with assets and deficits in separate columns, the process worked well for folks who were more linear thinkers.

With each new method came a specific outline of how it was to be utilized. I recall being trained as a mentor, experiencing anxiety about following each process completely and not adding or leaving anything out. As I started as a trainer, I was surprised with how much animosity some mentors had about the various methods of leading TRs: some openly rebelled against using the methodology at all in their groups. I had complete confidence that the process worked, but it was not working for some. So I went back over the theological reflection process. I remember thinking about the IAGO acronym. It hit me that this was a process, not unique to theological reflection, and not unique to academia. I began to tell my training groups, "You know, this theological thing you think is so foreign is something you use all the time! Say you go to a movie with some friends and after the movie, y'all go get coffee or a glass of wine. What do you do? You talk about the film, maybe a scene that made an impression. What was there about it that made it stick out? What was comfortable about it, what was uncomfortable? Why?" There was always a palpable exhalation in the room. "But, but, what about all the steps?," someone would ask. "Well," I would respond, "do they help you get where you want the group to go? If the steps are getting in the way, did you really need them? Now, don't get me wrong," I added, "the process, the basic structure works, absolutely."

I wonder if the theological reflection process as we experience it in EfM would have taken hold if it had been introduced in a less liturgical church. Form and structure have been such a critical element in Episcopal worship. We take the prayer book and its forms of worship with utmost sincerity. Changes, big and small in our services, are done with careful deliberation. So when we talk about being careful with the steps of theological reflections, we're very familiar with the concept. Steps and their order matter, and process is essential. Yet who cannot thrill at the energy that happens with the appearance of the Holy Spirit in music and preaching, and the power of the words in the Eucharist. Well-done reflections, like well-done services, fill us with that sense of presence.

The natural world brings systems and structures: the order of life. And the supernatural brings the presence of the Spirit. When the two are in balance, the Church and our reflections are at their best. All structure and no Spirit is rote, lifeless, and without energy. All Spirit and no structure is formless, chaotic, and without resolution. Our goal in worship, in reflection, and in life actually, is to bring the two together.

When we combine natural and supernatural, we invite the unexpected. And we must have the humility and the courage to hold onto that tension. Making room for the Spirit is a risky proposition. "What if it all falls apart? What if I see myself losing control of the group?" It's been my overwhelming experience that we have to walk to the edge to give the Holy Spirit space to come in. Of course, we do have to know what we're talking about; that's why we study and practice. And yes, we have to let go, but maintain the essential structure at the same time.

Here I was, realizing that leaning heavily on process was helping inexperienced mentors find necessary structure, but that it was also getting in the way. I wanted to help mentors break out of the "process is the most important thing" box. I began to wonder if I wasn't a TR heretic. I wanted the mentors to experience leading reflections with a broad brush, not a long, complicated recipe. But was I going against the accepted line of training? Then, the

Reading and Reflection Guide came out. Here it was, in black and white, the way I had been explaining it, only now it was adapted, not IAGO, but IECA—Identify, Explore, Connect, and Apply. Much of the same idea but more in line with the TR process developed over all these years. To this day, I still spend an hour or so with foundation training groups going through "TR101" and I still hear the sighs of relief and the nods of understanding. More and more mentors are comfortable in leading conversational TRs without six pages of newsprint. And they realize they need more facility with the process, not less.

I participated in my first theological reflection forty-five years ago. I have seen it adapted in seminary small-group seminars and I have used it myself with junior high school youth groups, using episodes from *The Simpsons* TV show. I would say it's not following every step of every method. It's not how long or how short the reflection is, it's not even if you think you got to the end or not. The most important part is that you can see/feel the energy that the event is engendering, and the "aha's" that come from that energy—that imperceptible energy that the group creates when it is so clear that the Holy Spirit is present. It may be beyond my ability to describe it, but I certainly have experienced it.

During The Episcopal Church's General Convention in 2003, when Gene Robinson was certified to be the bishop of New Hampshire, I spent time going around the floor to the deputations (I was a deputy from Virginia). I'd introduce myself as a trainer in the EfM program and said I was taking a very informal survey. "How many of you have taken or are taking EfM?" Certainly a few deputations looked at me as if I had crawled out from under a rock, but many, many hands went up in the affirmative. I thought to myself then, this program has changed the very nature of this Church. Learning in community, traditions, history, and theology created a vocabulary to grow in the Spirit. Charlie Winters once said that he hoped his educational program for the laity might reach 2,000 people. Little did he know that it would be a major player in empowering the laity of the Church.

ADMINISTERING EfM WITHIN GOD'S STORY

The Story Through Numbers[1]

Joshua D. Booher

Managing the budget of a self-sustaining program in changing times while making sure funding does not stand in the way of accessing the program is a dance for the EfM staff. Booher, EfM's associate director, has been navigating these waters as a staff member since 2014 even as he continues his ministry as mentor and trainer.

The first thing to understand about Education for Ministry (EfM) is that it is a program, in a center (Beecken Center), in a school (the School of Theology), in a university (the University of the South). As such, the EfM budget is not completely independent and must work as a part of the Beecken Center's budget, which must work as part of the seminary's budget, which must finally work as part of the university's overall budget. Therefore, events in distal parts of the university can, and do, affect the EfM budget.

Another consideration for the annual budget is that EfM is generally required to fully fund itself. It does not receive operational funding from the Beecken Center, seminary, university, or any of the dioceses. As a result, all of its overhead costs have to primarily be covered by registration fees, training fees, and diocesan contracts.

In any given year, none of these sources of income is guaranteed. EfM estimates the budget based on current trends. The

---

1. This article is a response to questions that are frequently asked of the program. It is not meant to be a comprehensive look at the finances of the EfM program.

estimations are further complicated by the proposed budgets being due early in the year (Jan/Feb) for a fiscal year that runs July to June. A lot can change in that five-to-six-month gap.

COVID-19 is a recent example. It arrived in March 2020 after the budget was submitted but before the fiscal year began in July. When the country shut down, many of our groups did not renew as they were waiting to be able to once again meet face to face. This change impacted the registration numbers, the number of books that were needed, and the revenue required for training. Further complicating matters, the previous year's annual budget is only half completed when the next budget is submitted. In estimating the budget, we work closely with an annual budget that ends a year before the new budget takes effect. Each year, the staff does their best to calculate a reasonable budget to keep the program operating.

The earliest that I have been able to definitively document a registration fee was the 1979–1980 cycle. At that time, the EfM registration fee was $200 per year. Participants were able to pay their registration fee in two installments (fall and spring). In today's terms, that $200 fee is equivalent to $866.55.[2] As a self-supporting program at the university, EfM has lost $500 in financial power per participant over the past forty-five years. This financial constriction creates a balancing act challenge. On the one hand, EfM has to raise tuition enough to cover the overhead costs. On the other hand, it needs to keep fees low enough to make the program affordable for the typical person wishing to enroll. This is not always easy.

The decision to stop providing texts free of charge—the yearly texts and interludes books—to the participants was another challenge. Several factors went into the decision to require participants to purchase their own texts in addition to the enrollment fee. First, EfM had been receiving requests for years to provide e-books as an option. Second, the printing business changed

---

2. "Inflation Calculator," Federal Reserve Bank of Minneapolis, accessed August 5, 2024, https://www.minneapolisfed.org/about-us/monetary-policy/inflation-calculator.

with the onset of the COVID-19 lockdowns. Supply chains were impacted, costs rose for the printing supplies, and many printing houses closed. As a result, book costs rose sharply and lag times became very long. (One of our Year Four books was backordered for eighteen months and we never received the shipment. EfM had to send participants e-books in place of the physical texts.) Subsequently, as prices rose for producing physical books, the publishers stopped offering discounts. This essentially doubled the cost EfM paid for texts. In response to the rising costs and the inability of the program to guarantee obtaining the texts in a timely fashion, the decision was made to stop providing the texts as part of the registration fee.

There were several benefits to this decision. First, it allowed the participants to purchase the texts in any format they wanted. They could buy e-books on the device of their choice. If they preferred physical texts and wanted to save money they could borrow the texts or buy used copies. Many participants began buying their texts early in the summer to get a "jump start" on the next year's readings.

To help offset the new cost of the texts, we reduced the registration fee by the amount we were formerly spending for texts. This essentially passed all of our savings back to the participants. From the participants' point of view, however, the cost of EfM had gone up: the price they were actually paying for the texts was significantly higher than the corresponding reduction in registration fees.

Most financial areas of the budget are primarily funded by participant registration fees and are generally hard to untangle. One area that can be fairly easily separated is the cost of mentor training. Before COVID-19, these costs included trainer travel, honorarium, and incidentals. At that time, EfM had the ability to underwrite some of the mentors' training costs. Once again, however, COVID-19 impacted EfM's standard practices. When local conference centers re-opened after COVID-19 shutdowns, their costs had risen dramatically due to their reduction in bookings as well as their increased operational costs. As a result of conference center fee increases, EfM's costs to host training sessions more than doubled. In effect, EfM was no longer able to underwrite any of the mentor training costs. Being aware of the difficulties these increased training fees created, we are looking for ways to make face-to-face mentor training more affordable.

One last question that often arises in EfM is how to help people who cannot afford to pay the yearly fee. When I was mentoring a face-to-face group, I dealt with issues many other mentors faced with their participants: medically disabled people living on $5,000 a year; elderly people living on retirement income; young people working a first job while paying student debts; and so on. I approached this issue from multiple fronts. I reached out to former participants who I knew valued their time in EfM and asked if they would be willing to donate money for scholarships to people with need. They all agreed to do so. During the discussion with these donors, I established some parameters—gifts were anonymous and donors would not be asked to contribute sequentially. I also went "old school" and, at each gathering, I placed a basket in the middle of the table asking for donations for the scholarship fund. Additionally, I asked the parish's vestry to put a line item in the annual budget for scholarships if they valued the role EfM played in their parish. My final note is that I never asked any participant to "prove" their need.

In closing, the one great challenge facing the EfM program now is the number of registered participants. During the first five years I worked for the program, EfM's enrollment was declining at a rate of about 200 participants per year. For the enrollment cycle after COVID-19 hit (2020–21), the program lost more than one third of its participants and has not been able to increase its enrollment since then. This statistic is not unique to EfM. EfM's declining numbers mirror those of The Episcopal Church as a whole. In 2014, The Episcopal Church had an average Sunday attendance of approximately 634,000.[3] By 2022, the average

---

3. "The State of the Episcopal Church in 2022," Graphs About Religion, accessed August 15, 2024, https://www.graphsaboutreligion.com/p/the-state-of-the-episcopal-church.

Sunday attendance was down to 373,000.[4] While these figures are concerning, there is hope. Both EfM and The Episcopal Church have a lot to offer. EfM provides a way for our faith to impact our daily lives. Through study and reflection, we grow into who God is calling us to be. EfM allows us to model a life that other people want for themselves!

---

4. Ibid.

The Evolution of Training Mentors and Trainers in EfM

Elsa S. Bakkum

Education for Ministry has long recognized the gifts of those involved in the program. EfM's training network is a group of accredited leaders who work with mentors to deliver the program. Calling on her experience as an EfM mentor, diocesan coordinator, and trainer, Bakkum was an effective associate director for training for twelve years using the strengths of EfM trainers themselves, as well as those of outside professionals, to equip and empower the training network. Her leadership encouraged diversity and support to enhance the learning and spiritual formation of EfM communities.

The development of the Education for Ministry (EfM) program is the story of an amazing gathering of forces from which the curriculum for the training of trainers and mentors evolved. Challenging training sessions, often over a period of many days of work in far-flung locations, required long-distance travel. They had an initiatory quality that kept trainers up to date, sharp, and challenged.

Collectively, the training community has driven much of the creativity and audacity that coalesced into this unique approach—moving theological thinking from the exclusive domain of clergy, religious vocations, and the academy into the domain of all people. During my thirty years as mentor, coordinator, trainer, and staff member in charge of EfM training, I collected historical testimonies and will include many of those stories in the words of the EfM founders and leaders as well as summaries of training practices and traditions.

In the Beginning

In September of 1973, the Rev. Dr. Charles Winters, professor of theology at the School of Theology, circulated a proposal for a program of Theological Education by Extension (TEE). He obtained a grant from The Episcopal Church Foundation and launched EfM in 1975. The proposed program sought to develop lay and clergy alike who were capable of thinking theologically, not just about God, Jesus Christ, and the Holy Spirit in Christianity, but also about the impact of faith in one's everyday life experiences. In 2019, Rick Brewer, a trainer of trainers, explained, "Winters didn't care if someone was Manichean, he cared that we understand what that is, notice if we have a Manichean view, and, if we are willing, to search and find answers to our own questions."

The Very Rev. Urban T. Holmes, dean of the School of Theology at the time, actively participated in this new program's learning cycle of "Experiencing, Imagining, Conceptualizing, Judging, and Action." It is strikingly parallel to the four current movements of theological reflection: Identify, Explore, Connect, and Apply.[1] The practice calls for stopping in the midst of everyday life in order to make space and time for a deep level of reflection. Training and theological reflection (TR) follow this lead in a way similar to the approach of parables—as invitations to create space for faithful attentiveness in order to step into new considerations and perspectives (mystery), rather than immediate morals or conclusions.[2]

Flower Ross joined the new EfM staff in 1976. She was the first to envision how to train EfM mentors and approached the

---

1. *Reading and Reflection Guide*, vol. A (2013).
2. Maxine O'Dell Gernert, "Receptive Spirituality in Urban Tigner Holmes III: An Approach for Spiritual Renewal in the Ministry," 1993.

task with the idea of "not knowing." Ross had been trained and accredited by the Association for Creative Change, an organization that was involved in training and accrediting trainers in human relations, organizational development, and conflict management.

The Episcopal Church in the late 1960s participated in leadership development programs that significantly grew out of what became known as the Human Potential Movement. These groups directly or indirectly drew from the work of Kurt Lewin, Abraham Maslow, William Shultz, Paulo Freire, and others as guides for their small group experiences.

Ross knew that the program had to have a way for people to form themselves into a group with trust before they would be willing to talk about their own lives. She had worked with storytelling before and thought that such a process could help develop trust among the members. These stories became spiritual autobiographies where participants could focus their attention on the parts of their everyday lives and how they were related to their spirit, demonstrating that reflecting on very ordinary decisions could indeed be fruitful. She found that using a metaphor helped with this process.

Sissie Wile, former director of training, upon Flower's death noted, "The models Flower designed for training were creative and based on principles that have grounded EfM for more than thirty years. The emphasis on having trained mentors to lead groups has given participants confidence in EfM because of its consistency and accountability."

According to EfM director Edward O. de Bary, Ross developed the original model for theological reflection in EfM. This included three sources of meaning: Action, Tradition, and Position, inspired by theologian Bernard Lonergan and the work of the Rev. Harry Pritchard. Ross's travel to Nicaragua, Western Canada, Alaska, and Australia led to the addition of the fourth source—Culture.

The process of engaging the sources of meaning followed the action/reflection practice of "Do, Look, Think, Plan," also called EIAG (Experience, Identify, Analyze, and Generalize):

Do. Action or activity
Look. Identification
Think. Examination or exploration
Plan. Generalization and application to the future[3]

Similar sequences that informed the present EfM Model of Four Movements are:

EIAG	EfM Four Movements	Laurie Green	Bernard Lonergan	Bernard Lonergan via Kenneth Melchin	Urban Holmes
Experience	Identify	Experience	Be attentive	Experience	Experiencing
Identify	Explore	Explore	Be intelligent	Understand	Imagining
Analyze	Connect	Reflect	Be reasonable	Judge	Conceptualizing
Generalize	Apply	Respond	Be responsible/ Be in Love	Decide	Judging and Acting

Other organizations that emphasized experiential learning and were heavy influences on EfM training were Life Training via John de Beer and the Mid Atlantic Training Centers (MATC). EfM, throughout its life, has been built on adult education principles, especially in being learner centered, valuing the life experience of the participant. Subsequent directors of training in the EfM program (with various titles) were John de Beer, Gordon Okunsanya, Gail Jones, Liz Workman, Johnna Camp, Rick Brewer, Sissie Wile, myself, and Beth Cavey.

Competencies

The concept of competency began to be used for trainers as the intern trainer process was implemented. The first mentors of intern trainers used five areas of competency to help assess the

---

3. *Common Lessons and Supporting Materials (CLSM)* (2006), 16-5.

new trainer's readiness: Theological Reflection, Group Skills, EfM Program, Design, and Self-awareness. (Rick Brewer, 2012).

In March of 2012, a task force of trainers created a list of six trainer competencies—proficiency in the attitude; knowledge and skills expected of an EfM mentor; preparedness for training events; establishes and maintains an appropriate learning environment; administers training events and completes effective evaluations; and contributes to the community of trainers. These competencies and their related subpoints guide EfM staff in inviting and accrediting new EfM trainers of mentors.

Facilitation

Training in the EfM context focuses on the facilitation of small groups for mentoring EfM seminar groups and leading training groups. Facilitation is an underappreciated skill in the Church and in the larger world. Yet, facilitation is key to holding space for a small group in which to function cooperatively and to promote learning.

Content and Process

Training in EfM focuses on the distinction between content and process: "Most discussion topics emphasize the content—topics [that] are 'there and then' oriented. They are thoughts about something external and do not involve us directly at that moment. In focusing on the group process, we look at what our group is doing in the 'here and now,' how it is working in the sense of its present procedures and organization."[4]

Training Practices—The Gold Fish Bowl

Following the theological inspirations of Lonergan and Holmes, EfM training has always included opportunities to learn from the

---

4. *Common Lessons and Supporting Materials* (CLSM), 16–18, 2005.

experiences within the training context. One of these is a process known as the Gold Fish Bowl, which places trainer candidates into three levels for TR: facilitators, practice trainers, and trainer staff/coaches. The process was meant to distinguish the roles of mentors and trainers and was followed by discussion to encourage learning from the experience. This practice has been called debriefing, processing, reflecting back, learning from, feedback, and being on the hot seat. The purpose of these opportunities was to notice what happened, process the experience, and name the learnings.

Learning Experiences

Sometimes, the space of the Gold Fish Bowl and debriefing did not promote learning. A system of judgment and hierarchy crept into the EfM climate under which some trainers and mentors unnecessarily suffered during their time in the "hot seat." Some prospective trainers became alienated and lost to the program. The development of various theories of positive psychology and recognition of the shadow side of the intense groups of the '70s and '80s encouraged training staffs to shift priorities to more collegiality and respect for the expertise that mentors and trainers brought with them into their first encounters with EfM. In 2012, under the guidance of Bud Holland and Jim Papile, EfM training adopted the term "Learning Experiences" to describe group processes conducted within foundational trainings of trainers. This replaced the Gold Fish Bowl process and was subsequently adopted.

"Plan Tight and Hang Loose"

Early on, the importance of trainers as facilitators responding in the moment to the needs and learning objectives of mentors led to a mantra of "Plan Tight and Hang Loose." Trainers designed training for the ideal situation, but recognized that a specific group of trainees would often require adjustments to the training outline in order to prioritize learning, as adults vary in their experience and the speed at which they grasp new ideas and processes.

Open Source

From the beginning, materials used for EfM training were freely shared within the EfM community. At first they did not include the designation of an author; however, in recent years this practice has shifted to acknowledging the originators of materials both to recognize the authors and to identify the source for additional information.

Lay and Clergy

While EfM trainers and mentors were made up mostly of clergy at the beginning, there was also a tradition of lay trainers and mentors. As a lay woman, Ross set the precedent as the first training director. EfM is one place in The Episcopal Church where the distinctions between clergy and lay are not always a part of first introductions. Recognition of gifts of leadership, facilitation, and spirituality are highlighted in EfM training experiences.

Conclusion

Many people approach Bible study as an opportunity to learn the "correct" interpretation of passages and "right" theological categories. However, there is no one systematic theology, but rather, new thinking that develops new systems in every generation.

EfM's use of metaphor to universalize life experience or themes discovered in a group pondering over a biblical or historical story makes it possible for groups to speculate, to interact with the elements of the multifaceted metaphor, and to dwell within it until discoveries are grasped. New meaning is discovered rather than recited, and new life choices are unveiled whether they come from difficult life experiences such as guilt, anger, and frustration, or from joyous experiences of love, discovery, and freedom.

Future Training Implications

Elizabeth Cavey

EfM is in constant transition, incorporating new core texts and ways of connecting. In order to empower mentors and to support them during times of transition, EfM training must also evolve. Cavey, currently serving as EfM's trainer in residence for mentor empowerment, describes changes that have been made to training procedures and outlines possibilities for the future.

In January 2024, I began my dream job working as the trainer in residence for mentor empowerment for EfM. I built upon the extraordinary work done by my predecessors, especially Elsa Bakkum. These leaders tapped into the wisdom of the EfM community to build a network of gifted, dedicated trainers.

My position shifted its focus this year. Rather than only focusing on the quality of trainers, we are now focused on what mentors need to feel fully empowered to deliver this program to seminar groups throughout the country and the world. Quality training is a large portion of this focus, along with building community, as we imagine the future of EfM.

Quality Training

EfM offers a high-quality training experience. We are continually evolving our ability to help trainees experience learning rather than passively receiving learning. Our emphasis is on experience and broad reflection—not just theological reflection—and we encourage mentors to integrate their learning into their ministry.

The heart of our training philosophy is experiential learning—incorporating what we study into how we do our work, reflect on our experience, and adjust to meet evolving needs. This emphasis on experience and reflection creates an atmosphere of mutual discovery and support, and mentor training feels more like a retreat that renews ministry rather than a test to be passed.

Mentor accreditation is also being reimagined. We are looking to refocus our approach to better resemble continuing education models where once accreditation is received, it is maintained through extended formation experiences, workshops, and webinars.

Building Community: Mentor Training

One aspect of mentor training is how quickly community forms within the group. Each training cohort is unique and builds its own sense of group-self with the trainer. We are working to create more opportunities for community building beyond annual training. Diocesan coordinators, trainers, and other mentors can play a role in these efforts. I dream of a mentor community that continues to grow, expand, and diversify in ways that support the growth of this community.

Building Community: Communications

Reflections is the email group for EfM mentor communications. It is used to share resources and ask questions about mentoring. It is a tremendous resource and it is my personal mission to transform this vehicle into something enriching and uplifting for all mentors.

EfM Week x Week hit the scene in fall 2023. Karen Byers and I co-host weekly videos with guests that address subjects that can help mentors facilitate seminar groups. The videos are posted online in a place where mentors can access them and refer back to them.

Online information sessions began as an introduction to the new online training platform, rolled out in early 2024. These will continue as monthly sessions open to all mentors to address mentor needs, updates to the program, and opportunities to build relationships with fellow mentors. Going forward these sessions will be posted online in a place mentors can access.

The Future of Training

In the years before COVID-19, the majority of training happened at retreat spaces around the country. We quickly adapted to online training during the COVID-19 isolation years. Post-COVID-19 is a time of creatively balancing the ease and accessibility of online training with the benefits of embodied presence at onsite training.

Going forward all training will have an aspect of online study before group learning. This past year everyone experienced the "Mentor Training and Discernment" foundational online module. One of the benefits of this standard online study tool is that we all now have a common language, which improves our communication, builds community, and enhances what trainers can do in group training. Everyone returns to the same starting point, checks their supplies and gear, and goes on their unique mentor journey forward. We will continue to expand the online offerings to better support all training.

Being mindful of costs however—in time, money, and accessibility—online training will be a major part of EfM's future. We continue to strive to balance the administrative demands with the flexibility desired by mentors.

The future of training all comes down to balance between the needs of individual mentors and the need for support systems that can care for the whole of the program. You will continue to find me performing this balancing act in service to this beautiful program, God willing, for years to come.

The Diocesan Coordinator: A Continual Calling of Volunteer Leaders

Cynthia C. Hargis

Diocesan coordinators are the liaisons between the bishop's office, local mentors, and the Beecken Center—the administrative center for EfM at the University of the South. Hargis, currently serving as EfM's diocesan relations coordinator, provides training and administrative support for coordinators, mentors, and staff. She creates community with her warm hospitality and spiritual insights.

"Then I heard the voice of the Lord saying, 'Whom shall I send? And who will go for us?'" (Isaiah 6:8)

I came to work for the Education for Ministry (EfM) program not really knowing what it meant to be called or what constituted ministry. I had accepted another position at the University of the South when I saw a job announcement for secretary to the field director of the EfM program. The job offered more money, so I applied. On July 1, 1991, I began my work as secretary to the Rev. Dr. Edward O. de Bary.

Edward O. de Bary spent about a third of his time planning trips and traveling to Episcopal Church dioceses to support those that already sponsored EfM or to represent the program to those that did not. He would try to visit four to six dioceses each time he traveled. He attended diocesan conventions and General Conventions. He met with bishops, other diocesan staff, mentors and their groups, EfM trainers, and clergy in parish settings. Sometimes coordinators or others would plan special events and invite Ed to speak.

As part of the contractual relationship with dioceses, Ed worked with the bishops to appoint coordinators to administer the program and support the EfM mentors and participants in their dioceses. There were approximately eighty-seven coordinators volunteering their time for the program when I arrived in 1991. Ed was responsible for recruiting, training, and supporting those coordinators. Ed managed the diocesan, parish, and international contracts until he passed the diocesan and parish contract work to me along with the title of EfM diocesan coordinator.

Ed's title eventually became EfM program director and, with him, I learned more about the program's structure, systems, curriculum, theological reflection, training methods, and constituents. I learned more about The Episcopal Church and how the dioceses are structured and operate. Ed invited me to work on a coordinators' training conference staff with him. His administrative duties, oversight of the curriculum, and travel left him little time to develop materials and resources for our coordinators or to offer them enough support.

After working with Ed on that coordinators' training, I realized how important the coordinators' work is to the health and growth of EfM. They show up steadily when needed and called. They come from all walks of life, from many professions, and with a wonderful blending of talents, gifts, experiences, creativity, and desire to serve. Many of them are EfM graduates. Most coordinators bring a deep love for the program, which they want to share with as many people as possible. They want to do their absolute best work for the program, their dioceses, their churches, their families, and their communities. Many say their lives have been transformed by EfM and they delight in making that possible for others. So, they go about their work, doing the seemingly little things with great love and great attention to detail.

Today, we have eighty sponsoring dioceses that have been faithful to the program since the late 1980s when Ed sold contracts to those dioceses. Approximately fifty of the eighty-three coordinators we have today are also mentors. We have had as many as ninety-two contracts during my tenure. We also have several parish contracts in place for groups that do not have a diocesan sponsor.

It took several years before I understood the depth and breadth of the calling to the work that would change my life and spiritual walk as it has done for countless others. I realized that the coordinators needed an advocate whose job it would be to recruit, develop training and resources, train, and support their ministry. Those duties were added to my portfolio.

When I became the leader of our coordinators, a manual for coordinators and a coordinator job description were in place. As I learned with and from our coordinators, I expanded and adapted both. The coordinator position is an unpaid volunteer leadership ministry. The coordinator's purpose is to help the program and diocese promote EfM within the diocese, to act as liaison alongside the sponsoring diocese and EfM staff, and to serve as a resource for mentors, groups, and newcomers in the diocese.

We look for people with strong organization, management, promotional, hospitality, and communication skills. Experience in EfM and knowledge of diocesan organizational structure are important. Knowledge of EfM's curriculum, methods, structures, and procedures benefits the program, diocese, our constituents, and the coordinator. People with these qualifications and characteristics are vital to helping staff maintain the quality of the program and promote it across the diocese. Diocesan coordinators are instrumental in helping us recruit, encourage, and support mentors and their groups.

We ask coordinators to look for opportunities to publicize the program in appropriate media in their locales. They may make presentations at diocesan conventions, parish gatherings, ministry fairs, and other functions. Many of them reserve booth space at diocesan conventions and display the EfM textbooks and brochures so that newcomers can get a taste of the program. Some coordinators introduce the program by planning and hosting onsite introductory sessions for newcomers or Zoom gatherings that include new folks, EfM mentors, participants, and graduates.

Many coordinators help prospects discern whether EfM is right for them at this time in life. Coordinators help newcomers understand that EfM is not Bible study, but a regimen of reading, reflection, preparation, and participation.

We ask that coordinators stay in touch with their mentors and their groups. The coordinator may be called on to help search for new group members when participants graduate or leave so that the group can remain viable. They may be helpful in locating a new mentor when the incumbent mentor steps away or retires. As a primary point of contact in the diocese alongside diocesan staff, the coordinator often helps newcomers find and connect with existing EfM groups. Some coordinators host Zoom gatherings where mentors and participants can come together to support one another.

As we slowly return to our pre-COVID-19 training schedules, we will invite veteran coordinators to help us host multiple mentor training events. The coordinator will be onsite for the entire training and will handle registration; collect registration fees; communicate with and pay the training venue; and work with venue staff to set up training spaces. The coordinator will welcome trainees and trainers upon their arrival. They will help people find their lodgings, meeting space, and worship spaces. The coordinator will help with any eventualities and emergencies.

During my thirty-three years with the program, we have been able to recruit able, willing people, many of whom I believe felt called, just as I do, to do this work and do it well. The call to do this work well and in a way that is worthy of these volunteer leaders prompted me to spend four years in graduate school at night while working full time for EfM. I spent those years learning what it means to be a leader who knows that in order to have followers, you need to care for them, and you do everything you can to equip them—listen, pause, gather data, analyze data, reflect on the data, and then respond. I also help them find sources of help and teach them that flexibility and a sense of humor are required. As a team, we plan well, we hang loose, and we are kind to ourselves and each other. This is our motto.

Working with our sponsoring bishops and diocesan staff members has also been a pleasure over the years. They are faithful in their support of the program, renewing their sponsorship year after year. As I write, this year's sponsorship fees are arriving steadily each day. The bishops and their staff are responsive, gracious, supportive, and they value the EfM program. The conversations, the correspondence I have shared with them, and the testimonials I have read as they honor mentors, graduates, and coordinators make this very clear. One bishop wrote to thank us for "the gift and blessing that is EfM." We are incredibly grateful to our diocesan partners for helping us continue this important work.

There have been many changes and challenges while I have worked for EfM. I have worked with several directors: Edward O. de Bary, Johnna Camp, Sissie Wile, Karen Meridith, and now Kevin Goodman. Each leader has brought new ideas and faced shifts in technology, systems, curricula, policies, procedures, finances, staff, and so on. We are celebrating fifty years of EfM because these leaders and a very resilient, loving, and dedicated staff have been willing and able to adapt, learn, grow, and continue to lean into change. Many of our EfM family—mentors, participants, trainers, coordinators, and alumni—have also remained willing to weather change alongside us.

I am encouraged that our present executive director has included EfM staff, diocesan coordinators, diocesan staff members, trainers, mentors, participants, graduates, and the School of Theology staff and faculty in planning for the next fifty years. Task forces on communication, training, curriculum, new course offerings, administration, technology, and more have worked together to examine and reimagine every aspect of the program. We have formed cohorts and teams to provide support, training, and encouragement for the people who deliver this program. All this change has been fast paced, exciting, and a bit scary. It has also strengthened and encouraged a faithful, steadfast, and enthusiastic EfM family for the years ahead.

    I am excited about our return to a new and beautiful space in the recently renovated Hamilton Hall on the School of Theology's campus. I am excited about our upcoming EfM curriculum with a wider range of offerings. I am excited that we will have better technology in place that will grow with us and allow us to learn and teach in new ways. I am excited that we are working together as an entire community to hold each other accountable and to discover better ways of managing our work, sharing information and resources, and training folks. I know that the cooks, recipes, and ingredients of our products may continue to change, but I believe the flavor, texture, and aroma will remain tasty and filling for many. Finally, I am grateful to have spent such a large part of my life working and learning alongside all of these people. Thank you for answering the call to this important ministry. Blessings and peace to all.

Education for Ministry in the Diocese of North Carolina: This Coordinator's Journey

Marcia Houck Moore

> Dioceses that support EfM have a diocesan coordinator, but the job of coordinator is not identical from one diocese to another. Moore has been the coordinator for the Diocese of North Carolina for nine years and was the first to offer an onsite training once the COVID-19 restrictions were lifted. Moore shares what the coordinator journey has been like for her.

The path of the establishment and growth of Education for Ministry (EfM) in the Diocese of North Carolina and my own story as participant, mentor, and coordinator in the program have parallels that echo every odyssey, every journey, every search for meaning, purpose, and belonging known to man.

Restlessness. Uncertainty. Exploration. Questioning. Searching. Doubting. Discerning. Risk-taking. Identifying. Committing. Discovering. Awakening. Growing. Opposition. Success. Hills. Valleys. Plateaus. Community.

I was officially appointed to the position of EfM coordinator for the Diocese of North Carolina on September 1, 2016, by our bishop suffragan, the Rt. Rev. Anne E. Hodges-Copple. I experienced this appointment as a great compliment and honor. What I want readers to know is that those who came before me set the tone and values that established the EfM program in North Carolina with its foundation in community-building and support. My predecessor and dear friend, Shelley Kappauf—one of the original co-mentors of the first EfM group at St. Andrew's in Greensboro, North Carolina—accepted the coordinator position from the Rev. Celeste Johnson Geldreich in 2005. This story begins and continues with gratitude and grace.

Let me start at the beginning of this story.

The first 200 years in the life of the Diocese of North Carolina were devoted to planting and building new churches, to providing worship, to adapting to the needs of life in a new world, and at one point early on, to rebuilding and maintaining itself. In the years following the revolution, the diocese almost ceased to exist. The Church of England was exceedingly unpopular as it represented the English monarchy with its authority and oppression. The Diocese of North Carolina was not restored until 1817. From that point on, the diocese struggled, survived, struggled more, and grew through the chaos of the Civil War, Reconstruction, Jim Crow, and into our modern era.

EfM was created in 1975 by a small group of faculty at the School of Theology at the University of the South, Sewanee, Tennessee. EfM was carried out into the world and into Episcopal parishes, first in the South, as a means to provide theological education to the laity. The EfM program was received enthusiastically and grew rapidly throughout the United States and eventually internationally, with mentors being trained and certified, and seminar groups springing up in dioceses all over the country.

The Diocese of North Carolina was and is one of the dioceses that participates in the governance of the University of the South. The date of establishment of EfM is assumed to have occurred in the early to mid-1970s. The Revs. John and Tricia de Beer, currently residents of the Diocese of North Carolina, recall that when they came to this state upon leaving Sewanee in the mid-'80s, EfM was alive and well in churches in this diocese.

Education for Ministry was introduced to St. Andrew's in 2004 by the new rector, the Rev. Wendy Billingslea. All of us, including the co-mentors, felt our way along, learning the process of theological reflection together.

It quickly became apparent that one of the great strengths of EfM was how the process of worshiping, learning, and reflecting in a group builds bonded communities of fellowship and faith. It was within this still-new, learning cohort that I was invited to co-mentor a growing EfM program at my church.

That was the first year of my seventeen-year journey as an EfM mentor and co-mentor. There were challenges and victories along the way. There were individuals who struggled with the materials or with each other, some who embraced and loved theological reflection (TR), and some who saw no use for it. There were some who were seeking something not to be found in EfM. What also was revealed to me was the great importance of scholarly scripture study—the great sweep of Church tradition—and how the whole process works in and through the Holy Spirit. It brought me to the understanding of the strength of relationships formed in those sacred communities; connections that will not be broken. It was through discernment, prayer, and grace that, somewhere during those seventeen years, I awakened to the awareness that EfM is my calling, my vocation, and my ministry.

To this day, I cannot name the sense I had that serving as coordinator for the diocese was what I should, and would, eventually be doing. Again—a nudge? A call? An awakening? As life for all of us moves through its expected phases and stages and when Shelley communicated she would not be doing the job of coordinator indefinitely, my immediate response was to let her know I would be very happy if it was passed on to me.

In early 2016, I began "apprenticing" as a co-coordinator with Shelley, shadowing her as she planned and hosted mentor trainings, communicated with mentors throughout the diocese, and helped me become familiar with some of the administrative tasks. In September 2016, I was appointed to the position of coordinator. It felt like a natural fit and I was thrilled to serve in what

I believed (and still believe) is the way I've been called to help folks find themselves as God's own, and in the process, furthering God's kingdom among us.

There was no gradual easing into the job. Immediately, I jumped in as planner and host of a mentor training scheduled for that same month. I think this is why a colleague once described this job as being a "holy party planner!"

The established expectation in the diocese was that mentor trainings were scheduled twice a year and almost always were held at a local retreat center run by Franciscans, which was comfortable, accessible, and welcoming. We always had two, and often three classes, running simultaneously and we welcomed mentors from all over North Carolina, as well as from a number of surrounding dioceses and states.

Having the sole responsibility for this mentor training was daunting and, at the time, the biggest part of my role as coordinator. There were many hats to wear, usually several at one time (a fine metaphor for a TR), involving the tasks of scheduling, communicating, and juggling, all while being flexible to changing needs. The overriding priority was to be sure there was an environment that invited all the elements of hospitality, renewal, learning, networking, and inspiration for the participants and trainers. An additional priority as coordinator was to establish closer relationships with the mentors in the diocese, as well as with diocesan staff with whom I would be working.

I knew some of the mentors simply from their participation in trainings, but it was important to convey to them that I would be helping and supporting them in their jobs and with any problems that would arise. This required establishing familiarity and trust—my goal in all of my interactions. As the EfM program has evolved, this aspect of my job has become an all-encompassing value.

I'm constantly aware that the active support of EfM from our bishops has been an ongoing gift and blessing. In recent years, our diocese has identified formation as one of its program priorities. With the help of Jenny Beaumont (also an EfM trainer and mentor), our missioner for adult and lifelong formation, we have been able to hold up EfM as a cornerstone of adult formation and have promoted its accessibility and visibility in programming. Becoming familiar and friendly with diocesan staff has been invaluable, in terms of receiving their help with setting up online registration and payment systems for training and with communication in the form of publicizing and marketing. As a result, I've been able to establish an EfM page on our diocesan website that contains announcements, schedules, and information about available seminar groups, along with contact information for EfM staff, diocesan staff, and mentors.

As mentioned, Jenny has been a tireless advocate in our diocese for the foundational role EfM plays in adult formation. During the pandemic, it became clear there was a need to find a way to keep mentors connected to EfM and each other. I started hosting periodic Zoom-based forums for mentors, and in the last several years, Jenny has been instrumental in helping expand the frequency and scope of those get-togethers. They are now held every other month.

I realized early on that, in my role as helper and point person for "all things EfM" in my diocese, I should be well informed and armed with an understanding of administrative processes, emerging technologies, protocols, and expectations.

Once again, Jenny stepped up, offering her technical know-how as a great resource and filling in where I'm not as strong. She has set up a Dropbox platform just for EfM mentors in our diocese that contains everything a mentor could possibly need or want: prayers, liturgies, forms, schedules, articles, contacts, links, and on and on. Mentors can download documents for their own use and add their own contributions.

The number of seminar groups in this diocese has gradually declined over the past twenty years. This is partially due to attrition; partially due to changes in peoples' expectations, commitment, or obligations; a general drop in church membership; and most recently due to the cultural changes brought about by the COVID-19 pandemic. Even though this is a nationwide phenomenon, we are committed to stopping it or reversing it.

Consequently, recruiting new EfM participants, new mentors, and establishing new seminar groups becomes even more important. I've had to learn new marketing skills and strategies while encouraging a healthy community among current mentors. I promote all the programs and features that can attract new enthusiasts and provide renewal and retention for experienced participants and mentors. In this vein, I have tried to be an ambassador for EfM, talking by phone, Zoom, and email with individuals considering joining groups or being certified. I visit churches in the diocese and speak with groups, hoping to communicate information and share my own love for the program. I have plans for the coming holidays to bring mentors together for a social gathering that will provide a reminder of our close and loving connection in spirit, fellowship, and fun. One of my ongoing goals as EfM coordinator is not only to increase numbers of certified mentors and seminar groups, but also to find ways to expand access to our program to all areas of our diocese.

At this point in my story, I can't go any further without holding up the individual who has faithfully walked beside me on this journey—Cynthia Hargis, EfM's diocesan relations and online coordinator. Her sharing, teaching, supporting, encouraging, and loving ministry has been my light when there was darkness. Cindy's faith and devotion to her vocation has been priceless. My advice to coordinators is to remember that she is your starting point and one of the greatest resources you will have.

This fall of 2024, my life in EfM will come full circle as we move into the future. At the end of the 2022–23 year, I stepped away from mentoring an EfM seminar group. Even though I continue as diocesan coordinator, I realize that there are issues, trends, and discussions going on in the greater EfM community that I was missing—those revolving around current curriculum, readings, theology, and procedures. In order to be the best advisor and supporter for mentors, I need to be "in the loop." I'm so excited to be a participant in an online group made up of trainers and coordinators. Once more I will be worshiping, reading, learning, and reflecting in an EfM group and will again have the shared experience of grace and fellowship as I move forward.

We all know that at fifty years, the EfM program has much to celebrate. I'm so grateful for those who have found meaning and belonging in their seeking, for all the lives that have been changed, and for this program that continues to provide spiritual sustenance in a challenging world. We also are aware that our beloved program is at an inflection point, brought about by the realities of economics and culture in that same evolving world. What will bring growth and success? What is not working? What should we embrace? What should we let go?

What we know from EfM itself is that we have all we need: our tradition and wisdom, our culture of sharing and learning, our own positions and experience, and our actions of work and prayer together, led by the Holy Spirit, as we continue to serve as Christ's hands in the world.

Waters Under the Bridge: A Time of Transition

Sissie Wile

Transitions are always challenging but are also full of opportunity and growth. Moving from a long-term director to a new generation of leadership creates changes for a program and staff. During these moments of "already and not yet," it is necessary to take time to honor what is ending and prepare for what's next. Wile, former EfM interim executive director, led the program through the transition with creativity and grace.

In the early 2000s, Education for Ministry (EfM) was transitioning from the leadership of an executive director who had been in place for many years to a new executive director. During that time, I was invited to come to Sewanee, Tennessee, for "a year" (as I told my husband, Fred) to assist the staff in some of the administrative details generated during the changes in leadership. During weekend visits, Fred got to know Sewanee and we developed many friendships; therefore, when I was invited to become the assistant director of training, I accepted, and that one year turned into seven. I was the assistant director for a while and later assumed the role of interim director while still overseeing the training network.

During my employment, I knew that my time in Sewanee would not be permanent because my interests and responsibilities remained in my home state of Mississippi, as my grandchildren lived there. I considered my time in Sewanee as a bridge between one era in EfM and a new one. I wanted to serve in a manner that would contribute to the program; I wanted to keep the "waters" flowing under the bridge.

Being a lifelong learner is a particular characteristic common to everyone in the EfM community. Specifically, mentors and trainers want to provide opportunities for others to explore not only deeper theological topics, but also the practice of reflection. Using small groups as our venue for meeting, mentors and trainers must be aware of the dynamics that help make a small group work effectively.

I have always appreciated the strengths that trainers bring to EfM, including the many skills that they learned in their vocations. For example, trainers skilled in the facilitation of small groups and experiential learning brought those skills to EfM and created mentor training designs that focused on learning in community to reflect on experiences. Richard Rohr affirmed experiential learning in his book, *Falling Upward*: "Faith is not for overcoming obstacles; it is for experiencing them—all the way through.... We do not think ourselves into new ways of living, we live ourselves into new ways of thinking."[1]

With the assumption that new ideas stirring in the "waters" could invigorate the program, professors were invited from the School of Theology and the University of the South in Sewanee to join trainers in the trainings of trainers (ToT) and offer ideas on ethics, spirituality, and current pedagogical methods. From the professional training world, we were introduced to program theories that encouraged self-awareness, such as Appreciative Inquiry, the Enneagram, and Emotional Intelligence.

While there was some concern among trainers that speakers made ToTs more didactic than experiential, they were willing to be exposed to new information and to explore how the various topics could be useful in EfM training. Hopefully, we all learned a little bit more about what characteristics make up our personalities and what buttons push us. As trainers, self-awareness is

---

1. Richard Rohr, *Falling Upward: A Spirituality for the Two Halves of Life* (San Francisco, Jossey-Bass, 2011).

the beginning of understanding how we might grow and deepen our skills.

The practice of organizing periodic EfM task forces began to emerge from the "waters." A task force brought a few trainers together for a brief time to address a given subject. Its work was summarized in a report that could be distributed among trainers so that all trainers could benefit from the creativity of the task force. A common practice up to this time had been to spend time in ToTs working on program development. Using task forces for this purpose could maximize time in ToTs for experiential work.

EfM mentor training had once been a requirement for graduating seminarians, but the EfM staff often heard grumblings from them about the time required to take mentor training. While the seminary wanted future priests to start EfM groups in their parishes, not all priests are suited to be mentors. In response to this, we designed EfM immersion—a one-day introduction to EfM led by trainers. EfM immersion is offered each year during seminary orientation to introduce seminarians to the basics of EfM and invite participants into experiential activities followed by reflection on those activities. Seminarians are encouraged to start EfM groups but are also encouraged to find laypeople who will maintain groups in their parishes. Seminary graduates, both at the School of Theology and in other seminaries, are given scholarships of $100 to be applied to their first mentor training leading to accreditation.

Before the new executive director was hired, the Very Rev. William Stafford, dean of the School of Theology, asked EfM to develop a strategic plan. The Very Rev. Dr. Charles E. Kiblinger was hired in 2007 as a consultant to facilitate the work of the strategic planning committee and to write a final report to be presented to the dean. It would be the job of the new executive director to implement this plan.

Kiblinger oversaw extensive interviews with EfM staff, students, mentors, coordinators, and trainers throughout the country. In the summary of his consultation, he wrote, "I continue to be amazed by the vibrancy of this program throughout the

Church. The average life of church-wide programs is about seven years. This one has lasted more than thirty years. While there are issues that need attention for the future of the program, it continues to enjoy broad support and a stellar reputation." Those words were written in 2007, and in 2025, EfM continues to create and act on its vision for the future.

The deep undercurrent of the "river" was the EfM staff at the School of Theology. Managing diocesan coordinators, registering groups, maintaining accreditation of mentors, distributing materials, and answering scores of questions with grace and hospitality kept the "waters" moving. The vice-chancellor of the university, wondering why I had not hired an interim assistant, asked me, "Do you think you walk on water?" I knew I didn't walk on water, but the team members of the EfM staff assured me that we could keep the "waters" flowing until another director was hired. That person could have the option to choose their own staff. It was one of the greatest gifts in my professional life to work with them!

The EfM community has always drawn creative, passionate, and faithful seekers who are committed to their own spiritual journeys and to being journey partners to others. During the years I was on staff for EfM, the "waters" under the bridge were not always calm; in fact, at times they were troubled. Nevertheless, I believe that EfM, even in troubling times, has been able to see opportunity in chaos and to thrive in an environment that is always open to renewal and greater understanding. I give thanks for the many EfM participants I have met in the United States and around the world who reaffirm that the Spirit of God continues to hover over the waters and bring forth new life. And in that spirit, EfM moves into the next fifty years!

Insights: Reflections from the EfM Staff

The EfM staff has shown extraordinary dedication to necessary details and a sense of community that has maintained EfM through various transitions. They are the bedrock of the program, providing guidance to all constituents who call on their leadership. The stories they tell of EfM over the years are insightful, informative, and sometimes humorous.

Bobbie Ashley
Registrar and Database Coordinator, 1999–Present

At the time I began my work with EfM, some of our offices were in the basement of the program center on the School of Theology campus. There was a lot of paper at that time: checks, applications, and the manual processing of credit cards. The fax machine was our major source of receiving forms and other information, and the typewriter was still a thing!

We now scan everything we receive and don't have any paper files left. Even the historic files have been digitally scanned so there is no loose paper. Registration in the last few years has been converted online.

Staff is family; there are just eight of us. Births, death, marriages, and divorce—we've been through it all together. It means a lot that we can count on one another for support. Since Kevin Goodman has been the executive director, we have been reading the interlude materials and have been doing theological reflections. He has shown us what EfM is truly about.

Dawn Baker
Materials Coordinator, 2003–Present

I joined the EfM staff in 2003 under the management of Cindy Sherrill. Cindy was gracious, but she was clear that folks had to get things done and so she held people accountable. One mentor described her as the "iron fist in the velvet glove!"

I answered the phone. When things were especially hectic with registrations, I knew that my work included the "interruptions" of phone calls. I was also in charge of the books and kept track of sending those books to the approximately 4,000 mentors. Additionally, I was in charge of the day-to-day finances. The COVID-19 pandemic made financial management especially challenging and I realized the need to be a "good steward."

I continue to enjoy dealing with mentors and my teammates. My devotion to my responsibilities gives me little rest, but provides me with a deep satisfaction in caring for a system that maintains EfM as a valuable resource for the world.

Donna G. Layne
Operations Coordinator, 2015–Present

In November of 2017, I became the registration specialist for the mentors with the last names L–Z. I enjoy this position because I get to know the mentors. They call my direct line and I answer their questions about books or changing membership processes. Sometimes they call because they want to talk to a "real person." This is what the EfM program is all about—people who check on one another or listen to someone who is having a bad day. With so many institutions providing only automated responses, it is vital that EfM has a real person answering the phone.

In 2024, the new executive director, the Rev. Kevin Goodman, came onboard. Exciting things are happening here. We are working on a new curriculum, new short courses, and the fiftieth anniversary celebration of the EfM program! We are offering Zoom and onsite training. We are back in the newly renovated Beecken Center in the School of Theology. What is most important to me personally is the staff meetings that we have each Tuesday. We pray, check in, read interlude books, and theologically reflect. As a result, we are a team who knows one another on a deeper level. It's amazing what our small number of eight accomplishes on behalf of EfM. Such dedication will continue to sustain EfM through challenges for years to come.

Sarah E. Limbaugh
Events Coordinator for the School of Theology, 1983–2024

When I joined the EfM staff, Cindy Sherrill was my supervisor and I was Cindy's secretary. I was also responsible for maintaining the EfM book inventory and for shipping the books. At the time we worked in the basement of what is now called the Bairnwick Women's Center. Edward O. de Bary had been hired as the EfM director a few months before me.

On my first day, I was a nervous wreck. My phone was the main phone for EfM, and it rang a lot. I was told to answer it "Bairnwick Center, this is Sarah." The staff had organized a welcome gathering for me and, of course, the phone rang. I picked up the phone and said, "Bairnwick Sarah." Everyone laughed!

While working in that basement office, we did our due diligence to help with the plumbing issues in that old house. We had been told by Physical Plant Services that we needed to do a regular "flush" of the toilets in order to help the plumbing run smoothly. Every so often, someone would go to the third-floor bathroom, then staff would handle the bathrooms on first and second floors, and the staff in the basement would all open the doors so that we could hear the signal to "Flush!," which we all did simultaneously. I don't know if it helped the plumbing but we had a great time doing it!

Deborah Shrum
Administrative Assistant/Conference Coordinator, 1994–2020

I was so grateful that Edward O. de Bary offered me a job working for EfM. On my first day at my new position, a training of trainers session was happening at our offices. The director of trainers, Gail Jones, invited the support staff to have lunch with the trainers. I was introduced as a new person on staff at that lunch. Sammy Sturrup, a tall Black man from the Bahamas, suddenly picked me up and twirled me around three times. I was stunned. Since then, I have become accustomed to, and happy with, the exuberant behavior of Sammy and the other EfM trainers.

Mary Stuart Turner
Supervisor of Administrative Staff, 1981–2006

When the School of Theology's library was moved to the University of the South's DuPont Library, EfM was given four floors of "stacks" in the building to use as storage for the program's books. That allowed for a bulk order (semi-trailer load) of books, saving the program money. We organized the stock logically with Year One on the first floor and Year Four on the fourth floor. The eighteen-wheelers would arrive around 7 a.m. and the administrative staff, plus a few of the staff's children, would meet the truck and form a "fire bucket line" to move sets of books from the truck into the building.

Beyond the Mountain: EfM Partners Around the World

After EfM's beginnings in Sewanee, Tennessee, people from around the world heard of the program through personal contacts and were touched by its potential to change lives. These pioneers took this novel idea to their homes in Canada, Australia, Hong Kong, the Bahamas, New Zealand, the U.K., and Europe.

EfM Aotearoa, New Zealand

Tricia Carter

> He aha te mea nui o tea o? Make e ki atu, he tangata, he tangata, he tangata
> *What is the most important thing in this world? It is people, it is people, it is people.*

This ancient Maori proverb sums up the story of Education for Ministry (EfM) in Aotearoa, New Zealand (EfMNZ). To tell the story of EfM is to tell of its people, both within the wider Church and the nation.

    Aotearoa (New Zealand) is a group of islands at the southern end of the Pacific Ocean. It currently has a population of five million people, 18 percent of whom identify as Maori. These are the first peoples of New Zealand, the tangata whenua (people of the land). There are two official languages within the country, Maori and English, and they are at times interchangeable, which can make reading New Zealand resources or visiting a little confusing at times. While the bicultural foundations and the place of *tangata whenua* are acknowledged, there are other layers. The largest city in New Zealand is also the largest Polynesian city in the world. It includes residents of Tonga, Samoa, Niue, Fiji, and the Cook Islands. Further immigration from Europe, Africa, India, and Eastern Europe truly makes Aotearoa a cultural and religious melting pot.

It was into this melting pot in 1979 that Education for Ministry was first introduced, making it one of the longest international partnership arrangements with the EfM program. It arrived in New Zealand via an enthusiastic ministry educator from Christchurch who took a summer break at the University of the South in Sewanee, Tennessee. On returning home, news of this exciting program was shared across the Anglican Christian Educators network. A course that focused on action/theological reflection as part of a small group process of predominantly lay ministers was a new possibility, and in metaphorical terms, the touch paper was lit.

Formal theological education outside of seminary was very hard to access for laypeople, and there was no uniformity of education across the different denominations, or even dioceses within the same denomination. The one umbrella organization was the New Zealand Association of Theological Schools (NZATS). They supported the introduction of this new program and entered into a license agreement with the University of the South to provide materials so that EfMNZ could begin "down under."

The day-to-day running was left to the educators' network within the Anglican Church under an administrative and executive board. Theological Education by Extension (TEE), run by David Moxon, was responsible for the oversight and training as the network grew. Trainers were recruited. They visited Sewanee and mentor training was offered nationally to set the solid foundations.

Local clergy were encouraged to gather small groups within their parish setting and people were identified to train as mentors for the groups. One of the issues with being so far from the University of the South was the maintenance of standards for the trainers. It was not practical to send all the trainers to Sewanee, so a uniquely New Zealand proposal was made. The trainers would be accredited as a group with a representative (a different individual each time) going to represent them at the training. One year the representative would travel to the United States and on alternate years a Sewanee trainer would travel to New Zealand and work with all the trainers. This model later spread to Australia and combined training events for New Zealand and Australia have been held. This solution was a wonderful seeding ground for a two-way flow of creativity. The visit of key leaders from EfM Sewanee kept the relationship alive and real.

As EfM groups grew around the country, it became apparent that there were some curricular challenges. Years One and Two, which were biblical-based texts focusing on the first and New Testament, were a comfortable fit. Year Three, with its Christian history focus, was more problematic. Questions were raised locally about the relevance of the distinctively American focus. One common question was beginning to be raised by participants. Could the Aotearoa New Zealand story be reflected in the texts?

In response to this, the EfM Board commissioned a historian, the Rev. Allan Davidson, to write a companion book to supplement the American story in 1989. It was initially planned as an additional three months at the completion of the four years of study. *Christianity in Aotearoa: A History of Church and Society in New Zealand* was initially published for EfMNZ and subsequently became a foundational text for all those studying Church history at seminary.

Later, recognition of the unique nature of theological reflection methods and its strengths was revisited by the NZATS. It was looking for a way to recognize prior learning and bring it together with other aspects of ministry training. It developed the Associate of Christian Ministry Diploma (ACM). This diploma had three areas, Education in Ministry, Education in Theology, and Education in Community. Completion of EfM was considered sufficient to qualify for the whole of the Education in Theology component. It was the only course being taught that achieved this outside of university papers. This pathway advanced awareness of EfM nationally and encouraged a boost in enrollment in local groups.

Participation continued to grow throughout the 1980s and 1990s with there being little competition for this area in the education sector. Groups also spread into the wider Pacific, as far as Fiji, under the New Zealand training network. By 1992 there were 15 accredited trainers to cover the country's training needs.

Under the direction of Paul Dyer, who had been a foundational board member since 1983, it was proposed that a formal independent trust be established to be the board of governance moving forward. After much work, this deed was finally completed and signed in February 2001. The initial board was split into two wings, an administrative executive and an accreditation executive. By the time of the signing of the trust deed, these had been merged into one board executive with a representative of the trainer network to fill a space on the board. With some minor revisiting in 2008 and 2014, this trust deed is still the foundation document for governance. The board is led by a chairperson who is elected annually. The board was designed to include representatives from across denominations and education networks and included both lay and ordained persons. Methodists, Presbyterians, Salvation Army, Catholics, and Anglicans have served on the board over the years.

EfMNZ has been blessed with a very stable administration and leadership over its forty-five years. The initial board and the trust board have seen very few changes. The role of chairperson across the two boards has been held by the Rev. David Moxon, the Rev. Paul Dyer, the Rev. Peter Williams, Bill Atkin (interim chair), the Rev. Judith Wigglesworth, myself, and the current chair, the Rev. Leanne Munro. This stability in leadership has done much to enhance the reliability and reputation of EfMNZ and has helped maintain the story throughout the board's life.

Expansion of the program stalled with the arrival of the global pandemic of COVID-19. EfMNZ was shut down almost completely. No face-to-face groups were held as the country went into almost total lockdown. Groups did not meet, and many mentors and trainers took the time to reassess their commitments moving forward. There had been little facility for online groups prior to the pandemic and it proved a difficult time to start afresh. Some groups did continue meeting by Zoom, but outside of the main centers, many rural communities struggled to access high-capacity Internet connectivity.

After the pandemic, EfMNZ finds itself in a place of serious self-reflection about a way forward. Many of those involved in leadership have been there almost since the beginning and have made the decision to step down or retire to make room for a new generation and new opportunities. It is time for a new beginning but the core goal remains.

In honor of the celebration of the fiftieth jubilee of EfM Sewanee, I offer thanks for the many opportunities that this partnership has offered to the New Zealand Church. We are thankful for the professional relationships built, friendships made, theological ideas shared/challenged, and the opportunity to be part of a much wider global family. Our partnership means hundreds of New Zealanders have graduated from this program and have been truly educated for ministry. The people of the mountain have truly blessed the people of the Land of the Long White Cloud.

EfM Bahamas

Yvonne Symmonett

Education for Ministry (EfM) has been life-changing for Bahamian participants. EfM was introduced in the Bahamas in 1980 with the support of the late Rt. Rev. Michael Eldon, then bishop of Nassau and the Bahamas, including the Turks and Caicos Islands. The late Rev. Samuel Sturrup and the Rev. Kirkley Sands were certified as EfM trainers in April of 1980.

Flower Ross, manager of training for EfM in the early 1980s, launched a training session in New Providence at the Hon. Janet

Bostwick's cabana on Adelaide Beach on June 30, 1980, with Sturrup serving as co-trainer. There were ten groups in total. As the coordinator, I initially observed that EfM was slow moving. Many of us are not readers, but as soon as we met weekly in groups and combined the readings with our personal stories, the positive effect on our reading skills was amazing.

An offshoot of EfM Bahamas, since our decrease in numbers, manifests itself in biannual house retreats. These retreats are conducted by a retired priest, who presides over a mass and engages in discussions from presented readings.

EfM Canada
Annette Cowan

EfM in Canada had auspicious beginnings. As the story goes, in the mid 1970s the Diocese of Kootenay was looking at parish renewal and specifically at baptismal ministry. The bishop at that time, the Rt. Rev. Fraser Barry, and the dean, the Very Rev. Jack Greenhalgh, brought in a consultant to look at how best to approach parish renewal. On one occasion, the bishop, the dean, and the consultant were driving to a conference when they began to discuss baptismal ministry. As the bishop and the dean were talking, the consultant, who was in the front seat of the car with the bishop, threw a pamphlet over the back seat to the dean and said, "You need to read this." The pamphlet was about an educational course for laity from the University of the South in Sewanee, Tennessee. And as the saying goes, "the rest is history."

The dean was tasked with looking into the program. After several phone calls to the university, he invited someone from Sewanee to come to Canada. To the dean's amazement, the offer was accepted. In 1977, Flower Ross led the first mentor training in Canada. Mentors were accredited and EfM groups began. In 1985, EfM Canada signed a contract with the School of Theology of the University of the South.

The seed money for EfM came from the Diocesan Anglicans in Mission Fund. Initially, policy, process, and procedures for EfM came from the University of the South. It would be much later that EfM Canada would develop its own policies and procedures.

It was suggested that an advisory board be set up to help run the program in Canada. The first board consisted of four members, all from the Diocese of Kootenay. With the development of Zoom, board members were added from across the country.

During the 1980s, Canada had two trainers, both of whom lived in the Diocese of Kootenay—the Very Rev. Jack Greenhalgh and the Rev. Christine Ross. They traveled many miles to lead training sessions in most of the dioceses in Canada. More trainers were added in the 1990s—Patricia Bays, Cathie Hall, David Fletcher, Rob Ross, Norman Knowles, Diane Clifford, and Stewart Payne. Later trainers were Tim Smart, Patricia Martin, myself, Lynn Dillabough, Jennifer Solem, and Carol Kysela. Accreditation was given to Canada to have their own training of trainers in 1997. In 2011, the program director at Sewanee gave accreditation to Canada to train its own new trainers.

Many have talked about the first books used for EfM. The off-white books, the white books, the mauve books, and the RRGs. Along with the reminiscing was, "Do you remember when there was just one form of TR?" accompanied by a slight shudder. The evolution of the program brought angst among some trainers, mentors, and participants, but it also brought new thoughts and new ways of engagement.

In 2007, EfM Canada's first two online mentors were accredited. They were Christine Ross and Catherine Hall. Later additions Paula Porter Leggett, David Harrison, myself, and Jennifer Solem were trained as online mentors.

In 2020, all in-person sessions came to a halt as a result of the COVID-19 pandemic. The online groups continued and the face-to-face groups did their own version of EfM Online. In one remote area where there was no Internet access the group met over the telephone. In 2020, all in-person training events were canceled. The following year we held trainings via Zoom. Modules were developed so that the trainers could use each module during the training. It was a bit daunting at first, but soon people could see the benefits of holding training events via Zoom.

Because of Zoom, training events were opened up from coast to coast. Mentors were delighted to meet other mentors from different parts of Canada. In 2021, a lot of the groups were still uncomfortable about everyone meeting in person, so they developed a hybrid system for seminar sessions. EfM Canada has continued with training via Zoom. A number of the dioceses saw the cost/benefit of having trainings done this way so this practice has continued to the present day.

It has always been important for EfM Canada to have Canadian content. EfM Canada hired an academic to create some Canadian-specific content—the history of the Church in Canada and Canadian cultural concerns and issues. In 1993, Archbishop Michael Peers delivered an apology to the Sacred Circle for the Anglican Church of Canada's role in residential schools. EfM Canada did a series of studies relating to our Indigenous brothers and sisters, which were used as interlude books. Some groups invited their indigenous neighbors to speak at their EfM groups and congregations. One bishop challenged EfM to engage in "Truth and Reconciliation." With regard to gender issues, EfM Canada has removed questions about gender and the current registration form asks for preferred pronouns. Trainers and mentors are encouraged to be aware of special regional concerns and to communicate them with EfM Canada so that the program can be adapted to address their specific needs.

Throughout the years, the EfM program in Canada has seen many applications beyond small group seminars—some dioceses use EfM as an education tool for lay ministry programs; some dioceses use it as part of formation for the diaconate and for locally trained priests; and most dioceses recognize the importance of having laypeople who can think theologically.

It is surprising to realize how much of the Church leadership comes from those who have taken EfM. It is heart-warming to hear that because of EfM, and a little local encouragement, people now have the confidence to lead the prayers of the people, to read a lesson, or to officiate at lay-led services. It is heart-warming to hear how a former participant was better able to hear their call to the priesthood. It is heart-warming to hear how, because of EfM, a graduate was able to start a home church.

Like most institutions, EfM Canada finds it hard to find people willing to lead. In the Church, membership is down. In parts of Canada there are parishes that cannot afford a priest. Bishops are looking to EfM to help fill some of the leadership gaps.

In the near forty-year history of EfM Canada, there have been 4,033 people who have taken all, or part, of the program. There have been 140 mentors trained. It has seen four directors. Each one brought their own unique gifts and styles. Each has had their specific challenges in carrying out the duties. The constant, however, has been the love of EfM and the love of God.

EfM Europe

Marguerite Casparian

As far as I know, EfM Europe started in Italy in 1993. When I went to diocesan gatherings after 1995, others had heard of EfM in the United States but no groups had formed yet.

In 1992, Ivan Cendese, an Episcopal priest from Utah, was on an eighteen-month sabbatical with his family in Florence. While attending services at St. James, he stirred up some interest in EfM and helped Marjorie Willis and Marie Buti go to mentor training in Lincoln, England. In 1993, a group of about ten people started studying together but found theological reflection (TR) difficult. The following year they split into two groups, one meeting midday and one in the evening.

When my husband, Peter, and I arrived in 1995 (when he became rector) both mentors were anxious to hand over their groups to me and reunite them. I had been a mentor for eleven years in Lawrence, Kansas, and then Lexington, Kentucky, and really loved and felt comfortable with TR. We used their old books, which I remember as the yellow books, because they felt they needed to regroup and begin again together. As I remember, Marie had brought those books over from the United States the previous summer. It was a wonderful group of people eager to learn and share.

In 1996, our family came back to the United States for a visit and I returned to Florence with the next year's books. There were now two groups, one in the morning at St. James and one in the evening at the American consulate. Our consul general was part of that group that, because of everyone's changing lives, only had one thoughtful and caring year together.

I can't remember the year, maybe 1999, when the School of Theology transferred the administration of EfM in Europe to England. Our group of mostly fourth-year students filled out monthly report sheets and I, as mentor, filled out even more. By the end of the year, England's administration wanted me to go to London (at my own cost), stay in a hotel (at my own cost), and take their mentor training, which at that time seemed exorbitant for us and impossible for St. James. Before that change in practice, I had been taking the required training when I returned to the United States during the summers. So, with only a couple of students, we decided to have another year of TR with a small group, and anyone who wanted to read further borrowed the necessary books. It wasn't ideal, but we had a wonderful community that continued to challenge and support each other.

Those nine years in Florence were magical. The church was full of English speakers—some married to Italians, some on sabbatical, some working there, and some who emigrated from several African countries. People from each of these groups participated in EfM, bringing a richness I'd never had before in a group. We had a Muslim and a Jew join us, which of course led to profound conversations.

For the last four years, Peter, now retired, has been serving churches in Taormina on the island of Sicily and Assisi on mainland Italy. There are small groups of people keeping these two Anglican churches open. They do it for their own community and to be a place of worship and temporary community for travelers.

There is a possibility to form new groups here but it has its challenges. In Assisi people get together on Sundays, but because they live a long distance away, reconvening another day would be very difficult. And they are all tired of online meetings. They need face-to-face conversation. In Taormina there is a monthly Bible study that could be turned into EfM, but there is no natural mentor/leader in the group. They rely on the leadership of the monthly changing clergy. Also, with everyone on a strict budget, they would never be able to pay the fees.

I have long thought that a more abbreviated study with the concentration on TR would draw people to EfM in a different way. My last group in Texas has graduated but meets monthly, rereading MacCulloch one chapter a month (because who has ever had enough time with that book?). It's a fabulous group that roams from discussion into a loose and natural TR. No one is a mentor or leader. There is one person who emails a reminder of the date and time that has been mutually decided upon at the last meeting. And because no one needs to be reminded of the wise guidelines of formal EfM, we call each other to task if need be.

This Texas experience makes me think that an already strong group, like the ones in Taormina and Assisi, could learn the EfM methods and rhythms and use them in a less structured way. After doing an abbreviated TR, one of the women said to me, "No one has ever taught me to think that way!"

Thinking in metaphors and practicing theological reflection have become so natural to me that when a mature adult says they've never thought that way, I am baffled. EfM has such a gift to give!

EfM Australia

Greg Davies

EfM began in Australia in 1977. The director of the General Board of Religious Education (GBRE) at the time—the Education Board established by the General Synod of the Anglican Church of

Australia—was the Rev. Alan Baxter. He introduced the program to the board, which then agreed to introduce the program to the Anglican Church of Australia under license from the School of Theology at the University of the South.

The role of national director for EfM in Australia was the director of the General Board of Religious Education. They were George Hearn, 1978–81; Noel Delbridge, 1981–85; Trevor Smith, 1986–99; and Bill Ray, 1999–01. In 2001, the GBRE resolved to dissolve and thus the license was transferred to the Diocese of Brisbane, which appointed the following directors for EfM in Australia and Hong Kong: John Noble, 2001–02; Trevor Smith, 2002–15; and myself, 2016 to present.

All directors of EfM promoted the program to the dioceses of the Australian church and gathered a team of trainers and mentors, which enabled the program to flourish and provide a valuable pathway of ministry formation for the laity.

A number of dioceses subsequently used EfM as a basis for authorized lay ministry and recognized its enormous value in equipping laypeople for ministry. The program was also valued by many participants as a pathway that led them into ordained ministry, while for others it affirmed their Christian ministry and led them into a ministry with EfM itself as mentors and trainers.

At its height in 1998, EfM Australia had seventy-four groups established across twenty-two of its twenty-six dioceses.

In 2015, the financial viability of the EfM program in Australia was problematic and faced closure. However, with the new revised program then being offered, combined with some administrative restructuring, EfM continued to be offered around the Australian Church.

It has to be acknowledged that without the support of the General Board of Religious Education, and the changes within the Australian Anglican Church more generally, growth of EfM stalled and has sadly been on a steady decline since that time. In 2015, I was appointed as national director of EfM and have been able, with a small group of volunteer EfM trainers, to continue to offer and maintain the program in Australia and Hong Kong.

With the onset of COVID-19, significant challenges faced EfM as to whether groups could continue. Most, if not all, groups were able to adjust and use the Zoom platform during this period. As a result of this experience, a number of groups continued to meet on Zoom or with a combination of online and face-to-face seminars. This development has been a lifeline for EfM in Australia, as it has enabled EfM groups to form outside the traditional parish setting. Participants now gather from a variety of parishes or faith community settings, which in turn has brought greater diversity and accessibility to those who are seeking to explore their Christian faith at a deep and reflective level.

With a renewed and expanded EfM being offered in 2025-26, EfM Australia is hopeful that it will continue with renewed energy and passion for a faith and ministry formation program that has given so much to so many Christians in Australia during the past forty-seven years. I look forward to its continuing presence and gift to the Australian Church in the years ahead.

EfM United Kingdom

Christopher Halliday

EfM was started in the United Kingdom in the late 1980s, after the Rev. Chris Lee spent a sabbatical from ministry in the United States looking at adult Christian formation. I was invited to Sewanee for a mentor training and, upon returning to Gloucester Diocese, I was able to persuade the diocese to be the first and only diocese of the Church of England to sponsor EfM.

I became the first accredited mentor and then trainer after attending a training of trainers event in 1992. Subsequently Edward O. de Bary came to the UK and led a training, thus beginning the first official EfM group. In 1998, there were thirteen groups and 130 students in the UK.

During the next 10–15 years, EfMUK was centered on a few individuals who built and maintained groups. In Manchester, Gary O'Neil and Ian Stubbs established several groups. In the southeast, Haydn Wilcox established three groups, and Joanna Hobart had groups in the Gloucester area. When Gary O'Neil moved to Birmingham, he again established groups there and the Manchester groups continued with a number of mentors joining the program.

EfMUK ran its own mentor training events under the guidance of Joanna Hobart, Haydn Wilcox, and Gary O'Neil.

During the years, EfMUK has had three directors—Chris Lee, Gary O'Neil, and myself since 2019. The director has been supported by management groups consisting of mentors, trainers, and group members with a part-time, paid administrator. EfMUK has a board of trustees and, since the pandemic, the trustees have been tasked with rebuilding the management structure.

EfMUK has always used the materials and texts provided by the program's leadership with the proviso that some texts might be swapped out for more appropriately Eurocentric materials. The decision as to which texts might be most appropriate has been left to mentors. With the current curriculum revisions being proposed, EfMUK will again consider which core texts are essential for continuity with headquarters and which might be swapped out for "homegrown" material.

EfMUK is currently at a low point. We have four active groups, three in England and one in Scotland. We also have links with the EfM group in Munich and are hoping to foster a group in Frankfurt. We have a training scheduled for Paris in 2025 with the express intention of centering a group in the Episcopal Cathedral in Paris. We have the potential for two additional groups in England.

Despite our best efforts, we have found it impossible to get diocesan lay development officers to consider the "off the shelf" offering from EfM. We feel that this is partly a prejudice against what is perceived as a "liberal" program, and partly because locally appointed officers feel they have to justify their existence by creating their own programs.

The trustees and the management group will have to decide in the coming year whether to continue to be a part of the worldwide program given the cost constraints that will accrue from the new contract and the new curriculum. We have the ability to carry on as we are for the foreseeable future and continue to hope that we can attract people to the program. Given the nature of life in the Church of England, unless and until we can once again persuade a diocese that they should sponsor EfM, we will have little or no support.

PROCLAIMING GOD'S STORY

Realizing Then Reconciling a Multitude of God's Voices

Phoebe A. Roaf

EfM's first-year participants encounter many surprises while studying the Hebrew Scriptures from a historical/critical perspective. Roaf's journey from EfM participant to bishop in The Episcopal Church provides a particular lens on the program's effect and importance. Her insights give hope as we struggle to find unity of purpose amid a diversity of beliefs.

In my experience, much of a spiritual journey can be understood retrospectively. That has certainly been the case as I reflect on how Education for Ministry (EfM) has enhanced my faith and influenced my vocation.

I don't have any memories of a time without God. I grew up in a household with an Episcopalian mother and a Baptist father, and an awareness of the Lord's presence and provision was infused into all aspects of life. Church attendance was mandatory in the Roaf household and conversations about God were not limited to Sunday mornings. Family members regularly expressed gratitude to Jesus for the many blessings we received. They articulated how their faith motivated them to be of service to others. "From everyone to whom much has been given, much will be required; and from one to whom much has been entrusted, even more will be demanded" (Luke 12:48) was a constant refrain. The adults in my life regularly asked how the Lord was present in the issues they faced, a precursor to the theological reflections (TR) I would engage in years later as an EfM student.

Church was an environment where I felt safe. As a child, I was nurtured and encouraged by Episcopal and Baptist congregations. Because of these positive experiences, I never left the Church. Summers spent at Camp Mitchell on Petit Jean Mountain outside of Little Rock, Arkansas, morphed into leadership in the Episcopal Young Churchmen (EYC) at the parish and diocesan levels in the late 1970s and early 1980s. During my senior year of high school, I served as president of the diocesan EYC in Arkansas. This led to stints as a Sunday school teacher, a lector, a lay eucharistic minister, a member of the altar guild and the vestry, and an assistant youth group leader in multiple congregations. In addition to these volunteer opportunities, I longed for a deeper understanding of God. I wanted my intellect and my heart to be fully engaged in my relationship with the source of all being. I became a student of the Bible, seeking to make sense of ancient texts and discerning their relevance for my life.

I was intrigued when I learned about EfM in 1995 when I relocated to Little Rock to begin law school. There was an active EfM group in my congregation and I was struck by how enthusiastic the participants were. Something about the structure of the program—worship, Bible study, reflection, the sharing of stories in a small group, and the peer-led format—was deeply moving for everyone involved. When the EfM mentor let me peruse the Year One three-ring binder, I was hooked, despite my reservations about the amount of reading involved. My heart overruled my head and in the fall of 1996, I entered my second year of law school and Year One of EfM.

My first year of EfM was overwhelming. I had no prior knowledge of the four-source theory of the Hebrew Scriptures. Like many Christians, I was unfamiliar with much of the Old Testament aside from the psalms. Some of my fellow first-year classmates experienced a crisis of faith because of this knowledge. The fact that the Torah was composed of multiple sources of written and oral tradition had the opposite effect on me. The realization that the compilers included multiple versions of the same story and it was up to me to sort out the apparent contradictions in the text was liberating and miraculous. I was also reassured by the messiness of the characters depicted in the Hebrew Scriptures. I saw aspects of my own life reflected in the trials and tribulations of our Jewish forefathers and foremothers.

EfM provided my first opportunity to write my spiritual autobiography. A different set of questions about our faith journey was assigned each year, which meant that I was constantly learning something new about myself. Spiritual autobiographies were much more straightforward than TRs. It took some time to get the hang of TRs, especially using the old formulaic method of mapping the four quadrants (action, culture, position, and tradition) on sheets of butcher-block paper. But the concept of how God was engaged in my life was something I had experienced in conversations with family members as a child. Processing TRs in a small-group format with people who held different theological perspectives was lifegiving. EfM spoke to the part of my soul searching for answers to questions I didn't know that I had.

I finished Year Two of EfM before moving to New Orleans, Louisiana, to begin a legal career. I postponed joining a new EfM group because I wasn't sure how much spare time I would have to devote to the class. After a two-year hiatus, I started Year Three and subsequently graduated. I was grateful for the flexibility that enabled me to temporarily suspend my studies until a more opportune time.

As satisfying as my EfM journey was, I sensed that God was inviting me to go deeper. EfM played a pivotal role in acknowledging my call to ordained ministry, a call I struggled to accept for more than ten years. And EfM was instrumental in my transition from lawyer to seminarian. Not only did I enter seminary with a firm grounding in the Old Testament and the New Testament, I entered with an understanding of church history, ethics, and contemporary theological issues as well. EfM also helped me become comfortable discussing my faith with people from various backgrounds and identifying how God was present in the events of everyday life. In retrospect, EfM helped lay the groundwork for a rewarding seminary experience.

I returned to New Orleans to serve as associate rector at a large parish and spent three years gaining confidence in my priestly voice. I led Christian formation classes but I wasn't connected to an EfM class during that time. When I relocated to Richmond, Virginia, to become rector of a congregation in 2011, a local retired priest suggested that we start an EfM group at the parish. It had been ten years since I graduated from EfM and I thought it would be a great way to introduce my parishioners to a program that had been meaningful to me. In 2012, I became a co-mentor of an EfM group with this priest. We served as co-mentors from 2012 to 2018.

Our EfM group was ecumenical in nature, including students from several local Episcopal congregations as well as Baptists and Pentecostals. The theological diversity of the participants led to vigorous discussions at times. The retired priest and I were well suited to facilitate these conversations. He was my parents' age and had been ordained forty years longer than I had. Because of our different life experiences, we didn't always agree. One of the benefits of our shared leadership was modeling how to respectfully disagree.

Being a mentor was rewarding in a different way than when I was a student. It was a privilege to see the light bulbs go off as people grappled with the scripture. Many students had never received permission to ask questions of the text and determine what was central about God for themselves. For example, Year One students were often astounded at the violence in the Old Testament. That led to discussions about whether the God portrayed in the Old Testament was the same God who sent the incarnate Jesus to Earth in the New Testament. But these conversations weren't primarily academic in nature. Over the years, I witnessed EfM participants make a deeper commitment to the Church. Not only did they assume new leadership roles, they also matured in their faith. I never ceased to marvel when a participant claimed an authentic relationship with Jesus instead of accepting their parents' understanding of God.

I became bishop of the Episcopal Diocese of West Tennessee in May 2019. Our diocese has sponsored EfM groups for many years and I have happily continued this tradition. The EfM framework enhances my current vocation by encouraging me to be curious about the perspectives of others and to always ask how God is at work in the situations I encounter.

Embracing the mystery of God and continuously asking questions are at the heart of the Christian journey. This is especially true for twenty-first century bishops as we navigate an increasingly post-Christian, post-denominational landscape. Now, more than ever, we are invited to collaborate with others in shared models of mission and ministry through mutual discernment. Although there are no easy answers to the issues facing the Church, EfM reminds participants that every generation has faced challenges. Sometimes, a challenge becomes an opportunity when considered from a different point of view. The survival of God's Church is ultimately God's business and we are privileged to play a small role in this unfolding journey. The lessons gleaned from the first 3,000 years of Christianity, according to Diarmaid MacCulloch, can serve as guideposts for our time. The EfM framework helps me embrace the challenges and opportunities of life with humility and hope.

Holy Ground in Cyberspace

Kay Flores

Education for Ministry (EfM) relies on creative imagination and adaptability. Before Pathwright, before Zoom, and when Blackboard was becoming popular, EfM sought ways to create community beyond rooms and walls. Flores, an EfM mentor, trainer, and former diocesan coordinator, was a pioneer in EfM's efforts to bring the people of God into cyberspace.

My experience with EfM Online began when my friend, the Rev. Ann Fontaine, suggested I go to an EfM open house at a nearby church in Casper, Wyoming. I went to the open house with the intention of signing up, but the group's regular meeting times conflicted with a commitment to my teenage children, so I declined the invitation. Shortly after, she told me that she and a friend, Dr. Norman Peterson, were thinking about offering an EfM group online. I don't remember saying yes to EfM, but that didn't matter to Ann. During the summer of 2001, Ann said I should enroll and send in my check. I did what Ann said, and that fall, we started the experiment: the pilot project of EfM Online.

I did not realize at the time what an amazing experiment this was. Until that pilot project, EfM only met face to face. Lynne Wilson, the canon for ministry development in the Episcopal Diocese of Wyoming, had asked Ann if EfM could be offered via the Internet to leaders of isolated and rural churches.

Ann lived in Lander, Wyoming, with a population of fewer than 7,000. She had been an EfM mentor since the early days of EfM and was an active trainer in the program. Norm Peterson, who lived in Cheyenne, the largest city in Wyoming with about 53,000 people, was also an EfM mentor. He had just retired as a professor emeritus from the University of Wyoming, College of Education, after serving as the department chair for secondary education. Norm was a proponent of distance- and life-long-learning. He also had experience with Blackboard, a course management system used by universities and colleges.

In 2001, EfM was more than twenty-five years old. Mentors and trainers all knew that the small, face-to-face groups were an important component of EfM. Many people believed that there was no possibility that an online group could offer the kind of community that face-to-face groups offered. One of the developers of EfM, Edward O. de Bary, once told me that EfM Online was only useful for introverts. Even Ann had her own doubts. She later wrote, "I thought it would be possible to carry out the program but did not believe it would be as good as face-to-face EfM. I could not have been more wrong."

We started with a group of eight people who lived around Wyoming in various circumstances. Carole Buckingham lived on a ranch thirty miles down a dirt road from Kaycee, a small town of 250 people. The next town with an EfM group was sixty miles away from that small town. Distance and Wyoming weather did not make that a practical option for a ranch family with children. Judy Likwartz had started an EfM group in Pinedale, Wyoming, another small town, but after two years, was unable to find enough participants to support a group. Jean McLean lived in Basin, Wyoming, but traveled frequently for work. Jim Peck was retired in Jackson Hole, Wyoming, and traveled often. Several people were in the process to be ordained in Wyoming's mutual ministry program.

We were all on dialup Internet when we started. Through the magic of Blackboard we could see the same computer screen, but Blackboard had no audio or video. We typed our thoughts. Carole remembers that her Internet was so unreliable that she prayed just to stay online for an entire session. We each experienced our own challenges with Blackboard and with staying connected to the Internet.

We experimented with theological reflection (TR) online together. We found that starting with an image worked well with the available technology, so we often began our TR with sacred art. We branched out into images from culture and later moved into the dilemma method. We did not attempt a microscope theological reflection for several years because of the technological limitations.

Blackboard offered an asynchronous discussion board where we each posted our weekly comments and responded to other participant's thoughts. A variety of theological viewpoints were present in the group and we had some interesting conversations on that discussion board.

Our mentors planned three in-person gatherings that year. We shared meals, worshiped, and engaged in theological reflection. Our first in-person gathering was in September 2001, while the world was still living in the shock of 9/11. The next gathering was impacted by a blizzard. On those occasions when we met in person we realized that we knew each other so well, although we could not hear or see each other in our weekly engagements online. We had built a virtual community!

The next year, one of the original participants moved out of state. A person in a neighboring state heard about the program and asked to join us. Each year, we gained new people. Our EfM Online group was no longer limited to people in Wyoming. We still held one or more gatherings each year and participants from other states flew to meet us and to experience the beauty of Wyoming.

After a few years, we needed two online groups. Then other dioceses wanted to start online groups. This expansion required the development of training for online mentors. The first training sessions for online mentors took place on the campus of the School of Theology, the University of the South, in the spring of

2004. We taught people about the technology and, more importantly, we shared how to translate traditional EfM into an online world. We tried to emulate the feeling of being virtual by moving the participants to offices around the building.

The University of the South was not offering any courses online in the early days of EfM Online. As a result, Ann and I were listed as the EfM help desk. We figured out how to help participants and mentors handle the challenges of pop-up blockers, cache-clearing, and updating from afar.

We chose to call this project EfM Online rather than online EfM. It was not a new thing—it was the same EfM that so many people loved, just delivered in a new way. Eventually, we began offering training for online mentors online, both domestic and foreign.

Over the years, we worked on several iterations of Blackboard. Eventually, this included audio and video. As the technology evolved, some participants balked at asynchronous discussion boards. As a result, EfM Online switched to Zoom around 2018. Fortunately, that switch meant EfM was prepared and ready for the COVID-19 impact in 2020.

During March of 2020, I was reluctant to travel from Washington State to Nebraska to lead a training. I had been out of the country just weeks before, and in those early days, we did not know much about how COVID-19 spread or whether I could be contagious without knowing. I was not ready to travel, so I proposed a new way of training. I was able to offer a "Foundations" training from my home in Washington while the participants were either at home or onsite in Nebraska. It was successful, and as 2020 progressed, all training sessions pivoted to online.

Today there are many groups meeting online. Some choose to always meet online for convenience, even if they live in the same community. Other groups have participants around the country and the world. In 2024, most training sessions were held online.

The EfM Online pilot project of 2001 has helped EfM to grow. EfM mentor Jane Dowrick, who is also the EfM coordinator in the Diocese of Virginia, described her group's experience this way: "In March 2020, like the rest of the world, our EfM group learned that we could no longer safely meet in person because of the COVID-19 pandemic. I can't recall how I learned about Zoom, having never used it before, but to Zoom we went as a group. I found Zoom to be easy to use and affordable. On Zoom we are all looking at one another, able to see our expressions and reactions. On Zoom, the quality of sound can be enhanced by using earbuds or headphones, or, in my case as a hearing aid wearer, with Bluetooth sound right into my ears. At first, we had to learn how to have a naturally flowing conversation in a Zoom room. There were some rocky moments when we weren't sure if we were interrupting one another, but we eventually figured this out. I think the most important thing I've noticed about meeting online is how very present we are with one another. I believe that Zoom has helped us become more adept at being there for one another. This is a delightful surprise. I know there are still many who can't imagine meeting online at all, much less for the past four years. And we intend to continue meeting online because of various circumstances of group members. Meeting online has been a wonderful game changer!"

Norm Peterson's wife, the Rev. Carol Peterson, recently told me, "Norm loved EfM and really enjoyed being a mentor. Even though he died several years ago, he would be thrilled to see how many people's spiritual lives continue to be enhanced through their participation in EfM and especially the online option."

Ann Fontaine died in 2018. In 2007, she posted an article on the Episcopal Café titled *Holy Ground in Cyberspace*." In it, she wrote, "Originally, we thought [EfM Online] would be great for rural, isolated students. We have discovered that it is great for those who travel for work, those who live in cities and don't want one more night out, and those who have children at home. The intimacy and depth of sharing is beyond my dreams. When we do find time to see each other in person we are like old friends."

In the midst of bandwidth, WiFi, and Zoom, we found that God is present online too!

Send Them Out!
EfM and the Ministry of Church Planting

Katie Nakamura Rengers

Education for Ministry has been transforming congregations and communities since its inception. Rengers, former trainer and staff officer for church planting with The Episcopal Church, shares how she uses EfM to build new communities of faith, including leading groups into unexpected places.

Recently I participated in a think tank on church planting in mainline denominations. As what usually happens at these sorts of things, we ran through the gamut of challenges—a shortage of leaders with church-planting gifts; institutions that are more concerned with survival than with mission; and so on. We then dreamed about what we would love to see—more lay-led, clergy-supported models; church plants that reach a greater diversity of people; and others that inspire traditional churches to new possibilities and new practices.

That evening at dinner, one of my colleagues said, "Tell me about your own church plant, Katie. How did you get started?" "Well," I said, "Back in 2014, I had this Education for Ministry group..."

My colleague is an evangelical Lutheran, so I started by giving my Education for Ministry (EfM) elevator speech. Then I described how, ten years ago, seven folks in their late twenties and early thirties gathered weekly to read the Old

Testament and do theological reflection together, and how that quickly became twelve, then sixteen, then twenty. It was shocking how fast our group grew; after all, who would have guessed that younger adults would commit to such a rigorous, time-consuming endeavor? Yet EfM spoke to a longing we all felt—for community, accountability, vulnerability, and transcendence—that we didn't think we were receiving in the inherited Church.

It was this group of energetic young people, inspired and empowered by scripture with a fuller understanding of Church history and tools for theological reflection, who formed the core team for the Abbey, the first new Church community in the Diocese of Alabama in a decade. Rather than a "traditional" church model, we opened a religious coffee shop that provided space for EfM, worship, community, and generosity.

It used to be that regularly starting new churches was part of the Episcopal ethos. In the post–World War II period there were widely regarded practices for doing so, inspired by the Church growth movement that emerged in the '60s and '70s. For Episcopal dioceses, this usually meant identifying a growing suburb (most often majority white) and sending out a talented priest (almost always male) with a team of laypeople from surrounding churches. This "launch team" started celebrating regular Eucharists and eventually built a physical structure to house the new church's worship and programs. In other words, there was a "recipe" that, when done right, usually worked.

Since the '90s, however, Episcopal church planting has lost steam, as it has in most mainline denominations. There are many reasons for this. First, waning missional energy corresponds with the Church's numerical decline (which became really noticeable about three decades ago). A mindset of scarcity has set in, both in terms of finances and in terms of leadership. The logic is understandable. If your existing churches have fewer people and less money, why send any of them/it out to start a whole new church?

Send Them Out! EfM and the Ministry of Church Planting 141

Another reason for ebbing church-planting energy is increased awareness of the Euro-tribal churches'[1] hand in colonialism, both in terms of how we may have contributed to displacement and annihilation of Indigenous peoples and in forcing other immigrant groups to assimilate. (For example, after the Japanese internment, "go to church" was part of the advice my grandparents were given about how to best reenter society and minimize discrimination against them.) It's a tricky space and a holy space—rediscovering mission and evangelism in a declining Church while simultaneously working to repair the breach to which many of our historic efforts contributed.

There is a third reason we have shied away from church planting (and likely many more, but I'll stop at three). It's hard! The "recipe" of past decades rarely works anymore. The rate of failure is high. Expectations are often unspoken and sometimes unreasonable. Like any entrepreneurial effort, a church-planting team strives to create a worshiping community where nothing existed before, and in a centuries-old denomination, it can be hard to work up this kind of energy.

The difficulty is more than just the energy of creating *ex nihilo*. Planters and planting teams who are steeped in mainline customs actually have to unlearn quite a lot. They are often coming from an established church where there is an established history of liturgical expression, atmosphere, programming, and community norms. A church plant, on the other hand, is not yet defined at all. It invites its founders to leave what is known, safe, and comfortable in favor of discomfort and dislocation. It asks us not to re-create a mini version of our beloved home parish, but to respond to, and partner with, how God might be speaking in a new way to new neighbors.

In the last decade, the triennial General Convention has prioritized support of new communities with "people historically underrepresented in The Episcopal Church." This emphasis on

---

1. Alan Roxburgh uses the term "Euro-tribal churches" to refer to denominations whose history includes migration from Europe to the United States. See his book, *Joining God, Remaking Church, Changing the World: The New Shape of the Church in Our Time* (Morehouse Publishing, 2015).

people of different ethnic, cultural, and socioeconomic backgrounds gives even more uncertainty to when and how a new church—even though rooted in the Episcopal tradition—will come to express its newfound shared rhythms and norms.

Humans tend not to like uncertainty, and this makes church planting quite an interesting and specific call.

When we planted the Abbey—our church within a coffee shop ministry in Birmingham—friends from previous churches where I had worked wanted to support the endeavor. I've lost count of how many of them came for worship two or three times. During their first visit, they were often ecstatic. "It's so different! It's so welcoming! You worship around a coffee table, just like Jesus! There are people coming in from the streets, just like Jesus!" But by the second or third visit, the rose-colored glasses came off.

After three visits, during the last of which a stack of foldable metal chairs crashed to the floor during Communion, like a set of dominos, one friend said to me, "I love you. I love the mission of this church plant. But this is just too much chaos for me to feel worshipful."

In other words, being part of a chuch-planting team requires a tremendous amount of spiritual maturity and a particular kind of spiritual preparedness for "being sent." It requires the ability to separate what I "like, love, or prefer" from what is fundamentally needed in order to do the Church's work of restoring all people (including myself and my neighbor) to unity with God through Christ. It requires a tolerance for failure when an endeavor was undertaken in faithfulness. It requires personal sacrifice, for the sake of growing in my own discipleship and vocation as a lay or ordained leader.

Of course, this necessary spiritual maturity is not unique to church planting. In the words of our Presiding Bishop Sean Rowe in his address to the 81st General Convention, The Episcopal Church faces an "existential crisis."[2] We share this crisis with

---

2. Ruth Graham, "The Episcopal Church has Elected its Youngest Leader in Centuries," *New York Times*, June 26, 2024, https://www.nytimes.com/2024/06/26/us/epicopal-church-bishop-sean-rowe.html.

all mainline traditions, which are feeling the quake of cultural, religious, and institutional shifts all at once and, which for now, are experiencing their aftershock in terms of hemorrhaging numerical decline. Distrust of institutions and loneliness are on the rise. Demographics in many American neighborhoods are rapidly changing. Culture is moving away from twentieth-century models of Sunday worship. Even at the largest, most well-resourced parishes, we are moving from relative comfort to dislocation. Spiritually, mature Christians will be in hot demand as we strive to be flexible and resilient in the midst of what many are saying is one of the most pivotal religious shifts in the history of our country.

During the COVID-19 pandemic, I had a Zoom conversation with one of our Episcopal church planters and one of their church's key lay leaders, "Dan." Even before COVID-19, they had intended to plant an outdoor church—a Sunday eucharistic community with no permanent building that was committed to worshiping God out in God's creation. I asked Dan, a longtime traditional Episcopalian, what drew him to this new expression. "Well, Katie," he said, "It used to be that I enjoyed all the beautiful organ music, and the altar, and the prayer books, and such. But as I've gotten older, I find I just don't need those things anymore. They're very nice and I still love and appreciate them, but I don't *need* them anymore."

I was so touched by what Dan said that I found myself doing a personal theological reflection. In terms of "Tradition," I thought of one of my ancestors in ministry, the Rev. John Yamazaki, the rector of Saint Mary's Mariposa. Yamazaki took only a small, foldable travel altar with him into the desert where he and his entire congregation were incarcerated during World War II. Everything else—high altar, sacristy, candlesticks, piano—they left behind (along with their homes, businesses, and pets). Few can reflect on the biblical exile, in which temple worship disappeared, like Japanese-American Christians.

Culture is a bit complicated. Episcopal Church culture has (I think unwittingly) formed many people to believe that certain practices and adornments are necessary for proper worship. Worship must be in a sanctuary. We must drink from a common cup. The bishop must be part of the apostolic line of succession. Secular culture doesn't care much for church tradition, but it reinforces a sense of entitlement to personal preference in worship. "I need Eucharist every week in order to feel close to God." "I have to have my five minutes of silence before church starts to center myself." "Praise music just doesn't do it for me; I have to have my hymnal fix."

And, of course, personal belief. I, Katie Nakamura Rengers, believe that it's going to take a lot of spiritual maturity for Christians to make the sacrifices and take the risks needed for us to ensure future generations of the Good News of Jesus and for us to thrive into the future.

Since I started supporting church-planting efforts on a Church-wide level, I hear a similar story of lament from many dioceses. "We don't know how to start new churches. Our people and our parishes aren't prepared for church planting." And, related to all things missional, "Throughout the last few decades we've utterly failed in forming disciples for mission!" I used to accept this diagnosis as truth, but more recently I have begun to question it. What if we, in The Episcopal Church, are more prepared for this missional moment than we realize? What if we have done a better job than we think in forming disciples of Jesus?

When I was in middle school, the ska punk band the Mighty Mighty Bosstones released their hit, "The Impression that I Get." The last verse goes, "I'm not a coward, I've just never been tested. I'd like to think that if I was, I would pass." What if, in terms of missional church planting, our disciples just have "never been tested?" Or, to use a more biblical/theological phrase, they've just "never been sent"?

The biblical concept of "sending" in terms of clergy and lay deployment is worth its own essay. Here I will just say that I think the future of church planting in The Episcopal Church necessitates us recovering the apostolic practices of sending and being sent. Our current models of clergy calls and even lay leadership are more rooted in capitalism, professionalism, and consumerism than in apostolic vision. Yet we can easily point to the biblical examples of Jesus sending out the seventy and of the church in Antioch sending out Paul and Barnabas. To follow in their footsteps, we will need to relinquish current mindsets of scarcity—scarcity in terms of people, money, and preparedness.

I'd argue that EfM has been preparing disciples for this particular moment in the mission of the church for the past fifty years! EfM equips people to ask deep questions about what it means to follow Jesus and love our neighbors, and what God asks us to sacrifice in pursuit of the Living Bread. Through the four sources, it helps participants identify and name the similarities, differences, and tension points between what experience, culture, faith tradition, and personal belief are speaking into a given situation. For example, is the worship and way of "doing church" that I personally like something that is contained in scripture or in tradition? How is culture influencing the way I receive this worship? Where does the source of one authority end and the next begin? Who is the church mainly for—those inside of it or those outside?

A few years ago I published a blog post that got a fair amount of attention. It was titled "The Kind of Leaders We Need," and in it I made the point that The Episcopal Church (and other mainline churches) tend to opt for ordained leaders who love and will serve the status quo, often while actively filtering out the leaders who will actually help navigate the uncertainty of this post-institutional, post-pandemic age. Of course, this doesn't mean these leaders don't exist, but it means that they don't tend to be ordained. And I wonder if, through lay training programs like EfM, many of these people are right before our eyes!

As I look back through that blog post, I observe how many of these characteristics are nurtured through the Education for Ministry program.

- We need leaders who love Christ's church, but who aren't "in love" with any one expression of it. Missional leaders must be able to see who isn't being reached and what aspects

of the tradition aren't working for their context. They are just as curious, if not more so, about where the Holy Spirit is showing up outside their community as how She appears inside.
- We need leaders who know what it's like to be on the margin and who have developed that experience into strong relational skills. Most are familiar with Henri Nouwen's phrase, "the wounded healer." At this moment, we also need "marginalized includers." We need leaders who have carefully examined their own story and can use this to relate to others on the outskirts of society and church.
- We need leaders who have the courage to take risks, not just to talk about taking risks. Missional leadership isn't a profession, it's a full-bodied and "soul-ed" leap. It can't be preached, it must be led by example.
- We need leaders who know how to be in a healthy community and how to invite others into it. In a time of increased isolation and loneliness, we need leaders who have experienced community and can nurture it.
- We need leaders who are comfortable in uncomfortable spaces. This includes uncomfortable conversations, anxious topics, frequent disruption, and unpredictable situations.

And, finally: We've got to stop waiting for the leaders to come to us, and we need to start seeking them out!

Through its regular weekly gatherings, reliance on the telling of, and listening to, spiritual autobiographies, committing to exploring tough and uncertain topics through theological reflection, and incessant asking of how God is revealed in our daily lives and experiences, EfM has the capacity to be an incredible training ground for missional leaders.

What might be possible if our dioceses would actively seek out EfM graduates, not just for ordination or lay leadership in existing churches, but for the work of starting new expressions of our ancient faith—expressions that are adaptable and flexible and particularly attuned to reach the growing number of people who are completely disconnected from church? Increasingly, they are also disconnected from community and transcendence.

I began this piece by telling you about my coffee shop church plant that was launched by a young adult EfM group. For the first six months, the coffee shop struggled to figure out its identity as a third-space community. What was supposed to happen the other forty hours a week outside of Sunday worship and EfM gatherings, when they were just a coffee shop? How would we encourage people to not just buy their coffee and sit alone, but to engage with each other as a spiritual community?

And then, George showed up. George had been a mentor for EfM for years and had recently retired from his day job. He began showing up at the Abbey every morning; he'd purchase a black coffee, chat with the baristas, then sit down with his laptop or a book. After a few weeks of this, I began to notice something intriguing. George was no longer sitting alone. In fact, he'd developed a little "club" of Millennials. Some were the baristas, some were his friends from other places, and some were fellow customers he'd met and welcomed to his table. They'd be talking about church-y and non-church-y things, their feelings, their problems, their love lives. George had pretty much planted his own microchurch right before our eyes, over nothing more than a table and a cup of coffee.

The microchurch of George was contagious. It began to transform the way our baristas interacted with other customers and the way customers responded to the Abbey's space and to each other. Strangers became more likely to talk to other strangers in the coffee shop and unexpected friendships formed. We no longer experienced community only on worship and program days but all week long! Finally, we could say that our coffee shop ministry was synonymous with *ekklesia*, with church!

I am convinced that Education for Ministry is a great hope for the present and the future of our Church. We are more prepared than we think for the challenge and possibility the Spirit is sending our way! Now, let's send some of these incredibly formed graduates out on their mission!

EfM in Prisons

Anne Moats Williams

There is no place where God is not there. The apostle Paul experienced the power of God's Spirit penetrating prison walls. Sometimes it is easy to succumb to the assumption that adult theological education is not feasible outside the Church. As a mentor and trainer, Williams has served the incarcerated by leading EfM seminars within prison walls and she shares her insights with us.

"*The Bible begins with two accounts of the creation set side by side.*"

That sentence appears on page 87 of *The Bible for Today's Church,* which is one of the books in the second edition of *The Church's Teaching Series* written by Robert A. Bennett and O.C. Edwards. It started my journey with Education for Ministry (EfM) and eventually into prison ministry.

When I first read that sentence, I was both appalled and angered. Appalled that as a lifelong Episcopalian in my early forties I had never heard of such an important aspect of scripture and angered that no one had bothered to teach me such an important detail.

During the same time, I was beginning to serve on several diocesan boards and committees. Once I realized that my theological knowledge was lacking, I was sure that ignorance about basic Christian subjects would become clear.

What I did after that was search for a remedy for my lack of knowledge. I found several alternatives but the one that hooked my interest the most was EfM. The program was new to my diocese, Iowa, so I signed up for mentor training in 1990. That meant that in my first years in the program, I was a student-mentor. After several years, I mentored groups in two other towns and once, I was doing three groups every week.

As I became more aware of who I was as a Christian, I had a meeting with my bishop, Christopher Epting, to explore what I might do. I had reached a point in my life where I could devote more time to ministry. He asked, since I lived in a town that had a prison, if I had considered prison ministry. My answer was, "Oh no. I can't see myself doing that. I'm a woman. It's a male prison. I'm small. No." I actually said, "I'm small."

I began to do hospital ministry, which was a good fit for me since I had studied in the medical field in college and had a master's degree in several psychology-related areas. That ministry combined my knowledge of hospitals and their procedures, psychology, and theology. In other words, I was comfortable working in an emergency room since I understood the medical side.

In November of 1996 I attended our diocesan convention and a man came up to me and said, "Anne, I've been going into Anamosa State Penitentiary (ASP) along with a couple of others to do evening prayer once every three months. We're going in next Sunday. Would you like to go with us?"

I thought for about three seconds and said, "Yes." The truth was, I couldn't come up with an excuse not to. So that is when I began prison ministry and because I was an EfM mentor, I immediately had a goal of starting a group inside.

Starting a group in a prison setting isn't easy. The first hurdles have to do with establishing a relationship with the administration, security staff, and chaplain. They need to be sure that you are trained in their rules and procedures, can be trusted, and that the program you want to bring to the inmates is one that will enhance the prison, not cause problems. Unfortunately, religious volunteers are somewhat of a weak link in the thinking of prison administrations and security, mostly because we want so badly to help the inmates. That can make us easy targets for manipulation.

In my case, starting with an established volunteer group helped me go into the chapel for a while before even suggesting the idea of EfM. For several years, the only ministry we did was discuss the Sunday's lectionary or participate in a book study. We slowly worked our way from being inside once every three months to every week.

After nine years, I finally was allowed to start an EfM group in 2004. This year marks the twentieth continuous year of the program at Anamosa State Penitentiary—even COVID-19 didn't stop us. The chapel was open most of the pandemic time except for a couple of months—November, December, and January of 2020–21, when the pandemic hit this institution hard. All inmates were restricted to their cell during those months and the chapel was completely closed.

When the restrictions were finally lifted, all of the chapel programming was resumed but without outside volunteers. But since I was on staff at that point, EfM could resume. We finally finished the 2020–21 year in the fall and were able to start the 2021–22 year late, but we did it.

As of this date, ninety-two men have been in the program. Because of transfers, releases, and one death, twenty-six men have graduated! This year there will be another full group.

Throughout the years, whenever someone asked the EfM staff at the School of Theology if the program could be done in a prison, they would refer the person to me. Subsequently, I developed a list of general rules for doing prison ministry to share with potential prison mentors:

- Always ask specific permission about anything, and I mean anything, you take into the prison—what type of writing pen you can take in with you; can you take markers; what about paper clips, CDs, tapes, and books. At this institution, the only things someone can bring in without question are picture IDs and car keys.
- Never take out anything that you didn't bring in. The prisoners' game is to get you to take something insignificant in or out and then it escalates. For instance, "I don't have a stamp for this letter for my mother. Can you mail it for me?" Then

when they ask you for something clearly illegal—bring in a cell phone, drugs, or a weapon—they will come back with, "I'll report that you took out...." Because you don't want to be found out and perhaps banned from the prison, prisoners can manipulate you.
- Always, always be polite to the staff. They are not the enemy. They are doing a difficult job and if you do something against the rules on their shift, they can be in trouble. If you are told to do something by a staff member, do it. Don't question their authority in front of inmates. You can get clarification at another time. If you can't abide by the rules of the institution, you won't be able to go in again.
- Educational opportunities are relatively limited in prisons. It varies from state to state and from institution to institution, but in Iowa, there is almost no education available beyond high school. So just putting up a sign and inviting all to come to a meeting will get you many bodies, but several may not be right for the group. I have been doing some form of Bible study in prison for about nine years. As I began to think about starting an EfM group, I evaluated the men who were attending the Bible study and others who were regulars in the chapel. Given the academic nature of EfM, men that could not stick with the lighter type of Bible study were probably not good candidates. The staff chaplain is a good resource in evaluating who might be a good prospect.
- Reading competency is an issue; however, you don't want to exclude people who lack this skill from benefiting from participation in the group. So often, someone who didn't have a very good academic experience in public school, for one reason or another, really blooms in a program like this since it requires primarily reading and discussion but no papers, tests, or grades. Sometimes you can ask one of the other group members to be a mentor to an individual who may have difficulty with reading, either because of poor reading skills or because English is a second language. Sometimes,

inmates in the same living unit may organize a discussion group outside of the regular EfM time.
- Commitment to the program can be difficult for prison groups. I try to talk to each individual when they apply and again to all of them as the year starts in order to assess their availability. I want to especially stress that EfM isn't a light commitment. In addition to the three hours of class time each week, it takes about the same amount of time outside the class to prepare.
- It is a rare exception when the inmates can pay the fee. Expect to raise the money yourself. Try asking EfM graduates or put a notice in your diocesan newsletter asking for donations. I have been successful in raising almost all of what I have needed. Larger parishes in your diocese might sponsor an individual. If there is someone in the group who is an Episcopalian, their congregation might sponsor them. Your bishop may have some theological education funds upon which you could draw. One benefit to prison groups is that they get a discount. Consult the EfM staff about prison group fees.
- Bibles, prayer books, and hymnals can be obtained for free from The Bible and Common Prayer Book Society of The Episcopal Church, 815 Second Avenue, New York, NY, 10017-4594 (biblesandprayerbooks@episcopalchurch.org; 212-716-6131; fax 212-716-6120). It can take several months to receive them, so start the process several months before your group startup date.
- It is a given that prison groups are going to be ecumenical. That has wonderful benefits for EfM, but it also means that respect for one another's opinions and each person's background is vital. The group I have now runs the gamut from one highly educated Episcopalian, a Roman Catholic, very fundamentalist Christians, and occasionally a non-Christian. Be very clear in setting up expectations about religious affiliation when establishing norms at the beginning of the year and be ready to revisit the issue if needed.

Using "I" statements and not "everyone thinks" statements are crucial. Also, emphasize that the intention of EfM is not to make anyone an Episcopalian but a better Christian.
- On the whole, I've had fewer group dynamic difficulties with the prison group than I've had with any other EfM group. Because the educational opportunities are so limited in prison, EfM, being such a high-quality program, is its own best motivator.
- The sharing of food in a traditional group is usually part of the normal course of events. Prison groups can rarely have food. Depending upon your institution, you might receive permission to bring in food for a final celebration or graduation, or perhaps at Christmas. Just be very sure that you have permission and that you are sensitive to the rules about anything metal. Do not take in anything remotely alcoholic.
- The process of theological reflection (TR) is integral to EfM. Don't shortchange it. There are people who will struggle against the process and will never "get" it, but don't let that stop you. Use as many different types of TR as you can. Doing theological reflection is a huge benefit to people in a prison setting. Individuals are in prison because they made a bad decision; some based on what they can get away with (opportunism), or what feels good (hedonism), or "I'm going to do whatever I want to" (individualism). From the beginning, I emphasize that EfM is going to help them make better decisions. Theological reflection introduces Godly principles into decision making, and that resonates with the prisoners. You'll find that inmates will eventually look forward to TR more than the bookwork.
- Always remember that even though we want to trust and believe others, most of the people in prison are there because they should be there, at least for the time being. Be the presence of God to them, recognize the presence of God in them, help them live to their best potential where they are, but don't get conned.

I received this letter from one graduate:

This evening, I sit in my cell basking in the warmth of God's abundant blessings. YES! God's grace, wisdom, and embrace can find their way over the 40-foot walls of the Anamosa State Penitentiary to enrich the lives of many of the men incarcerated here.

As many in our diocese are aware, ASP is one of a handful of Correctional Institutions in the United States to have an active and robust Education for Ministry seminar group. Thanks to the tireless effort of Rev. Anne Williams, Deacon Melody Rockwell, and to a growing number of you in the diocese who generously support us with time, finances, books, and prayers, we are now in our ninth year! If any of you are familiar with how short-lived programs can be in a correctional setting, you would, as do many of us here, recognize the active hand of God in our studies and discussions regarding the Hebrew and Greek scriptures, Church history, and the world's great theological thinkers and ethics.

Today's discussion came with the added blessing of several distinguished guests. Bishop Nigel Peyton and Mrs. Anne Peyton, from our companion diocese in Brechin, Scotland, the Rev. Barbara and the Rev. Mel Schlachter of Coralville, and a return visit from our long-time friend and mentor deacon, Melody Rockwell.

I am certain that all present would admit to a little apprehension at the beginning. However, as the conversation began, it became—as it should always be for us of Christ's church—sisters and brothers coming together from various backgrounds, denominations, and understanding to bring meaning and life to God's Word and wisdom. The members of our group, both past and present, represent Apostolic Pentecostals, Baptists, Episcopalians, Jehovah's Witnesses, Methodists, Presbyterians, and Roman Catholics. The face of Christ's Church truly is universal!

> The topics covered today in our discussion were the Tower of Babel, New Testament Kerygma and Didache, the Emperors Constantine to Charlemagne, and Immanuel Kant and Fredrich Schleiermacher. Imagine for a moment, 19 people from diverse backgrounds as above coming together and offering differing insight and understanding from the same material, while challenging each other to go deeper into our faith and enriching all. If this is not God's handiwork, I do not know what is.
>
> Sadly, the time came for our new friends to leave and our group to break up for the day. As with each Monday and Tuesday, it passes by too quickly for us all. All of us here at the Anamosa State Penitentiary Education for Ministry group are profoundly thankful for the opportunity of new and lasting friendships and the wonderful support we receive from so many throughout our diocese. We pray that God's blessing will abound in all of your lives, just as they do here. Peace to all.

This graduate also said, when he graduated, that he didn't know what he was going to do after he finished EfM, and then he realized that EfM had prepared him for the rest of his life even though the rest of his life will be spent in prison. He is now a hospice supervisor.

Be the presence of God to them, recognize the presence of God in them, help them live to their best potential where they are, but don't get conned. This has been my motto during these almost thirty years of being a prison volunteer and a member of the staff: "So be wise as serpents and innocent as doves" (Matthew 10:16).

God Kept You Around for a Reason

Termaine Hicks

The prophets of Hebrew Scripture call on the people of God to seek justice and to be a light to others. Hicks, an EfM graduate, was accused of a crime he didn't commit. Understanding God's grace, coupled with the power of forgiveness, takes a lifetime of prayer and discernment. Hicks discovered grace, forgiveness, and discernment as a participant in an EfM seminar while incarcerated.

Twenty-two years ago in my neighborhood in South Philadelphia, I heard the screams of a woman being raped. I followed her voice to the alley. As I arrived, I reached for my cell phone to call 911. At that same moment, the police arrived on the scene and mistook me for the assailant. They shot me three times in my back before my hand even came out of my pocket.

What happened next happens far too often. The police lied. They planted a gun on me and said I pointed it at them. But that gun actually belonged to an off-duty Philadelphia police officer and was not reported stolen until the day after I was shot. Based on their false testimony, I was convicted and sentenced to twelve-and-a-half to twenty-five years in prison. I served nearly nineteen-and-a-half years of that sentence because I refused to accept responsibility for a crime I did not commit just to make parole. I couldn't do it, although I thought about it. I wanted out, but that would have been too big of a burden for me to bear. To walk around as a convicted rapist, register as a sex offender, and try to find gainful employment knowing I was innocent?

I believe I'm a pretty strong guy, but to try and function under those circumstances? Ain't no way!

There are so many different ways one could look at what happened to me and be outraged, appalled, angry, upset, and be justified to feel as such. I, however, was the one who actually experienced it. I was the one who was lying on the ground bleeding out, feeling his life slip away. And I choose to look at it from a different perspective.

You see, today could have easily been the twenty-second anniversary of my death. Today I could've been a memory to my family, a legend to my grandson. Or today could have been my twenty-second year confined to a wheelchair because one of those bullets hit my spine. Or, had I taken the deal of a 30–60-year sentence the district attorney's office offered me, I'd still be incarcerated because I pled guilty, and guilty pleas are a little bit tougher to overturn. I could still be sitting in the penitentiary if the New York Innocence Project had not taken on my case and fought like hell to prove my innocence.

Life will come at you. It will come at you fast. It will come at you unexpectedly in the form of an accident or deliberately by the hands of another human being. What are you going to do? And how are you going to assess your new reality?

I remember a conversation I had with the nurse whose job it was to bathe me after my surgery. I didn't know how many times I had been shot. And when I asked her if she knew how many times I had been shot, she sat the sponge down, looked me square in the eyes. "Baby," she said, "I don't know. But you have about seven bullet holes in your body. God kept you around for a reason. You need to figure out why."

She then pointed to every bullet hole, lifting up my arm and showing me exactly where every bullet entered and exited my body. One of the bullets made three wounds. It entered the back of my right arm, exited the inside of my right arm and entered my right lateral chest wall where it collapsed my lung. That hand was in my pocket when I was shot, not extended pointing a gun at a cop. "God kept you around for a reason," she repeated. "You need to figure out why."

A year after I was convicted and my case was on appeal, I was looking for a way to make sense of all of this. I took a quick inventory of what I liked to do and writing was the one thing that kept coming to the top of my list. As a kid growing up in the '80s, I fell in love with hip-hop and aspired to be a rapper. I used to write raps daily. But as I grew older, other things began to interest me. The time and energy it took to muse and to jot down lyrics was no longer there and I just stopped writing altogether.

In 2002, I wrote a pretty cool play titled *The Christmas Conspiracy*. In short, Santa Claus was this Russian drug lord named Nikoli Klauskis who created the whole Christmas season just to smuggle drugs across the world. Frosty the Snowman was his hitman, named IceMan, and Rudolph? Well, poor Rudolph was the transporter who was caught smuggling the drugs during a blizzard because his nose kept alerting the authorities as to his whereabouts. He got arrested and snitched on the whole operation. Needless to say, the men loved it and that officially put me on the map in the penitentiary as a talented playwright.

I wasn't completely locked in as a writer at this point. I was focused on getting my wrongful conviction overturned. Nothing mattered but my appeal, but the appeal process is a long one. It's a hurry up and wait—months, sometimes years—before a ruling comes down, and in my case it was denial after denial. Two decades of denials. Dozens of judges looking over my case, and still, denial. But God kept me around for a reason.

In between my denials, and to maintain my sanity, writing became my therapy. It gave me the ability to create an alternate environment from the bizarre one I found myself in—an innocent man, yet according to the law, a convicted rapist.

In 2007, I was transferred to Graterford State Penitentiary (GSP) to be closer to my family in Philadelphia, especially my son. I had been at Somerset, a state correctional institution outside of Pittsburgh, approximately six hours from the city, and, as a result, I did not see my son for the first seven years of my incarceration.

That was tough. In lieu of not seeing him in person, I wrote him a letter every single week for thirteen years and called as often as I could.

For a very long time I was in denial about what happened to me. It was hard for me to accept that I was actually shot, convicted, and sitting in the penitentiary for something I didn't do. It was the twilight zone. I was watching my son grow up before my eyes through visitations. But when he turned eighteen and was able to visit me on his own without being accompanied by an adult, and he walked through the visiting room door alone as a young man, it really hit me hard. I cried. That was a joyous, but tough, day.

It was at Graterford when I was introduced to Education for Ministry (EfM), and in the fall of 2008, I met the new facilitator, who had just taken over for a man who had recently passed away.

Thankfully by this time—seven years in—I was already an avid Bible reader, deeply immersed in my spirituality, and had a sound understanding of my relationship with my Creator. So when I was invited to sit in on one of EfM's classes to see if I'd be interested in a theological education, I thought, "Why not?" I was already in full pursuit of my purpose. God kept me around for a reason and I needed to find out why, and the program felt like the next natural step to take in this journey.

The fellow prisoner who invited me to sit in on my very first EfM class and who is serving a life sentence said, "Mayne. Just a heads up, this isn't your typical Bible study class." I didn't think much of it until the facilitator said the exact same thing to the group of twelve men, all of whom I already knew.

EfM is an intense theological four-year study that will no doubt first challenge your belief in all of the biblical/historical stories you've been told, read, or even watched on television and will essentially flip that all upside down.

It introduces you to the concept, with no lead up, that the stories in the Bible are a myth. Or a legend. Excuse me? A myth is a widely held but false belief or idea. And legend—a historical but unauthenticated story. What are y'all talking about? In my mind, if the Word of God said it happened, it happened.

It took some getting used to, hearing that the Bible is a book full of varying beliefs, conflicting accounts, and unauthenticated stories. You definitely need a solid, personal foundation before entering into a comprehensive theological study like this. Some guys didn't last long because of this critical thinking–based theological examination.

When I started Year One—the Hebrew Bible—it was by far the most challenging year for me. There were six of us in this group. By the end of Year One, and on to my graduation at the completion of Year Four, it was just me holding it down. I enjoyed it all. Embraced it all because God kept me around for a reason and I was determined to figure out why.

By the time of my EfM graduation I had written and produced about eight plays. And because my graduation ceremony was about two hours long and I was the last man standing, I asked if I could perform a play. The facilitator said absolutely. She'd heard all about my plays and now she would have an opportunity to see one. I named this play, "Soldiers in the Army of the Lord" because EfM's curriculum was definitely a battle. The performers were some of the group participants.

I played the lead. His name was Sgt. Holisroller but was affectionately called "Sgt. Holy-Roller" by his battalion. He was a no-nonsense, Bible-thumping drill sergeant whose dialogue consisted of biblical myths, legends, and scriptures. His duty was to encourage and equip them with the necessary tools to be effective soldiers in the army of the Lord.

While attending EfM sessions, writing plays, and working in the chaplaincy department, I was noticing how the prison population was getting younger and younger. These young men were coming through with long sentences and life sentences without the possibility of parole. After talking with a few of them I learned that almost all had gotten into a fight because of something small—someone scuffed their sneakers, said something to their girlfriend, or trash talked on the ball court. That led to a fight, losing that fight, then getting a gun to shoot and kill the offender. Now they're in the penitentiary with a life sentence, and a life sentence in Pennsylvania means you're never getting out. A fight they lost and that could have been prevented if cooler heads had prevailed. It cost them their freedom for the rest of their lives.

That messed with me. I empathized with their situation because it could have been prevented. I also noticed how they gravitated toward my plays. They loved watching them on the jail's video station. They would stop me and recite dialogue from their favorite character that I created. When word got out I was working on another play, I wasn't short of actors. These men were lining up to be in the next production.

So in 2008 I shifted my playwriting focus to writing short educational scripts to teach critical thinking and conflict resolution. The goal was to help curb gun violence and bullying within schools and neighborhoods and to hopefully prevent future kids from coming through the penitentiary or from killing one another.

I titled this collection of scripts "STEPUP," an acronym which stands for Selfless Thinking Expresses Potential *that* Uplifts People. I walk the viewers through the worst possible outcomes to the most feasible ones through a series of reenactments. I wrote several of these STEPUP scripts with the hope of having them produced while still incarcerated. That was not to be.

Finally, and I mean—finally!—I was exonerated. Talk about a whirlwind of events. I went from sitting in a cell, binge-watching TV in the midst of a pandemic, to a phone call from my Innocence Project attorney telling me that the judge had just vacated my sentence, exonerated me, and even apologized for the wrong done to me for two decades! Imagine that! My attorney was on the phone with the Department of Corrections working on my immediate release. Soon the guard tapped on the door to tell me that I was going home. And just like that, it was over.

It was nine months before I knew what I wanted to do in my ministry. I spent that time taking everything in—reuniting with family, getting acclimated to current society, and just taking my time. Once I was settled, I began to take another look at those STEPUP scripts I wrote while in prison.

God had kept me around for a reason and I finally figured out why—STEPUP. Violence was pervasive and now I was experiencing it in real time. Something had to be done. So I turned STEPUP into a 501(c)(3) nonprofit and produced *STEPUP to Help Curb Gun Violence*. Six months later I added *STEPUP to Say No to Bullies*. I started going into schools around the country teaching critical thinking and conflict resolution.

My goal is to have STEPUP films in every classroom across the country. STEPUP has a YouTube channel, @Stepup2008. If I can get to 1,000 subscribers, it will help me achieve this goal.

Three months after my exoneration I was asked by the facilitator of EfM from Graterford prison if I would consider becoming a board member for the Dennis H. Warner Memorial Foundation. The foundation is now named EAIF, an acronym which stands for Educational Assistance for the Incarcerated and Freed. Warner created this foundation to award scholarships to family members or released inmates from the state correctional institution. It allows them to further their education upon their release or to assist a family member's educational goals. I was honored to be considered for such a role.

Thanks to my life's experiences and my association with Education for Ministry, I've learned that if you're open to it, you will have all the tools necessary to discover why God kept you around.

EfM'S EMERGING VOICES

EfM and the Challenge of Gender: Past, Present, and Future

Tara K. Soughers

Learning to listen to many voices in the Christian faith and in culture is a deep value in the EfM program. Author, priest, and trainer, Soughers has been an advocate for meaningful dialogue with those we might be tempted to name as "other" for many years. Here she discusses a voice close to her own heart.

Few Episcopalians in 1976 would have been unaware of the General Convention that met in September. Even a young, fifteen-year-old Episcopalian from a small town in Indiana knew that momentous and controversial things were being discussed. The threat of schism, a word that I came to understand during that time, was being openly discussed. It wasn't discussed that much in my small parish church, at least in the hearing of its younger members, but it was on the nightly news. As the Church went through its convulsions, it seemed that the whole world was watching. In addition to dramatic changes in the Book of Common Prayer, the question of ordaining women was before the group for the third time. This time it was after eleven women had been ordained priests by three retired bishops in Philadelphia in July 1974 and an additional four were ordained in Washington, DC, in September of 1975. It was clear that those in favor of women's ordination were not content to simply wait passively for the General Convention to approve it.

Gender roles had long been contentious in The Episcopal Church. The first female deputy to the General Convention, Elizabeth Dyer, was actually elected from the Diocese of Missouri in 1946.[1] She was allowed to be seated and served in that capacity. By the end of that General Convention, however, it voted that the term "layman" was restricted to those of the male gender and women were prevented from being seated as deputies at General Convention, even if elected by their dioceses. That did not change until 1970, the same year that the ordination of women was first raised on the convention floor. With the precedent in place of interpreting male pronouns and gendered words in a way that upheld traditional gender roles, the General Convention refused to accept the gendered language of the ordination vows and canons as referring to women, even though comparable language was also used in canons relating to Baptism and membership where it was clear that masculine words and pronouns were being used to refer to all Christians. When the retired bishops stepped out of line and ordained women, they were charged with ignoring proper procedures and violating the collegiality of the House of Bishops. The House of Bishops first tried to declare those ordinations invalid, but because there was no prohibition against ordaining women in place and the House of Bishops had already passed a resolution indicating that they believed the women were capable of being ordained, they finally had to settle for the ordinations being considered irregular and bishops were asked not to allow the women to be licensed or to serve in their dioceses until General Convention approval.

At the General Convention of 1976, there was a valid concern that The Episcopal Church might break apart over this issue. It was clear that those favoring the ordination of women were willing to take matters into their own hands if the change was not approved. However, because of the way that votes are taken, it wasn't clear if there would be enough votes in the House of

---

1. The Episcopal Diocese of Missouri, accessed June 18, 2024, https://diocesemo.org/blog/elizabeth-dyer/.

Deputies to pass it. Opponents of women's ordination argued that it required a Constitutional amendment, which would then require the vote of two separate General Conventions to pass. Therefore, the earliest possible passage of the ordination of women would be at the General Convention of 1979. In a letter of advice to the Presiding Bishop John Hines, the Chancellor of the Diocese of Central New York Hugh Jones argued that what was needed was not a constitutional change but a resolution, a canonical amendment, stating that when the canons used gendered language, it should be construed as referring to both men and women. It was not clear whether even this would pass the House of Deputies, as opponents were sure to call for a vote by orders. In that case, each delegation would have one clergy and one lay vote and any delegation in which the clergy and lay members were in disagreement would be counted as a "no" vote. As the vote in the House of Deputies began, the tension was high, and it narrowly passed. For the clergy delegations, fifty-eight positive votes were necessary, and sixty were received. For the lay votes, fifty-seven were needed, and sixty-four were received.

I have spent a great deal of time detailing the history of women's ordination because it is one of the first of the major controversies that has beset The Episcopal Church in the past fifty years—the time in which Education for Ministry (EfM) has been a part of the way in which we, as a Church, have dealt with controversies. Many of the controversies that have rocked our Church have been, at their roots, disagreements around gender: gender roles, sexual orientation, women's bodily autonomy, and gender identity. What it means to be a man or a woman or neither or both, and what difference that makes in cultural expectations about behavior, presentation, and roles lay at the root of these controversies. In addition, controversies that are around gender are often the most emotionally intense debates. Church teachings in these areas have often upheld culturally imposed roles for women and men, often relegating women to a second-class status or to the status of children who cannot make their own medical decisions.

In addition, Church teachings have generally promoted the belief that gender is both binary and static. This belief led to the understanding that gender is determined at birth as either male or female based upon the morphology of the external genitalia, ignoring the fact that for somewhere between 0.018 and 1.7 percent of the population (depending upon the precise definition of intersex),[2] gender is not clearly defined at birth. The long history of trying to "make" intersex people into culturally acceptable men and women, with clearly defined genitals, demonstrates the problematic nature of Church teachings on gender. In addition, the presence of transgender or gender nonbinary people has also challenged traditional understandings of gender.

None of the issues around gender roles, same-sex relationships, abortion, or the immutability of gender have been resolved. While many thought that with the passage of *Roe v. Wade* more than fifty years ago, the issues of abortion had been dealt with. The overturning of that longstanding precedent by the Supreme Court in 2022 has demonstrated that those who want to maintain traditional understandings of gender are still at work in our culture as well as in our Church.

Education for Ministry has served an important role in the discussion of these contentious issues in its fifty years of existence. Although those who are in favor of traditional understandings of gender and social issues have often claimed that EfM is a "liberal" program, and indeed, I think that many of those attracted to the program lean more liberal than conservative, I do not believe that it is EfM that makes people accept the "liberal" point of view. Instead, I believe that some of the core values of the EfM program have led those willing to deeply explore difficult issues and topics to find a home with the program.

Two of these values are the expectation of treating all experiences with respect and the assertion that we are not in EfM

---

2. Leonard Sax, "How Common Is Intersex? A Response to Anne Fausto-Sterling," *Journal of Sex Research* 39, no. 3 (2002), 174–178, accessed June 18, 2024, https://doi.org/10.1080/00224490209552139.

to debate who is right or wrong.³ These values are often not the ones that conservative views hold as valuable. If one already knows the "right" answer, there really is no need to listen to those whose voices challenge your views, and if the answer is clear, then it can be frustrating to be in a group where one is not allowed to try to convert others to their point of view.

EfM is not a program designed to make sure that all people come to the right answer. In fact, practices such as theological reflection encourage a variety of different understandings and they require us to listen, without judgment, to people whose lives and experiences are different from our own. Although fairly homogeneous groups—in terms of gender, race, ethnic background, and class—can shield us somewhat from the dissonance that comes when tightly held truths are challenged by the experiences of others, honest conversation within such groups often demonstrates more diversity than we might expect. In any case, contact with the material, particularly interlude books, may also provide voices and perspectives missing in the local groups.

In our current time, societal understandings of gender, gender roles, and gender expressions are still highly contested. As understandings of these issues evolve and grow, the Church and EfM are going to have to grow and evolve as well. EfM, with its practice of deeply listening to others across differences and being open to transformation and conversion of life, seems to offer our community and the Church at large a model of how we navigate these issues. Theological reflection, in particular, asks us to consider a variety of sources in our attempts to make sense of the way in which God is calling us to live our own lives and to live in community with others. We are called to explore the wideness of the Christian tradition, not simply the proof texts that have traditionally been used to define gender and gender roles, but also admitting that the community of faith has always

---

3. Although these are long-held core values for the EfM program, the use of the Kaleidoscope Institute Material, particularly the Respectful Communication Guidelines, has highlighted these values in recent years.

encompassed a diverse and eclectic collection of "saints." We are called to examine our deeply held beliefs, wondering how we came to them. We are called to broaden our experience of the world through interactions with others who are different from us and whose lives have been filled with alternative experiences. Finally, we are called to take seriously our own culture and times, especially the scientific knowledge around gender that was not available in the time of Jesus or earlier in the time of the prophets.

For perhaps the most important value in EfM is the acknowledgment that God is not through with us yet, either as individuals or as a Church. EfM calls us to be open to growth and transformation. May we continue to believe that, through our work together as well as through the power of the Holy Spirit, we will continue to grow ever more into the people God is calling us to be.

Seeking Racial Diversity

José R. Fernández

Just as The Episcopal Church longs for racial diversity, so does Education for Ministry. Priest, scientist, professor, EfM mentor, and trainer, Fernández offers his experience as an EfM participant and encourages a path to naming the voices that are missing from the table.

"He is not one of them! He is NOT one of them! He is... he is... he is... like my son!" The words directed at me were heavy, charged with teary emotion and frustration. I would like to believe that they stopped the conversation, but they were more like a knife that cracked a block of ice exposing the formidable reality of racism among us. Everyone else stayed quiet; nobody knew what to say. I placed my hand on top of Jane's and said, "I love you, too, Jane. I love you, too." There was nothing else to say. The wisdom of Pat, the group's Education for Ministry (EfM) mentor, broke the silence and redirected the "Show and Tell" conversation to the discussion of the readings.

We never talked about it again, at least not in front of Jane. We never discussed the discomfort that sharing the church with "those people" was causing in the once welcoming white Episcopal community. We never talked about why some people considered the Hispanic children to be wild, unmannered, or that they behaved like savages. We never asked Jane why she referred to the Hispanics as "those people" but did not consider me one of them. I found it interesting that in the weeks to come, themes of charity vs. ministry, equity vs. equality, and words like sharing, neighbors, unconditional love, and respect permeated our theological reflections.

Some people apologized to me after the EfM meeting. The truth was that I did not feel offended or hurt. I felt Jane's love and understood where she was coming from. Perhaps a part of me had already become numb to situations like this. After all, I had been exposed to the deep South. I was in a biracial marriage, lived a pretty "white" middle-class life, and was very aware of my place and identity. I am brown, I have an accent, but I have always been treated like I'm not "quite" one of them—perhaps not brown enough to be Hispanic, or black enough to be Black. There is never a question about my genetic ancestry of 59 percent European, 31 percent African, and 10 percent Amerindian, the perfect genetic profile for a Puerto Rican, as documented by research. I got used to others treating me like I was not one of "those people," like I belonged to a different group that granted me a different level of privilege that I didn't understand and didn't know how to use.

Jane did not return to the EfM class the following year. I never knew if it was because of that night or because of the exodus of white people that subsequently happened in that church. I do, however, remember that during my fourth year of EfM, the group was the most diverse I had ever experienced. EfM was transformed from just a class into an EfM table—a place where spiritual growth was nurtured with a lullaby of acceptance, respect, and solidarity. A table of twelve people of diverse cultures, races, religious beliefs, and sexual orientations. A place where belonging was more powerful than segregation, where authenticity was celebrated, and our personal stories blended into the greater splendor of humanity. That table brought me hope, redefined my place not only as a Christian but also as a person, and gave me a sense of belonging and purpose. When I graduated from EfM in 2007, I wanted others like me to experience that, so it didn't take much from Pat to convince me to train as a co-mentor.

On the way to the School of Theology in Sewanee, Tennessee, headquarters of the EfM program, Pat tried to prepare me for what I was going to encounter at the training. I found her tone unusual, somewhere between alerting me and begging me to stay in my lane. I did not want to disappoint her or myself, so I was on my best behavior and embraced with assimilation the racial uniformity of the group. There was no doubt that the EfM mentoring community was a little different from my EfM table experience at home. I carried the torch of being the only person of color at that EfM training in the summer of 2007.

My journey within EfM often felt like navigating between worlds. Eighteen months after that first mentor training, I returned to the mountain to train and met another fellow mentor trainee from India who had come to serve as a priest in the United States. My joy at seeing another person of color was tempered by the realization that our experiences and theological perspectives were worlds apart. Despite his presence, the EfM training room was still far from representing the community outside its doors. For the next ten years, I participated in EfM mentor training, understanding that this program that I love so much was not a cross-sectional representation of the population around us. I also mentored many tables throughout the years—many wonderful tables with incredible people, whose stories and love I share and treasure, whose footprints have marked my heart and transformed my essence in unexpected and breathtaking ways. Yet, I was never able to replicate the diversity that I experienced in my fourth year of EfM or the sense of belonging that such an experience brought to my life, until I received a call that changed that reality.

I was in my office when I took the scheduled call inviting me to a one-week training of trainers. Elsa Bakkum, assistant director for training, explained how intentional she had been in creating a diverse group of emerging trainers for EfM. Her voice was reassuring and convincing, carrying a familiar tone of a lullaby of acceptance, respect, and solidarity that rocks a cradle of spiritual growth. I was intrigued, and so I accepted.

In 2017, I attended my first training of trainers, where I experienced a glimpse of what I believed EfM should look like—a vision of an inclusive table. This group was the closest to my fourth year EfM table. It consisted of ten people: seven trainees and three trainers. We were not all Episcopalians, five were female, five were gay, and four trainees were people of color. This was not a coincidence but an intentional effort to diversify the training community. It was a deliberate decision to widen the circle, to extend the table, and to make room for voices that had been absent for too long. The work together was energizing and the experience was transformative. The joy was exhilarating, but most importantly, there was an emerging hope for EfM to be more representative of the world and the people around us.

Every time I think about those seven friends who trained together, I smile with gratitude. The bond of that week of training is something we shared deeply, and whenever we see each other, there is a spark of hope and love that ignites within our hearts. We are drawn to each other like magnets, attracted by an unexplainable electromagnetic field of sacred and divine shared spiritual siblinghood. I always wonder, how did that happen? The answer is always the same: it happened because of intention.

The Judeo-Christian tradition rooted in our EfM curriculum invites us to be intentional. In the book of Samuel, when the prophet is sent by the Lord to find and anoint the new king among the sons of Jesse, Samuel is reminded that "people look at the outward appearance, but the Lord looks at the heart" (1 Samuel 7). Intention comes from the heart of all of us. It was the intention that motivated the Good Samaritan to care for the beaten man and it was the intention that Jesus praised when stating, "Blessed are the pure in heart, for they will see God" (Matthew 5:8). Yet, as James 1:22 invites us, intentions must be accompanied by actions.

I believe EfM can transform the world. I believe EfM should be the ecumenical formation tool for laypeople around the globe. I believe that EfM groups should look more like the people in our communities—diverse, vibrant, and truly reflective of God's creation. And I believe that these goals can be achieved only if we are intentional and act on them.

For EfM's next fifty years, I pray that, rather than forming EfM groups, we create EfM tables. Tables where intellectual food and wine overflow, where laughter and joy overwhelm, and where learning, sharing, and spiritual growth are available and accessible to all. I pray that each of us takes the challenge we face of needing to diversify this program as an opportunity—a call to step beyond comfort and use our divine intentionality to engage in the messy, beautiful work of building community. We must continue to be intentional about who sits at the table, seeking out voices from different racial, cultural, and theological backgrounds. We must seek out voices that challenge the status quo and push us toward a deeper understanding of who we are as people, who we are as Christians, and who we are as the Church. This is not about tokenism; it is about accepting and embracing the fact that our differences can become our strengths, and that when we create a space at the table for those who have been marginalized, our learning becomes richer, our conversations more honest, our sense of community more complete, and our humanity more splendid.

To make this happen, we must be courageous enough to look at who is missing and ask why. We must identify the barriers—whether they are cultural, economic, or simply a matter of feeling out of place—and commit to tearing them down. We must extend genuine invitations, offer support, and ensure that EfM is a place where everyone feels they belong, not just in theory, but in practice. And this is doable. All we need to do is turn intentions into actions and hold on to hope with the reaffirmation that the divine share of God within you is the same as the divine share of God in the person next to you, regardless of how that person looks.

I hold onto this hope. I believe in the power of EfM to be a force for change; to create spaces where each person is not just seen but celebrated, and where the radical hospitality of God's love can be embodied. The journey might not be easy, but it is worth it, and it will lead us to live into the Gospel call to love, justice, and reconciliation in new and transformative ways. And perhaps, as we experience such change, we will understand what it means to be drawn to each other like magnets, attracted by an unexplainable electromagnetic field of sacred and divine shared spiritual siblinghood.

Seeking Political Diversity

Gaines Campbell

In times of political and social discord, how do we navigate multiple points of view? Can our "position statements" allow space for other beliefs? Mentor and former trainer, Campbell offers his perspective.

In our world of political divisiveness, one would hope there could be some refuge in the love of God. But as we error-prone humans try to make sense of God, we create religious doctrine that can stray from God's purpose. Christianity, as just one of many religions that has done so, is even further subdivided into numerous denominations ranging from the extreme right of biblical literalism (conservative theology) to the extreme left of anything goes if you love God and neighbor (liberal theology).

Unfortunately, these left and right leanings often align with cultural left and right political leanings. Why this alignment exists is beyond the scope of this essay, but it does serve as a starting point for understanding why the Education for Ministry (EfM) program struggles with political diversity. For instance, since EfM is centered on liberal theology, most of the participants lean toward the left, theologically and politically. It is also beyond the scope of this essay to discuss the implications of how to be inviting to those who lean right theologically. Some people, however, are mixed, in that they, like me, lean left theologically but lean right politically. Their theology lines up with that of

EfM, but they are still in the minority politically and that can be a deterrent.

EfM is challenged in how to manage triggering comments and difficult conversations when it comes to political diversity. The challenges of that management are manifold, some of which are encouraging respectful communication guidelines; creating an environment to occasionally hold difficult conversations; creating a safe place for the minority to speak up with an opposite point of view; managing the conversation when triggering comments are made; and inviting all parties to live into the mystery that, in God's world, opposite points of view can both be right or can both hold a "truth."

When I first enrolled in EfM in 2000, none of these issues seemed to be present in my group. When I became a mentor in 2003, I was not aware of, or equipped, to handle any of these challenges. I cannot tell you the liberal/conservative makeup of the groups in my first three or four years mentoring because it didn't seem to be of concern. However, I began a new group in 2007 in which, unintentionally, the participants were mainly politically conservative. We did not necessarily have political conversations, but the conversations were bent toward the conservative point of view. I do not know how this affected the liberal participants because they never said anything to me, nor was I proactive in making sure they weren't withdrawing.

From 2013 on I have been in groups in which most of the participants were politically liberal. In fact, I was the only conservative in most of them. Personally, I was not there for political discussion and anytime comments were made that triggered me, I never spoke up for several reasons: I was not there to debate points or to point out my perception of the inaccuracies of what was said; I didn't want to derail the conversation that was currently at hand; I wanted to have thoughtful theological reflection without people feeling they had to be careful not to step on my toes; and I felt hiding my conservative view prevented the liberals from being ill at ease in sharing their talking points (which helped me learn more about the liberal point of view).

Comparing these discussions with my experiences of having political conversations with my conservative friends, I draw the following anecdotal conclusions: Many liberals are just as stuck in their point of view as many conservatives are in theirs; only the rare conservative and rare liberal are truly interested in why the person of the opposite side believes the way they do; when liberals or conservatives are in a group of likeminded people they rarely temper what they have to say and seem to buy into all the hyperbole of their group; and when I try to point out to my conservative friends that everything a liberal believes is not wrong, they don't want to hear it. (I suspect it's the same for liberals.)

This leads me to a perplexing question: Is it human nature to be dualistic? I believe it is likely that throughout human history dualistic thinking was a survival skill. This may be ingrained in humans and, in our modern culture, has moved into areas of thinking that aren't survival oriented. I wonder if most people want everything to be clear cut with no gray area and for all beliefs to be either right or wrong. It certainly can make things easier to analyze. It may take more complex thinking than we care to engage in to move toward non-dualistic thinking.

From another perspective, maybe we don't want to be open to gray areas because it may change our identity—the core of how we view ourselves. Even as I have become more open to liberal points of view, I cannot imagine that I would ever identify as being liberal.

Consider an issue like climate change. If you want to get your message out that humans need to change their behavior, is it possible to generate passion and mass attention if you admit you are not 100 percent sure of your beliefs? Many scientists who strongly believe that we need to take corrective action quickly also admit that their certainty level is not as high as projected in the media. For instance, well-known climate scientist and strong advocate for change, the late Stephen Schneider was often accused of not telling the whole truth. His response to those accusations was to detail the difficulty of giving a balanced perspective in his media interviews because they were short snippets that never allowed enough time for all the nuances of his beliefs.[1] So, does that mean our modern desire to receive all our news in short, quick flashes prevents us from hearing and understanding all the gray areas of beliefs? Is this one of the culprits that encourages people to stay in dualistic thinking? Or is it our dualistic thinking that causes our desire for short, quick flashes of news, because it is easier to process? Maybe we wouldn't stay on the news channel if too many nuances were presented.

What does all of this have to do with EfM? I believe we should encourage non-dualistic thinking to lead to an understanding that our world is not made up of rights and wrongs. Climate scientists use a whole range of terms like "very high confidence" to "very low confidence" (five levels)[2] or "virtually certain" to "exceptionally unlikely" (seven levels)[3] when describing their level of confidence and certainty in the predictions they are making. I wonder if we all should do this when making a belief statement. It could benefit us to reflect on it and assess the level of confidence and certainty we have in it.

How can we use this in EfM? I believe we need to establish a level of comfort with conflicting viewpoints, creating an opportunity for people to speak up when they disagree without fear of starting an argument. For instance, we need a means for people to say something like, "I disagree with what you just said, but so we don't go down a rabbit hole right now, I want to talk about that later." We need to train mentors to be proactive with their groups to prevent a small minority from feeling left out, leading them to maybe drop out or not return the following year. We need a politically balanced curriculum. We need mentors who are

---

1. Understanding and Solving the Climate Change Problem. "Mediarology": https://stephenschneider.stanford.edu/Mediarology/Mediarology.
2. Richard A. Moss and Stephen H. Schneider, "UNCERTAINTIES IN THE IPCC TAR: Recommendations To Lead Authors For More Consistent Assessment and Reporting," in R.Pachauri,T.Taniguchi, K.Tanaka, eds., *Guidance Papers on the Cross Cutting Issues of the Third Assessment Report of the IPCC* (IPCC, 2000).
3. David V. Budescu, Han-Hui Por, and Stephen B. Broomell, "Effective Communication of Uncertainty in the IPCC Reports," *Climatic Change* 113, no. 2 (2012): 181–200. http://dx.doi.org/10.1007/s10584-011-0330-3.

willing to lead difficult conversations and we need trainers who know how to train mentors in leading challenging discussions.

As a Christian-based group, we live into the mystery of the Trinity, and into the mystery that Jesus is both divine and human. These are both concepts beyond our human understanding. It is my belief then, in a world in which God is not bound by human limitations, that it is not so far-fetched to believe that we can also live into the mystery of non-dualism. Perhaps we are called to learn how to live into the mystery that two opposite ideas can both hold a truth, or both hold the whole truth. The hope is that seeking more political diversity in the makeup of our seminar groups will create opportunities for richer theological reflections, encouraging us to grow into a greater understanding of God's purpose.

Exploring the Challenges and Opportunities of EfM in Reaching Adults Across All Ages

Hannah Graham

EfM is a big commitment in both tuition and time. Young people trying to establish careers and families often do not have the luxury of committing to thirty-six weeks of seminar sessions, to say nothing of the reading and preparation. Mentor and trainer Graham speaks of EfM's meaning and value in her experience as a young mother.

Education for Ministry (EfM) is a program designed to deepen the Christian faith of its participants, equipping them to explore their beliefs and engage with their communities in meaningful ways. Reaching adults of all ages, however, has been a significant hurdle for the program, particularly in the face of modern-day demands and commitments.

One of the primary challenges is the time commitment required by EfM. Seminars are held weekly for two to three hours with an additional three to four hours of reading required to prepare for each session. This level of commitment can be overwhelming for full-time working adults, especially those with other responsibilities such as caring for children. Balancing work, family life, and personal spiritual development is a delicate act and many potential participants find it difficult to dedicate the necessary time to fully engage in the program. This challenge is compounded by the fact that adults in different stages of life have varying needs and availability, making it hard for EfM to cater to everyone equally.

Despite these challenges, the opportunities that EfM presents are profound. The content and insights gained through the program are invaluable, especially for those involved in shaping the next generation of Christians. The deep theological reflection and practical applications make EfM an essential tool for lay leaders, educators, and parents alike. Recognizing the need to reach a broader demographic, EfM will be introducing new structures like "EfM: Wide Angle" and "EfM: Reflections." These offerings have the potential to introduce the program to a broader audience, allowing more people to benefit from its rich content in a format that may be more accessible for those with demanding schedules.

Education for Ministry has continuously adapted to meet the changing needs of its participants, especially in response to the challenges posed by COVID-19. Gathering online became necessary during the pandemic, and this shift continues to allow people to connect across distances. The flexibility of cutting down on commuting to and from weekly groups and participating from home when childcare isn't available has made EfM more accessible to busy parents and working adults. The program now offers more online and hybrid models where groups primarily meet virtually but occasionally gather in person, providing a balance that accommodates the modern, fast-paced lives of participants. This adaptation has especially benefited younger adults, including those who travel for work.

My journey with EfM began in 2012 and has been an integral part of my lay Christian formation. Initially, I was asked to start a group in my congregation, not fully realizing the profound impact it would have on my life. Over the years I have served as a participant, mentor, and trainer, each role deepening my understanding of what the kingdom of God looks like on Earth. A particularly moving example of this was when my EfM class rallied around my family during a challenging time. My husband and I needed to sell our home and at the time had two very young children to care for. The entire EfM class showed up on a Saturday to help prepare the house for a showing. The support and love I experienced that day still brings tears to my eyes.

EfM has also taught me the importance of asking questions and wrestling with beliefs, an invaluable skill as I navigate the challenges of raising my three boys. The program has shaped my faith and equipped me to guide my family in their spiritual journeys.

Hope for the future of EfM lies in its ability to adapt and evolve. Introducing new program structures demonstrates a responsiveness to the needs of the modern adult learner. Through continued adaptation and a commitment to fostering deep, supportive communities, EfM will continue to be vital to Christian formation for many more years to come.

EPILOGUE

EfM: All the Pieces Matter

Kevin M. Goodman

This volume of collected essays celebrates the history, evolution, and experiences of people connected to Education for Ministry. Goodman, participant, mentor, trainer, and the program's current executive director, connects the program's history with what is next as lovers of the program work together to prepare EfM for the next fifty years.

I believe the greatest television series ever created was David Simon's and Ed Burns's *The Wire*. Across five seasons, viewers got to know and love all the characters, corners, and systems navigated by the citizens of Baltimore. We met cops, corner kids, and the leaders who moved product—sex trafficking, drugs, and money. We campaigned with politicians, worked the program with recovering addicts, and sat in classrooms with teachers and students. We waited for the morning edition, traversed the dock union, and confronted the horror of human trafficking. As we moved between housing projects, courtrooms, police stations, and church gathering spaces and, as we fell in love with the people who occupied these places, we discovered that all the pieces mattered.

All the pieces mattered.

In Education for Ministry (EfM), all the pieces matter. EfM participants gather in small groups in all sorts of spaces. Their mentors, loaded with perspective questions, accompany the participants through worship, study, reflection, and even eating. Coordinators partner with bishops and diocesan staff to get the word out, supporting these cohorts of transformation with encouragement, connection, and prayer. Trainers support mentors, empowering them with insights into group dynamics and theological reflection processes. Faithful leaders are accredited to do the work God calls them to do. Program center staff at the Beecken Center within the School of Theology at the University of the South strategize, organize, and administer what is needed to bring all of these pieces together into a sustainable and transformational program—a program that began fifty years ago when the School of Theology's faculty assembled their lecture notes into spiral-bound yellow books, hoping to empower all through education by extension to live into their ministry ordained at baptism.

All the pieces matter.

EfM is a universe of relationships and many of us wear multiple hats while ministering within the EfM program. Coldplay, the delightful band that inhabits the hearts and souls of many of us, sings, "You're a sky full of stars. What a heavenly view!" It takes all of us to draw out the gifts of God in each other so that we can all live and love fully as people of The Way.

I believe EfM looks great at fifty. Can you imagine the breadth of theological reflections that have taken place worldwide? There are unending sources for "Focus" in theological reflection. Consider the amount of worship that has happened beyond Sunday thanks to seminar groups praying together. As we move into the next fifty years of EfM, we could offer a prayer of thanksgiving for EfM's 120,000 graduates. With their wisdom and insight, and with God's help, we are blessed to be preparing for the years ahead. At fifty years, EfM is debuting the fifth revision of its curriculum, and for the first time in EfM's history, we are creating new formation products. As the world constantly moves and changes, we are called to meet people where they are. The journeys we find ourselves on and the destinations they inspire are shifting and changing at a rapid pace.

I wonder if you can recall a moment that sparked your journey of faith. For me, it happened one hot summer, between my junior and senior years in high school, while I was driving across I–10 in its entirety—from Jacksonville, Florida, to Los Angeles, California. I listened to the whole Bible on cassette. I heard strange tales of talking donkeys; women getting cut up and delivered across twelve tribes; flaming chariots of fire; a king dancing before God and many naked women; a dragon, a messiah, an apostle born with a thorn in his side; and a choir of blood-soaked survivors who were singing praises to the lamb. What kind of holy book was this? As soon as I graduated from college, I was invited to be a participant in an EfM group and my journey with EfM has been ongoing since then. The strangeness of those Bible stories still occupies a lot of my imagination, but because of EfM, I have better questions with which to engage them.

Kate Bush is a singer and songwriter from England. On *Lionheart*, her second album, in the song titled "Symphony in Blue," she sings, "When that feeling of meaninglessness sets in. Go blowing my mind on God." For me, these moments of meaninglessness are what I bring into the work of EfM.

My theological muse, Rachel Held Evans, in her book, *Inspired: Slaying Giants, Walking on Water, and Loving the Bible Again*, shares, "The church is not a group of people who believe all the same things; the church is a group of people caught up in the same story, with Jesus at the center."[1] In EfM seminars around the world, we have gathered for fifty years in an intentional space with a group covenant called "norms" to find meaning in our life's experiences. We look toward God's story, the history and tradition of the Church, and the voices of our culture in order to discover how to act like a faithful follower of Christ even if we don't understand who or what Christ is!

I wonder if you can imagine such a fulfilling life without EfM. I certainly cannot. I was nine years old when I first heard the words "Education for Ministry." In the late 1970s, the Rev. Bill Morris launched one of the first EfM groups at my home church, All Saints' Episcopal Church in River Ridge, Louisiana. River Ridge is about seven miles upriver from the French Quarter in New Orleans. My mother was in that first group. As a young gay man growing up in

---

1. Rachel Held Evans, *Inspired: Slaying Giants, Walking on Water, and Loving the Bible Again* (Nashville, TN: Nelson Books, 2018), 157.

The Episcopal Church, the only place I was able to find representation in the Church was within the practice of theological reflection. It was there that I learned my experiences mattered to God. It was in those moments that I began to understand that I was a part of God's sacred story despite what the world told me.

Representation matters.

Ruth Haley Barton, in her book *Strengthening the Soul of Your Leadership: Seeking God in the Crucible of Ministry*, shares this: "Solitude brought Moses to a place where he had slowed down enough to pay attention to the bush that was burning in the middle of his own life. At last, all other voices had quieted down enough that he could recognize a new Voice calling to him from this very unlikely place. Finally he was in a position to receive a word from the Lord. The practice of 'turning aside to look.'"[2] I can still see the smiles and hear the voices of the people in my first seminar group. Many have passed on but their hopes and dreams are alive and well in me. EfM creates the space for the sacred to be held and passed on.

Parker Palmer, a Quaker theologian, observes the following in his book, *Let Your Life Speak: Listening for the Voice of Vocation*, "We arrive in this world with birthright gifts, then we spend the first half of our lives abandoning them or letting others disabuse us of them. As young people, we are surrounded by expectations that have little to do with who we really are, expectations held by people who are not trying to discern our selfhood but to fit us into slots. In families, schools, workplaces, and religious communities, we are trained away from our true self toward images of acceptability. Under social pressures like racism and sexism, our original shape is deformed beyond recognition, and we ourselves, driven by fear, too often betraying true self to gain the approval of others."[3]

All of us are ordained for the work of God at baptism. The journey of faith is the opportunity to determine what gifts and

---

2. Ruth R. Barton, *Strengthening the Soul of Your Leadership: Seeking God in the Crucible of Ministry* (Downers Grove, IL: IVP Books, 2008), 62.

3. Parker J. Palmer, *Let Your Life Speak: Listening for the Voice of Vocation* (Hoboken, NJ: Jossey Bass, 2024), 9.

talents we each bring to the Christian community in hopes that they can be utilized within the context of where we work, play, volunteer, study, eat, live, and love. That is what we are called and ordained to do. EfM has always helped seekers of God prepare for ministry. Like the people I met in *The Wire*, we minister at school. We minister in the restaurant's kitchen. We minister at the copy machine. We minister at the recycling center. We minister at the local Walmart. Ministering is that vocation we pray to live into at the end of worship when we pray, "And now, send us out to do the work you have given us to do, to love and serve you as faithful witnesses of Christ our Lord."

As we emerge from the COVID-19 pandemic, there is something we have been seeking, but I have been unable to articulate it. Joan Chittister, in her book, *Scarred by Struggle, Transformed by Hope*, explains that "something" this way: "The great interruptions of life leave us completely disoriented. We become lost. The map of life changes overnight and our sense of direction and purpose goes with it. Life comes to a halt, takes on a new and indiscernible shape. Promise fails us and it is the loss of promise that dries in our throats. What was is no more and what is to come, if anything, is unclear. All the things we depended on to keep us safe, to show us the way, to give us a reason for going on, disappear."[4]

As we move past COVID-19, we face several choices. Do we go back? Or do we move forward? For many of us following the teachings of Jesus, a new sense of urgency has emerged. Perhaps it is because the entire world faced mortality together. As Noah and his family stepped out onto dry ground during the flood myth, we sensed a semblance of stability but the ground was still damp mud. As Kate Bush sings in her song, "Suspended in Gaffa," from her album, *The Dreaming*, "Suddenly my feet are feet of mud. It all goes slow-mo. I don't know why I'm crying. Am I suspended in gaffa? Not until I'm ready for you can I have it all?"[5]

---

4. Joan Chittister, *Scarred by Struggle, Transformed by Hope* (Grand Rapids, MI: William B. Eerdmans, 2003), 61.

5. Kate Bush, *How To Be Invisible* (London, UK: Faber and Faber Ltd. Pub: Bloomsbury House, 2023), 129.

All the pieces matter.

We read of drone strikes on an enemy sooner than people standing a few feet away have any idea about what has happened. Where is this place? We are bombarded by the latest headlines of desperation and death as the world often feels on the brink of World War III. Is this the apocalypse? We brace ourselves for hurricanes approaching vulnerable coastlines while being fed narratives of gloom and doom. Why don't people believe in climate change? We see forest fires raging out of control and the smoke, traveling from hundreds of thousands of miles away, hugging our skylines, making them disappear into foggy darkness. How am I related to people miles and miles away? We wake up in the morning to discover that gun violence has taken many more innocent lives and we seem to be lacking the resources or the willingness to do anything about it. Whatever happened to common sense? It all can seem so out of control. How am I as a Christian supposed to respond faithfully to all of this? These are the times when I thank God for EfM.

EfM looks good at fifty! Celebrating fifty years of EfM, the program that started it all earns "classic" status as new challenges and opportunities have provided growth and expansion of the program.

> **EfM: Classic.** Four years. One year at a time, a new array of small-group formation programs. Whether onsite or online, these intentional, monastic-like small groups utilize EfM's five core practices—living in community, regular prayer and worship, theological reflection, study of the Christian tradition, and vocational discernment.
>
> **EfM: Wide Angle.** Introduces God's salvation history and the work of the Church through story, study, and scholarship.
>
> **EfM: Reflections.** Short courses that last six to eight weeks and consist of study, engagement, and theological reflection.

EfM: Catechumenate. Engages the Episcopal tradition through ritual, study, and preparation for the journey of faith.

EfM: Fun. Uses manipulatives designed for adults to enhance seminar engagement and focus.

EfM: Pilgrimage. Draws inspiration from our partners in New Zealand to provide an invitation to intentional engagement when on the road.

Henri Nouwen, in his book, *Reaching Out*, says this: "When after many years of adult life I ask myself, 'Where am I as a Christian?,' there are just as many reasons for pessimism as for optimism. Many of the real struggles of twenty years ago are still very much alive. I am still searching for inner peace, for creative relationships with others, and for the experience of God, and neither I nor anyone else has any way of knowing if the small changes during the past years have made me a more or a less spiritual person."[6]

Lilli Lewis, the folk-rock diva of New Orleans, on her album, *All is Forgiven*, in the song "If You Really Mattered," invites us to consider, "I have one question for you. What would you do if you really mattered? How would you spend your days? How would you know who to walk away from? Who would you care for? What would you dare to lose? How would you choose your path? Use your last breath? What would you do if you really mattered?"[7]

What would you do if you really mattered?

Many of us discovered through EfM that we really mattered. That is a gift. That is grace even though I may not even know what grace is or how to define it. I have learned with others that all of God's people matter. Our stories are sacred. Our stories are a part of God's story. We are a part of each other's story. I hear this through the voices, stories, and experiences of people I have met along the way. And even though I don't see them anymore, I still

---

6. Henri J. M. Nouwen, *Reaching Out: The Three Movements of the Spiritual Life* (Garden City, NY: Doubleday, 1975), 11.
7. Lilli Lewis. "If You Really Mattered'," Righteous Babe Records, on *All Is Forgiven*, 2023.

think of them with love and affection. EfM is made up of intentional communities who study, form, shape, write, and administer the program in hopes that all of us discover that everything we do is part of the journey of faith. When we walk or waltz, whether we tumble and fall, whether we sing or sign, whether we jump or fly, all of it matters.

As EfM celebrates fifty years, my prayer for all of us who love this program is that God will continue to empower us to be good stewards of all that has been handed down to us so that we have the will and the confidence to pass it on to others who will live, minister, reflect, and study in EfM programs during the years ahead. And, listening to the hope from the ordination rite of a priest from the Book of Common Prayer—"May the Lord who has given us the will to do these things give us the grace and power to perform them. Amen."

APPENDIX: STORYTELLING

EfM Stepping Stones

Margaret Taliaferro

In the 1970s, Ira Progoff developed "Stepping Stones," a method of reflecting on and reexamining steps from the past that lead to the present. Progoff's "Stepping Stones" inspired EfM's original spiritual autobiography method. It is fitting that Taliaferro, EfM mentor, trainer, and coordinator, utilizes "Stepping Stones" to put EfM's fifty-year journey into context.

Date **Event**

1975 The Rev. Dr. Charles (Charlie) Winters submitted "A Proposal for a Program of Theological Education by Extension (TEE)."

The first Education for Ministry (EfM) groups began as a pilot program using lecture materials from the School of Theology's faculty (the "yellow books").

1976 Program officially launched as TEE—Theological Education by Extension. Flower Ross joined the staff as manager of training and developed the original theological reflection (TR) model: a three-source model.

Enrollment—500 students in eighteen dioceses.

1977 Ross and Winters selected five men to begin the training network. Cynthia Sherrill joined the EfM staff.

First EfM group established in Australia.

First EfM group established in Canada.

1978 Name changed from "Education for Ministry: A Program of Theological Education by Extension" to "Education for Ministry." The new name was copyrighted.

The staff began using a computer database for data (original records were kept on index cards in boxes).

The original program's intent was for a group to form and continue through all four years. Tuition was $200. Maximum number of students was set at ten. Over time, groups needed to take on new students to remain financially viable. Winters decided groups could function as "one-room schoolhouses."

1979 First EfM group established in New Zealand.

1980 David Killen became executive director of Bairnwick Center, a facility on the campus of the University of the South, which housed the EfM program. He was the director from 1980 to 1985.

John de Beer was hired as training director.

Cynthia Sherrill became administrative coordinator.

First EfM group established in the Bahamas.

1981 The Rev. Thomas McGillicut became EfM program manager.

John de Beer developed a training team to sustain the program and improve methods of theological reflection (1981–82). "The Microscope Method" was developed.

1982 Program began revision under Killen and the Rev. Dr. Ross McKenzie.

The Rev. Richard Brewer provided the idea to develop the *Common Lessons* and *Parallel Guides* for each of the thirty-three lessons in each of the four years. Brewer and de Beer and others developed and revised lessons over the years that followed.

Four-source model of theological reflection introduced: culture was added as the fourth source.

Enrollment reached 3,200 students with a network of thirty trainers.

1983	Edward O. de Bary developed a three-tiered contract schema for diocese sponsorship and established the diocesan coordinator role.
1984	Year One of revision released (the "white books").
1985	The EfM program moved to Hamilton Hall, joining the School of Theology that had moved to that location the previous year.
	Sherrill became director of administration for the extension center of the School of Theology.
	Tom Watson directed the program 1985–86.
1986	Dean Robert Giannini acted as director 1986–87.
1987	Dr. J. Carleton Hayden was named director until 1991.
1988	John de Beer left the EfM staff.
	The first bound version of a manual for mentors was introduced.
	Enrollment reached 5,000 students.
	First EfM group established in the United Kingdom—Gloucester Diocese.
1989	Gail Jones became director of the training and educational method.
	Reflection in motion was introduced.
1990	An index for the course materials was completed.
1991	Edward O. de Bary became EfM executive director.
	Clearer Vision Ministries, Inc., of Orlando, Florida, produced recordings of all materials for the visually impaired.
1992	Enrollment reached 7,500 students, 8,000 graduates, 800 mentors, and a network of sixty trainers.
1993	First EfM group established in Italy.
1994	John de Beer and Dr. Patricia O. Killen published the book, *The Art of Theological Reflection*.
	First EfM group established in Hong Kong.
1995	Liz Workman became director of training.

1999	Maroon binders, *Common Lessons and Supporting Materials* (CLSM aka "BOB"), released.
	Enrollment reached 7,000 students.
2001	First online pilot group was launched.
2004	Edward O. de Bary retired.
	Johnna Camp became interim director.
	Brewer became assistant director in charge of training.
	Sissie Wile became trainer in residence.
2005	Wile became assistant director in charge of training.
2008	Wile became interim director for EfM in addition to assistant director in charge of training.
2010	Karen Meridith became executive director.
2011	Elsa Bakkum became assistant director in charge of training.
2012	Curriculum was revised to include standard theological publications accompanied by the *Reading and Reflection Guide*.
	The *Reading and Reflection Guide* (RRG), Volume A, was published.
2014	Joshua Booher became assistant director in charge of operations.
2018	EfM switched from Blackboard to Zoom for online groups.
2019	*The Heart of the Matter* TR training manual produced with an expansion of the "Explore" questions.
2020	The COVID-19 global pandemic caused a halt to face-to-face encounters. All training sessions were moved online and groups either moved online or stopped meeting.
	The registration was down by more than one third for the 2020–21 enrollment cycle.
2022	Purchase of the theological publications became participants' responsibility.
2023	Kevin M. Goodman became executive director.
2024	First onsite training after COVID-19 was held.
2025	Revision of curriculum was launched.

A History of the Education for Ministry Program: 1975–95

Edward O. de Bary

Introduction

After nearly two decades, the Education for Ministry (EfM) program has found its place under the sun. It began modestly in 1975 as a program of the School of Theology of the University of the South. Today, EfM is a substantial presence throughout The Episcopal Church. It has become a worldwide program widely recognized for its excellence, influence, and importance.

EfM has influenced thousands of people, and it has made a significant impact on the life of many congregations. Through EfM people have discovered that ministry is part of everything we do. Some have decided to alter their lives significantly, chosen to begin new ministries, even to enter seminary.

This article appears as EfM enters its twentieth year. It is timely to put to paper some of the history while most of the participants are still able to contribute their critique, and many of the important documents still exist. This is the story of how EfM began as well as a partial chronicle of significant events and important figures who affected the development of the program.

I. Background

The Post–World War II Climate

In the aftermath of World War II the United States turned to new tasks. One was the reform of Christian education that our churches provided for its laity. Military chaplains had been very critical because they had found our soldiers and sailors in the armed forces ill prepared in matters of faith. Their critique was heeded and throughout many denominations there arose a new interest in religious education. In The Episcopal Church, beginning in 1946 under the leadership of Angus Hun,[1] there developed the Division of Christian Education. Thus, the decade of the '50s was a period of intense activity. When the decade of the '60s turned the Church's attention to social needs, this pattern changed. Nevertheless, educators had planted the seeds for the theological education of the laity. A process for informing the laity in theological matters was a possibility.

Working with Groups

One result of events prior to and during World War II was the dispersal of a number of German intellectuals from what was known as the "Frankfurt School" and officially called the Institute of Social Research.[2] This group of innovative thinkers scattered when Hitler came to power, and a number of them came to the United States. Some of these social philosophers

---

1. Carman St. J. Hunter, Christian Education in The Episcopal Church, *1940s to 1970s* (New York: The Episcopal Church Center, 1987), 2-3.
2. The term "'Frankfurt School' has come to be used widely but loosely to designate both a group of intellectuals and a specific social theory. The intellectuals were associated with the Institut für Sozialforschung (Institute for Social Research), which was established in Frankfurt am Main in 1923. It was, however, only with the appointment in 1930 of Max Horkheimer as director of the institute that the basis was laid for what was to become known as the Frankfurt School. Horkheimer (1895–1973) gathered together a team that included such now famous figures as Herbert Marcuse (born 1898), the radical philosopher and later ally of the student movement; Theodor W. Adorno (1903–1969), philosopher, sociologist, and aesthetic theoretician; and Erich Fromm (born 1900), the psychologist of international repute." Phil Slater, *Origin and Significance of the Frankfurt School: A Marxist Perspective* (London: Routledge and Keegan Paul, 1977), xiii.

were interested in learning how people communicate and how groups function. As a result, in part, of their work, the National Training Laboratories initiated a series of summer conferences in Bethel, Maine, to explore communications theory. When some of the Church leadership discovered this resource, a number of the Christian educators on the national staff of The Episcopal Church participated in the intensive workshops provided by the National Training Laboratories.[3] They were deeply influenced by the experience and sought to bring its benefits to the Church. As a result, there arose a significant movement. This produced a series of parish life conferences, communications conferences, and opportunities for training people to work effectively in small groups. Eventually whole networks developed to sustain this phenomenon, which also affected the educational, business, and military establishments.[4]

During the late '60s and '70s, the Group Life movement became less popular after some of its expressions tested the norms of social interaction to a point that could or would not be tolerated by the average American, much less by the average Episcopalian. While the work never ended completely, institutional fears fueled its repression. At the same time wiser leaders emerged who developed the most creative aspects and brought under control the possibilities for mishaps and stupidity.

At its best, the Group Life movement gave much energy to the Church and the processes of Christian education. Through Group Life conferences of one kind or another, many people learned a lot about themselves and about how groups and communities work or fail to work. These conferences produced leadership that possessed an understanding of the processes involved in working

---

3. Attending an NTL conference in 1965 at Bethel, Maine, proved to be a seminal event for EfM founder Charles Winters. As a direct result, he changed his teaching methods and began to evolve the seminar method used by the EfM program.
4. Two large networks formed—MATS (Middle Atlantic Training System) and ARABS (Association for Religion and Behavioral Sciences). While primarily organized out of church needs and networks, these organizations also served business and military training needs. They were especially concerned with group interaction and with such problems as racism, stewardship, leadership, and sexuality.

with groups and bringing about change. They saw themselves as agents of change. They participated in movements of liberation and equality in matters of race and sexuality. Often the old order, hierarchical and patriarchal, racist and sexist, was shaken by people who came out of this movement. The new leaders were assertive, and they had learned how to express their thoughts and feelings effectively. Those on the sidelines and those who were challenged, however, often felt threatened, and resistance developed. While this movement contained energy, it often lacked theological content. Its connection to the Christian faith and to the Church was not always apparent. Nevertheless, as a result, significant changes occurred, especially in leadership practices, stewardship, and education.

A chief setting for changes was the Christian education approach used by the Church. While the new methods were powerful tools to help people and communities change, the contents of their messages were often inadequate. People learned a lot about themselves, but they learned too little about their tradition and its basis in Holy Scripture. They learned how to produce change, but they were not grounded in history. As a result of changes brought about by the new methods, the movements appeared to be and sometimes were immature and naive. Often they did not have an adequate basis in reality, and they appeared to lack piety.

In part, EfM emerged from the efforts of people involved in the Group Life movement who sought to use its educational value, but also saw the need to incorporate the knowledge of the tradition necessary to provide a firm basis. In many ways, EfM was a way to rectify the omission of sufficient content by inserting into the work a substantial, scholarly, and adequate curriculum, and yet retaining the power and support of the community as an arena for learning.

One way or another, all who explored these paths had in common their interest in theology, Christian education, group work, and social interaction theory. Among them were Charles Penniman (director of the Educational Center, Saint Louis,

Missouri, who also served as a consultant to PECUSA[5]), Vesper O. Ward (who left the national offices of The Episcopal Church to become professor of Christian education at Sewanee), Henry Lee Myers (who succeeded Vesper Ward as professor of Christian education at Sewanee), William Yon (who later directed the training network in Alabama), Don W. Griswold (who later took training to South Africa), and John Heinz (who became rector of Trinity Church, New York).

These in turn produced a new generation of trainers and Christian educators who became key persons in the development and growth of EfM. Most important among them were Flower Ross (who became Charles Winters's chief associate in Sewanee) and her successor, John de Beer (who had been trained by Bill Yon and Don Griswold when they were in South Africa). Edward O. de Bary, later to become program director for EfM, received his early training while in seminary from Bill Yon, Hank Myers, and Charles Winters. He became a trainer for EfM under the guidance of Flower Ross and John de Beer.

The Seabury Series

In response to postwar demands, The Episcopal Church launched a program to prepare new educational materials to meet the Church's educational needs. Disagreement, however, occurred at the national level about the kind of materials to be produced under the title of the Seabury Series. There were those who wanted to move away from a dependence on written materials alone as the carrier of the curriculum. They understood the parish itself to be the curriculum. Others were more traditional, and they were impatient with the innovators. They wanted to develop a new curriculum and texts. Because of this disagreement, Vesper Ward asked the following questions of The Episcopal Church:

---

5. PECUSA is the acronym for Protestant Episcopal Church in the United States of America.

The staff would like to know whether the Department and the Church are asking us to spend our time producing unrelated materials about religion in the hope that somehow or other redemption will grow out of our efforts? Or are we expected to put our major emphasis upon human redemption through the dynamics of the parish and, in this process, develop educational resources that are related to living issues?[6]

As a result of this dispute, a number of staff persons left the national offices of The Episcopal Church. According to Henry Lee Myers, the argument had to do with how the program would be used and, among other things, revolved on the issue: Is a curriculum a set of materials to be sold, or is it a program to be marketed with training that encompasses the parish? The book publishers succeeded and the Seabury Series became a set of books with programmatic content. The programmatic aspects were not emphasized, although much was said about the need to train teachers. The dispersion of some National Church Center staff and the failure of the Seabury Series to address the need for quality theological education as a program (rather than a set of books) for the laity thus helped to pave the path for programs like EfM.

The Educational Center

The Educational Center, located in St. Louis, Missouri, exists slightly at the fringe of Christian education in The Episcopal Church. Early it developed a stance that was avowedly Jungian so that the work of this seminal psychiatrist was closely linked to the Christian educational materials produced at the center. One of the most innovative tools developed at the center was the "issue method" by which to approach the tools of theological

---

6. Hunter, *Christian Education*, 15; she quotes Division of Curriculum Development Minutes, October 8, 1951, page 6, cited in Dorothy Braun, "Historical Study of the Origin and Development of the Seabury Series of the Protestant Episcopal Church" (PhD diss., New York University, 1960), 173.

thinking and reflection. This method was used to analyze the theological questions posed by life and tradition. Unlike the more mundane use of the word "issue" (which usually denotes a dispute or problem), the Educational Center defined an issue as a tension that is true to life, to which all life is true, and that demonstrates how all people are caught in a constant grip of conflicting demands. Analysis using the issue method was used as a preparation for Educational Center courses.

Charles Penniman had been a consultant to Vesper Ward when the latter had worked for the National Church Center in New York City. Thus, when Ward came to Sewanee, he introduced this method to the curriculum. Others found it useful, and later John M. Gessell and Henry Lee Myers made this method part of the curriculum in Christian education for those who attended the School of Theology in Sewanee during the 1960s.

The issue method of organizing one's approach to theology was quickly adapted to EfM. Used from the outset, the method that emerged made considerable intellectual demands. Consequently, it was not popular with people who approached the reflective task more easily through images and metaphors. While the issue method provides a wonderful tool for clarifying values, it fails to seize the imagination sufficiently, something very necessary for those who prefer to reflect in nonlinear ways and who are better taught through images than by rationalizations.

Continuing Education for Adults

With the rise of scientific and technological developments, there has occurred a tremendous rise in continuing education programs for professionals of every kind. Today it is normal for medical doctors, attorneys, accountants, and clergy to attend programs and courses that continue their educational preparation. Many professions require that continuing education be pursued in order to maintain a professional license.

When Charles Winters observed this growing phenomenon during the 1960s, he recognized that the Church was not keeping up with the times. Christian education did not provide a very good basic education for the laity, and there existed virtually no sophisticated continuing education in matters of faith directed toward the average church person. Confirmation classes or catechetical instructions, sermons, and Lenten programs were not sufficient in either depth or length. Short of attending a seminary, few opportunities existed for a sophisticated and educated laity to obtain a preparation in faith commensurate with the other education they might have obtained. Winters's recognition of this need and opportunity was a key ingredient in the blend that formed the EfM program.

Program of Theological Education by Extension (TEE)

The churches in South America and Africa had developed a number of TEE programs. This phenomenon caught the attention of Thomas H. Markley, a student at the seminary in Sewanee between 1969 and 1972. He wanted to do a senior year of special study in the field and found a book about theological education by extension in Guatemala.[7] Some programs were more complex than others and most had their genesis in the need to prepare clergy when local seminary education was not and could not be available. Charles Winters later wrote about this book:

> As I studied it, I found it contained just what I needed. I did not think we should do it exactly as they had; it was still too dependent on shipping faculty bodies around and was too strictly tied into programmed learning texts.

---

7. The Presbyterian Seminary of Guatemala was a center of extension education. F. Ross Kinsler, ed., *Ministry by the People: Theological Education by Extension* (Maryknoll, NY: Orbis Books, 1983). David Killen's article, "Theological Reflection—a Necessary Skill in Lay Ministry," is in Kinsler's book, 225–35, and provides a description of how EfM was organized. In this article, he notes that there was a staff of twelve serving about 3,500 students and mentions the use of computers. Twelve years later, the staff has been reduced to nine-and-one-half persons, and there are more than 7,000 students in the program. Every desk is linked by computers, which have increased efficiency and lowered expenses. The growth of EfM has thus depended in part upon the availability of electronic media of communications at prices that made them affordable for church educational use.

Still, many of the principles of programmed learning I found to be helpful, and—especially—an article by Ted Ward, then at Michigan State, I believe, depicting the now infamous "two-rail fence" model of education. The penny really dropped with these suggestions.[8]

Thus was born the notion that the seminary might be able to launch a program of education by extension. The idea came to Charles Winters at a crucial time in the life of the School of Theology. The Church was in the midst of questioning the work of its seminaries and raising the question of their efficiency: too many seminaries for too few students appeared to be costing too much money.

Additional impetus for Winters came as the proposal for an extension program in theological education developed. In 1973 Ralph D. Winter, a professor at the School for World Mission at Fuller Theological Seminary, presented a paper and described a program "designed to allow the learner to participate in society productively while continuing his studies."[9] He suggested that a program of theological education by extension could train "minority" church leaders as well as "majority" church leaders. Thus, theological education might be more available to persons

---

8. Charles L. Winters in a letter to Edward O. de Bary, August 29, 1992. Ted and Margaret Ward, *Programmed Instruction for Theological Education by Extension* (Wheaton, IL: Cameo Press, 1970), is their larger work, but the two-rail fence appeared almost as an after thought.

In one of the Cameo workshops in Guatemala, Ward stated, "I think what you are talking about in seminary extension is like a two-railed fence. You cannot train high-level skills without field experience.... The second rail is cognitive input (book learning). What are these fenceposts? Seminar experiences! The role of the instructor in an extension program is to provide the seminars. The function of any good self-teaching material is to provide new information. These are different and complementary." Quoted from Ted Ward, "Programmed Learning Technique Workshop," *Theological Education by Extension*, Ralph D. Winter, ed. (South Pasadena, CA: William Carey Press, 1969), 321–2. An EfM addition to the model was a ground under the fence which represented worship, an essential element for a learning community in a church environment. A variant of this model is that of a railroad track. The tracks are the equivalent of the fence rails and the ties are the posts. The railway bed is the group of community life rooted in faithful worship.

9. Ralph D. Winter, "The Extension Model in Theological Education: What It Is and What It Can Do," a paper delivered to the American Association of Theological Schools, January 12, 1973.

in midcareer "not likely to be discovered or trained by the present seminary. The strategic task the Church needs accomplished just now requires a high-quality, fully-enfranchised extension of theological education. I believe the seminaries alone can best perform this task. But extension is the new tool the seminary must learn to employ." Winters and Urban T. Holmes, the dean at the seminary, cited this paper in correspondence, proposing the development of a program of theological education by extension.

Pressure on the Seminaries

During the 1960s the General Convention of The Episcopal Church authorized a study of its seminaries. The so-called "Pusey Report" (prepared under the leadership of Nathan Pusey, president of Harvard University) argued that our seminaries should be located in urban settings, should operate as part of a consortium of schools specializing in theological studies, should be large enough to be financially viable and should be able to take advantage of the richness provided by a large university setting. These conclusions pointed away from Sewanee, which had none of these advantages (although no specific schools were marked for closing). As a result of the report some openly questioned the need to continue seminaries that existed in isolated locations such as Sewanee and also suggested that the Episcopal Church had too many seminaries.

As a partial response to the Pusey report, Bexley Hall[10] moved to Colgate Rochester Divinity School in Rochester, New York, and the Divinity School of the Protestant Episcopal Church in Philadelphia joined forces with the Episcopal Theological School in Boston. The faculty in Sewanee was concerned, and the notion of an extension program in theological education became an attractive idea. It offered an opportunity to expand the mission of the seminary and give it a new lease on life. This came just at a time when the seminary was experimenting with

---

10. The Episcopal seminary at Gambier, Ohio, formerly associated with Kenyon College.

its curriculum and methods using seminars and student participation in the educational process; so the two programs seemed to fit together well.

A Proposal for a Program of Theological Education by Extension

In 1973 a proposal prepared by Winters was circulated by Holmes. It sought funds for Winters to use a leave of absence from spring of 1974 through fall of 1975 as an opportunity to test the possibility of an extension program, to visit other extension programs already in place, and to develop a pilot model.[11] The proposal was based on four assumptions:[12]

- The Church will find itself in a decreasing ability to afford stipendiary clergy and will therefore need more nonstipendiary ministries.
- The Church will need to have more nonpaid clergy because there will be fewer resources and therefore there will be less of a warrant for the training of full-time clergy as is now done in our seminaries.

---

11. Charles Winters's "A Proposal for a Program of Theological Education by Extension" was attached to a letter of September 21, 1973, from Urban T. Holmes to Richard L. Rising to solicit his support. Rising was also working on the problem of extended theological education, and Holmes added, "If there is any way in which I can help Charlie through you in pursuing this project, I would like very much to do it. It has my enthusiastic backing, if for no other reason than I feel some kind of expert guidance in theological education should be exercised in regard to these many local situations springing up all over the country. The whole thing strikes me as something of a reaction to the BTE's effort to consolidate seminaries, and I think we need to have some sanity injected into the proliferation of training centers." Holmes's warning fell on deaf ears. Twenty years later, many dioceses had their own training programs, leading to ordination. Other schools such as Duke, Emory (Atlanta), and Vanderbilt are seeking a piece of The Episcopal Church's theological education market. There exists no central registry of programs available to Episcopalians preparing for ordination, nor is there any official accreditation system under the aegis of The Episcopal Church.

12. Holmes's letter also alluded to the growth of local programs. These diocesan "academies" expanded rapidly in the 1970s and 1980s. Some were directed to laity, others to preparing deacons, and still others to providing an education for nonstipendiary priests. More recently these programs have declined since they are not well funded. The Educators and Trainers for Ministry (ETM)—now defunct—was formed and supported by the Board of Theological Education as a place for heads of these programs to gather. The association also included nonaccredited seminaries like Bloy House and Mercer.

- The Church is declining in numbers.
- The role of the clergy is changing.[13]

Winters cited a number of reasons that might favor extension education. He named the increasing cost of residential seminary education as a major factor, and asked, "How can the costs of theological education by kept within manageable limits?" Then he added a bold stroke. He suggested that there should be adequate theological education for the laity as well as the ordained and wrote, "The assumption that only an ordained person has the need or the ability to acquire a theological education is a blatant instance of clericalism." Finally, he suggested that there might be some good reasons for doing theological education where the classroom and the field are most closely related:

> Residential seminaries have traditionally been strong on theory, tradition, in short, classroom activities, thereby keeping scholarship alive. Recently we have been able to recognize more fully the need for reflection and have been acquiring some skills for this. It is in practical experience in the field and the integration of this into the total education process that seminaries have not been as successful.

Initially, Winters proposed an overall structure quite different from that which evolved for EfM.[14] There were two major compo-

---

13. Winters did not foresee the decline in the number of men enrolling in our seminaries and the corresponding increase in the number of women who would attend. The net result is that seminary enrollments of people seeking ordination declined about 25 percent between 1985 and 1993. Overall, enrollments remained about the same. The demographics changed as more women entered into the mainstream of professional church life and as new programs not directed toward ordination have emerged. In its early stages, EfM became a conduit that women could use to begin their theological preparation while various dioceses still resisted their entry into the ordination process. Many of our ordained women began their theological education in EfM.

14. After Charles Winters and Flower Ross left Sewanee in 1980, they moved to Loyola University, New Orleans, and launched another venture in off-campus adult Christian education. This program, prepared for the Roman Catholic Church, followed Winters's original proposal for EfM. It included possibilities for course credit and degrees. At Loyola, Winters also began using videotapes to enhance instructions. This program is

nents, weekly seminars with a cluster of about ten persons and periodic weeklong intensive sessions at Sewanee. He proposed that there be a set of reading materials carefully organized into manageable units with learning objectives and methods for feedback. Adjunct professors would be used for each group often. The model called for selecting priests as leaders. There would be an opportunity to explore the ministry of each student in a disciplined manner using verbatims, critical incident reports, and seminar discussions. The two-rail fence was offered as a model to explain the process.

Winters suggested academic standards such as are found in a residential program, including examinations and evaluations. He proposed that the MTS (Master of Theological Studies) be granted for the first two years with the possibility of an MDiv (Master of Divinity) if the person then enrolled as a full-time student at the University of the South for the final year. He supposed that the majority of the students would not be candidates for ordination.

The finances of Winters's proposal called for an annual tuition of $700, transportation to Sewanee three times a year, and paying the adjunct professors $2,000 per year. This, thought Winters, would hire a director-coordinator and also make a financial contribution to the operation of the School of Theology, thereby covering the program's indirect expenses. The proposal in this form was not acceptable to key members of the faculty, and it never left the drawing boards.

II. The Beginning of EfM

"Education for Ministry: A Program of Theological Education by Extension" originated from the 1973 proposal by Winters and Holmes. In 1974, Winters obtained a grant from The Episcopal

---

more expensive for the participant than EfM since there are examinations, academic credits can be obtained through it, and some students may qualify for degrees in religious science. Its numbers have never reached those of EfM, but it has become significant in the Roman Catholic Church.

Church Foundation[15] and used his sabbatical to design and begin the preparation of the materials for the program. Initial writing was done in Mexico.[16] There was opposition to the notion that this might be a degree program, or that it might substitute in whole or in part for the seminary experience as normative for those on the path to stipendiary priesthood. Thus Winters's concept was formed: this should be a program for the laity and without an academic degree. There was, however, no shift from the academic to the nonacademic because he always maintained that the two-rail fence model, bringing together academic education and personal experience, should be preeminent. The academic work and the personal development, the tradition and the workplace, should be given equal treatment.[17]

Developing the Materials

The content of the EfM materials first came from the work of the Sewanee theological faculty. Some lectures were taped, transcribed, and adapted from courses of the School of Theology.

---

15. Charles Winters's memo to the university treasurer, July 6, 1977, provides information about the grant: "Restricted account +7021 1010, Winters feasibility study, originally established from a $15,000.00 grant from The Episcopal Church Foundation, and augmented by a renewal grant of $10,000.00, was for the exploration of the need for a program of theological education by extension and the beginnings of the development of such a program. In the fall of 1975, the program began on a pilot basis with tuition fees and sponsoring fees being turned back into this account. The program became a regular operation of the School of Theology in fiscal year 1976–77. The funds presently in the restricted account are the surplus of grant monies and revenues accrued during the pilot phase. This fund will be expended before the close of fiscal year 1978–79 for the furtherance of the theological education by extension program."

16. In 1992 Winters wrote this author that he had given up plans for a degree program by the time he began the writing in Mexico. Opposition within the faculty had become too strong. Donald Armentrout, who was new to the faculty at the time, states that the opposition came from the late William Griffin (professor of Old Testament) and others who did not favor relying on seminar methods to teach adults and grant academic credits.

17. This tension between content and process, academics and reflection, erupted after Winters left and Edward O. de Bary joined the staff. De Bary argued that academic work should be given equal representation, but there existed a strong tide among many of the trainers led by John de Beer that process and reflection should come first. Trainers of mentors were prepared in the areas of process. Much less attention was given to the use of content until Richard Brewer, working with John de Beer, wrote the parallel guides for each lesson. Little emphasis on how to use these guides was given, however, and the training of mentors did not provide an equal focus on content and process.

These were organized in chapters with learning objectives and questions or tasks. Winters intended the students to learn the materials on their own, using weekly seminars as a discussion group. The materials for the Old Testament came chiefly from lectures and notes provided by the late William A. Griffin, professor of Old Testament. Marion Hatchett, professor of Liturgics, provided materials that had earlier appeared in *St. Luke's Journal of Theology*[18]; Urban T. Holmes's typescript book on ascetical theology was used as the basis for the work in that field. Other faculty provided syllabi, class notes, and outlines. The remainder of the text was the work of Charles Winters. One key to the entire process was the excellent editing by Ms. Georgia Joyner,[19] who

---

18. *St. Luke's Journal* was renamed *Sewanee Theological Review* in September 1991.
19. In 1992 Georgia Joyner reflected on her work with EfM:

> Looking back, nearly 20 years later, it seems a lifetime ago that I heard the rumor floating around Sewanee—the Seminary plans to launch an extension program in theology. My heart skipped a beat. Could this possibly mean me? Is this designed for such an average person, theologically illiterate and not a bit ambitious for ordination, but starving for some of the feasts I've watched seminarians devour? My diet was thin and my appetite huge. Prowling the shelves of the theological library until its librarians swept me out, auditing courses, listening to visiting lecturers, I picked up crumbs wherever they fell. But nothing fitted together.
>
> Gathering my courage, I wrote a note to Dr. Charles Winters. "Could you use an amateur volunteer?" I asked.
>
> On returning from a sabbatical trip to solicit funds, he had plunged into writing the program. I was given a desk in an adjoining office. A lesson a week was the agenda; 12 books were planned, each containing 12 lessons. The task was monumental. "I have a thousand pages of lecture notes here from Bill Griffin to start with," he remarked. "And this is only the Old Testament, of course."
>
> I did anything that came up. Jotted down biblical references in the margins of the reams of material his colleagues showered into his tiny office. Precomputer, cutter/paper, proof-reader, devil's advocate, and cheering section, I read each lesson that sprang from his typewriter. Playing guinea pig, I was the typical EfM student, standard BA degree only, no Greek, no Hebrew, and a lot of curiosity. But I was also pretty good at pretending l was somebody *else*. If I couldn't understand the text, I figured neither would other hypothetical EfM students. My task was to say so, and I did, writing comments in soft pencil on the typescript as each lesson emerged. Charlie's eraser evaluated my comments, sometimes to obliterate, sometimes to clear an especially dense theological thicket. He then passed the lesson to Barbara Hart's typewriter, which transformed it into camera-ready copy for offset printing.
>
> Book One: Genesis came back from the printer in August 1975, a good inch thick and weighing nearly three pounds. It seemed overweight, a bit wobbly, but, nevertheless, under its flag a pilot group of explorers gathered in Sewanee to make

freely donated her time. Indeed, at that time none of those on the faculty were paid for work other than regular salaries.

The course was organized into a four-year program, each year having thirty-six lessons. The year's materials were further subdivided into three two-part sections, each with six lessons. With each lesson there was the expectation that there would be a seminar meeting.

The seminars had another purpose, one beyond the discussion of the materials. In the seminars Winters expected students to integrate their lives with what they were learning. They were led by mentors who were paid $100 per month honoraria. To form the community and develop trust, students were first asked to share their spiritual autobiographies. Then, as the years progressed, they were asked to engage in theological reflection using techniques developed and taught to the mentors. The initial methods were fairly simple and relied heavily on the "issue" orientation that had been developed by the Educational Center in Saint Louis.

---

what we could of the new terrain. Book Two trimmed down to two more manageable volumes.

Charlie inherited Dr. Myer's study in Bairnwick on the ground floor: I called it The Womb. Dark-paneled, sequestered, and private, it was an ideal place to think, write, think, write, write, write. When he finished Book Six, I gave a party for the seminary faculty and their wives. We gratefully celebrated reaching the halfway mark and toasted the health of the growing child.

The staff had grown larger too, as need dictated. Flower Ross signed on to direct mentor training—a great burden lifted from Charlie. And David Killen had dropped in out of the blue, to provide additional relief. A theologian, he came to us with marketing expertise, exactly what we needed. And in the technical arena, the Bomb was born; the computer age had begun, and we welcomed it. Cindy Sherrill presided over a vast network of new equipment and a larger staff to keep track of shipping and receiving books, accounting, billing, and a thousand other details. We had become a business enterprise, requiring business methods.

Personnel continued to shift as the edition neared its end at Book Twelve. Charlie and Flower, now married, left Sewanee for similar work at Loyola University, New Orleans. John de Beer came on to direct mentor training and all its ramifications. Edward de Bary was appointed Program Manager. My work ended, I was given a farewell party and a big gift, which I appreciated. But it was hard to smile. My car kept turning the corner toward Bairnwick for several months; I had to keep a firm grip on the steering wheel.

A History of the Education for Ministry Program: 1975-95 217

The First EfM Groups

The first groups began in 1975 as pilot groups under the auspices of the seminary in Sewanee. This experiment proved successful and the EfM program was truly launched in 1976 under the acronym TEE (Theological Education by Extension). In that first year, according to a report dated October 1, 1976, approximately 500 students in eighteen dioceses were enrolled. Because of this initial and unexpected success, Winters decided to promote the program at the next General Convention of the Episcopal Church[20] scheduled for Minneapolis, Minnesota, in September 1976. At the General Convention he had an opportunity to present the new program. This was the first time EfM provided a booth for the General Convention's large display area, and this promotion provided additional impetus and growth.[21]

Growth and change raised practical questions. At the beginning Winters intended that each group form and continue through four years to completion without adding new students. To assure financial viability, each group needed a minimum of six students who each paid a tuition of $200. (In 1976 financial viability meant paying the mentor $100 per month for nine months, paying for the materials, and paying for overhead costs.) Winters decided that ten students would be the maximum possible for an effective seminar if each participant were to have enough time to enter fully into the discussion.

Over the course of time, students dropped out for various reasons. Groups faced the need to take in new students or collapse because they were no longer financially viable. Under

---

20. The General Convention of the Protestant Episcopal Church of the United States of America meets every three years. It has two houses—a house of bishops and a house of deputies. In conjunction with the convention, there is also a Women's Triennium and a large trade show. Each convention brings together several thousand Episcopalians from all over the world.
21. Since 1976 EfM has opened a booth each three years, except for the 1982 convention in New Orleans. A special EfM booth was designed for the 1985 convention in Anaheim and later converted into six displays which were used at many diocesan conventions and local area meetings. In 1988 (Detroit) and in 1991 (Phoenix), EfM participated in the booth arranged on behalf of the University of the South.

these circumstances, Winters decided that each EfM group could become a one-room schoolhouse. New students would always begin with Year One, lesson one, and move progressively through the program. As a result, students enrolled at more than one level in any given group, and a group might continue indefinitely as students cycled through the four years.[22]

An early set of decisions involved the problem of training mentors. The mentor was a key person who served as an important catalyst for the group, especially at the beginning. The primary skills required of mentors are twofold. A mentor must be open to a critical approach to the materials so that the student is not forced into a single interpretation. The mentor is not there to teach the materials, but to enable others to discover. This is why the more important aspect of a mentor's qualifications is the ability to work effectively with groups as an enabler rather than as an upfront presenter. Outstanding lecturers may make very poor mentors. At the beginning Charles Winters and Flower Ross relied on a pool of persons whom they knew in the southeast who had experience and training in working with groups. Soon it became necessary to initiate a regular program of mentor training to maintain the quality and integrity of the program.

The Name

The original name for the four-year extension program was "Education for Ministry: A Program of Theological Education by Extension." For the first few years, the second half of its title and the initials TEE were widely used. TEE quickly became associated with the yellow- and red-bound materials. Theological Education by Extension, however, is a generic title used in a massive way among the evangelical churches of the third world. Therefore, in 1978, Winters decided to emphasize the name, Education for

---

22. This turned out to be a very good decision for educational as well as financial reasons. New students received an introduction from those who had gone before them, and the discussion of previously covered materials proved enriching and deepening for the more senior students.

Ministry, under which the program was copyrighted. Usually, the letters EfM designate the program.

The Bairnwick Board

The growing program needed supervision and support, and a board of university officials was formed.[23] A resolution by the faculty of the School of Theology, dated September 1978, stated:

> Bairnwick Committee function and the relation of continuing education and extension education to the MDiv program. It was agreed that the Bairnwick Committee would be constituted as a board of directors for continuing education and theological education by extension. This board is ultimately responsible to the Dean and faculty of the School of Theology. The board will meet quarterly and the minutes of their meeting will be shared with the entire MDiv faculty. This board is responsible for personnel, policy, and budget, and not primarily for the building. It was noted that the faculty may make observations about the program at Bairnwick and also give advice. It was also noted that the printed materials should include some kind of phrasing that shows the distance between the School of Theology and the Bairnwick program. (This means that some kind of distancing phrasing is needed in the printed materials that come from Bairnwick.) The board is appointed by the dean and faculty of the School of Theology.

In December 1980 the board was discontinued by order of the regents of the University of the South and the vice chancellor. The dean was granted sole supervision under the direction of the provost and the vice chancellor. The university administration did not think it appropriate for a somewhat autonomous board to be

---

23. It included the seminary dean and faculty, the provost, and EfM salaried staff.

operating a program under its jurisdiction when there existed an administrative structure to handle such matters. Since relationships had become contentious, terminating the board was the obvious action to take.

Nevertheless, this was insufficiently explained, and for a time there remained a residue of bitterness around the matter, especially since finances were involved.

Bairnwick

Almost from the beginning, the EfM program was housed in the home that had formerly belonged to the Myers family. They had named their home "Bairnwick," and so the program, the board, and the center became associated with that name. Additional activities were assigned to this center for continuing education, namely, the programs of scholars and bishops in residence, and the arranging of small conferences. Bairnwick had kitchen facilities and living accommodations sufficient for fifteen people. It was an ideal facility to house small conferences and guests of the School of Theology. Bairnwick became an integral part of the experience of coming to Sewanee, especially for EfM trainers. The charm of the house, its reputation of having a ghost, Hrothgar's tomb, a basement that flooded, clanging pipes, and flushing all the bathrooms simultaneously on the count of three once a week in order to clear the pipes of rust were all part of the lore associated with the house.[24]

In 1985, the EfM program moved its offices across campus to the annex of Hamilton Hall. The School of Theology had moved to Hamilton Hall the previous year. It thus became possible for all School of Theology functions to be put under one roof in a building that was formerly part of the Sewanee Academy.[25]

---

24. The pipes were so old that the accumulated rust was flushed regularly in order to keep the water relatively clear. Hrothgar, a Sewanee Mountain legend, was a huge bulldog that once belonged to the Myers family; he was a well-known figure on campus.

25. The Sewanee Military Academy had been demilitarized during the course of the Vietnam War. When the local girl's school known as St. Mary's closed, it had become coeducational. In 1981 the Sewanee Academy merged with St. Andrew's School on the

Many, however, including the staff and Bairnwick's regular visitors, mourned the loss of the "old place."

The Second Step

According to an October 1976 report (unsigned but obviously written by Charles Winters) to the dean and the committee on Bairnwick, the rapid growth of EfM produced a number of problems. More people were needed to manage the program if they were to provide the needed services. Flower Ross, former director of Christian education for the Diocese of Alabama, had joined the staff as a full-time administrative assistant early in 1976, but her duties encompassed more than simply administration. She was asked to promote the program, travel extensively, train mentors, and coordinate various functions carried out at Bairnwick. Bairnwick was to serve as a continuing education center and host conferences as well as develop extension programs. The board also established bishop-in-residence and scholar-in-residence programs under the Bairnwick aegis, and a Christian education resource center. In addition, Barbara Hart and Mary Tom Watts (now a mentor and trainer for EfM) were employed on an hourly basis.

Even with additional staff in Sewanee, it could not do all the development work.

W. Jackson Wilson, rector of Christ Church in South Pittsburg, Tennessee, was the mentor for one of the earliest EfM groups formed. He had a close association with EfM from the outset, so he offered his services for expenses and a minimal honorarium to take the program to dioceses that expressed interest in the program.

This 1976 report also reflects problems that had continued to plague the program. These problems involved the production and printing of materials and finances. The university press in Sewanee was never competitive, and initially the materials were printed at Vanderbilt University.

St. Andrew's campus located just outside the university's 10,000-acre domain. These buildings on the Sewanee campus became available for other uses.

The financial relationship of EfM as a potential income producer to the rest of the university was also discussed in this early report.

> The present critical situation which the university faces may make it imprudent to utilize surpluses in any department for other than crisis needs. If the committee, the university administration, and the Board of Regents think it advisable, any surpluses from TEE might be designated, on an annual basis, to help alleviate the total budgetary crisis. To designate such surpluses unconditionally to current operating expenses of the Corporation, however, would seem to be unwise and a failure to utilize a possibility for creative use of funds.

The discussions involved the size of that surplus so that the real costs of the program were covered. Indirect costs were incurred whenever the university provided advice, counsel, support, financing, and facilities. The "present critical situation" referred to the financial crisis the university encountered in the mid-'70s, a crisis that occasioned a change of leadership for the university. At the time it was even more necessary to make every penny serve the university, and EfM was seen as a potential source of income. It was also the beginning of a period of rapid inflation, and this was felt by the university and the EfM program.

In 1977, Cynthia Sherrill joined the EfM staff as a clerical worker. Her abilities were quickly recognized, and she became administrative coordinator when Dean Holmes named David Killen as executive director in September 1980. In 1985 she became the director of administration for the Extension Center, thereby according her the title for the functions she had already largely assumed.

David P. Killen joined the EfM staff in the fall of 1978 as manager of administration and publications. He served as executive director from 1980 to 1985. May Daw came to Sewanee with her husband who entered as a student at the School of

Theology. She served as receptionist and coordinator of textbook shipments.

Major Changes

By 1979 the program was largely in place. Enrollments had leaped to over 2,000 students, and Charles Winters was busy completing the materials. Often he was working just ahead of deadlines, and occasionally behind them. Problems arose when he suffered a kidney stone and had to undergo surgery. This put him even further behind, and there were short delays. Students who had begun in 1976 waited with bated breath for texts to arrive. In the aftermath of completing the work and now wanting to wed his assistant, Flower Ross, the decision was made that they would leave Sewanee in August 1980.

The dean of the School of Theology, Urban T. Holmes III, announced these coming changes in the Fall 1979 EfM News.

> It is clear to me and my advisors that the program has grown to the point where I must take a more active leadership in Education for Ministry. To do this I will have to reallocate my time; so we plan to bring in an assistant dean for administration, who will help me in all facets of my work, including Education for Ministry.
>
> Furthermore, in lieu of a Director, we are creating as of September 1, 1980, the post of Executive Director of Extension and Continuing Education. Under this job will fall administration, publications, and programs (including the development of the new program we are "piloting" this spring[26]). We will also separate the management of training from training itself. It is our intention to employ for the present two staff trainers, one of whom will be resident in Sewanee. The management of training will

---

26. his new program was called "Awareness" and consisted of a series of short courses. Although David Killen was the key person in its production, his heart was never in it. It was Terry Holmes's brainchild, and the vision died with him. "Awareness" continued until 1985. Some of the materials were mediocre, and they soon became dated.

be under the direction of someone skilled in working within the Episcopal system, as well as knowledgeable in the training field.

Killen assumed the position of executive director in September 1980, and John de Beer was hired as staff trainer. William Hethcock was asked to manage the EfM training on a half-time basis along with acting as the field placement officer for the School of Theology. At the same time, Peyton Craighill became assistant dean for administration in the seminary.

Events soon made these plans obsolete. Hethcock became ill and was forced to curtail his activities. He served with the EfM program for only a short time. The EfM program was growing. It was decided to hire a program manager, and Tom McElligott was hired in August 1981. Terry Holmes had been on sabbatical during the spring of 1981. He never returned. His unexpected death in August of 1981 brought a new crisis to the School of Theology and to the Extension Center.

Formal Evaluation

During 1980, Doris Savage became a consultant to the program. She was asked to prepare a case study of the Bairnwick Center and EfM. An all-day meeting to receive that report was held on December 1 at the DuBose Conference Center in Monteagle, Tennessee, in conjunction with a decision to end the Bairnwick board. Those included in that meeting were the vice chancellor, the provost, the dean of the seminary, David Killen, Cindy Sherrill, John de Beer, and Barbara Stuart. Doris Savage reflected on some of the difficulties she saw:

> The Bairnwick staff has little contact with the seminary. The dean has little contact with the general staff, a negative for some. The assistant dean was at Sewanee three months before he visited the building. Some of the seminary staff have never been in the building.

The seminary faculty, which was largely responsible for the inception and execution of the materials used in the EfM program, have a proprietary interest in it and think it has been "taken over" by the university. Many say they did the writing and preparation for the program in good faith and that good faith has been abused by the university. They are unwilling at the present time to further involve themselves with the writing of new programs or the updating of the present ones. The faculty also complains that they are rarely informed about EfM, its operations and programs. They would like periodic reports from them.

The seminary administration complains that they do not always know what is going on at Bairnwick. They find themselves in the middle between Bairnwick and the university and spend much energy in that place. The feeling from the seminary, as well as the larger university system, is that they have little concrete information, which comes from the EfM program on which they are able to base decisions concerning that program.

Persons in the EfM program complain about edicts being handed down for which there is little explanation and that decisions are made without contact with or information from EfM. They think that the operational mode at the seminary is "don't offend anyone" and the administration finds themselves in a bind when they try to operate in such a mode and maintain quality. They wish to standardize expectations of all students and mentors without interference from other areas.

It is perceived by some at the university that Bairnwick does not see itself as a part of the university system or that they are aided in any way by the larger system.

Most of the problems of distrust are based on finances. The university thinks that the seminary and the center are unrealistic about the costs of running the program. To date there has not been a cost accounting, but that is in process and depends on the use of the computer when that is made available by the university.

The business acumen of the university and the seminary is suspect in the seminary and the EfM program. Some people think that the operation of a million dollar program such as EfM without a contingency fund, for example, is courting disaster.

The university perceives the program as an excellent, innovative and academically sound one. They have never received any negative feedback about the program itself. (The only negatives they have heard were administrative.)

A Time of Transition

The years leading up to Urban Holmes's death were difficult for the university. There had been a financial crisis. Now a new vice chancellor, Robert Ayres, and a new provost, Arthur Shaeffer, began working with this new program. Ayres was completely committed to the enterprise of theological education and especially to EfM. He quickly saw the public relations potential for the university because EfM was highlighting Sewanee in The Episcopal Church in a new and important way. David Killen, after the sudden death of Urban Holmes, sought to make Bairnwick relatively independent of the School of Theology and the remainder of the university since he feared that it might be choked financially.

The year of the interim deanship, 1981-82, was a period of marking time. Tom McElligott came on staff in August 1981 as program manager and left in May 1982. Barbara Stuart, who had served as his coordinator, moved away during the summer of 1982. Peyton Craighill, the associate dean, also left Sewanee in August 1982.

III. 1982-85: The Killen/Booty Years

John Booty came as dean of the School of Theology in August 1982. This was also when Edward O. de Bary joined the EfM staff, hiring Claudia Porter to serve as his assistant. The years of 1982 to 1985 were difficult. The staff in Bairnwick often felt embattled, while the university administration and the dean were unhappy with the conflict. The issues usually revolved around finances and personnel.

At this point, the program also experienced a downturn. The occasion was twofold. Rapid inflation had forced a 25 percent tuition increase over a period of three years and, more important, there was a change in the method of collecting the tuition. Prior to 1982 students enrolled and were then billed through the mentor. Payments were required in two installments, and the materials were sent to each group in three installments. It was a paper-intensive system that was difficult to enforce. Some students enrolled and materials were sent, but the tuition was not paid. Often students dropped out and failed to pay the second half of the tuition, yet the program remained obligated to pay the mentor's honoraria. By 1981-82 the shortfall was alarmingly high, so it was decided in 1982 that tuition should be paid up front, at the time of enrollment. This amounted to a significant shift, and there was a great outcry from mentors and students. The financial problems were resolved, but enrollments dipped.

Text Revision

By 1982, EfM was six years old. Many comments and suggestions had been received. Moreover, the language and the society were changing rapidly so that texts prepared for the mid-1970s were no longer acceptable, particularly when dealing with such subjects as liturgical reforms, women's issues, the death-of-God debate, and the use of inclusive language. One long response to the materials by Burley Brown, a mentor and history professor at Tulane University in New Orleans, was particularly influential.

The process of revision began in 1982. To limit faculty involvement in the revision process, David Killen suggested a committee that included two members of the faculty, two trainers, and members of the EfM staff.[27] This committee had the task of selecting a general editor who would then select the authors. The revision was presumed to be limited. Relatively little change was required of first-year materials, which dealt with the Hebrew Scriptures. Relatively more was anticipated for the Christian Testament (the second year), still more for Church history (the third year), and a total rewrite was anticipated for the fourth year, which dealt primarily with theology in the twentieth century. There was general agreement that more space should be devoted to the Christian Testament.

Applications for the post of general editor were received, and three people were interviewed. Ross Mackenzie was selected. He had served as professor of Church History at Union Presbyterian Seminary in Richmond, Virginia. Although a full-time Presbyterian pastor, Mackenzie also had close ties to The Episcopal Church. As the revision began, Richard E. Brewer suggested some innovative alterations to the program. Under the direction of John de Beer, Brewer took on the task of preparing the study guides (later known as "Parallel Guides") for each lesson, and the concept of the *Common Lessons* was put in place. The earlier materials had been presented in four years and divided into three portions for each year, each with twelve lessons. Thus there were thirty-six lessons for the year. This was changed to thirty-three lessons for the year, and a set of five *Common Lessons* was prepared. These lessons were grouped in four sets so that a student would not encounter the same common lesson each year, but in a given year all students would use the same common lessons. They dealt with group-life issues—starting up, theological reflection, spirituality, looking at ministry, and closing down.

The initial revision of Year One proceeded smoothly, but the first set, *Common Lessons: Series A,* provided the first indications

---

27. The original members of the committee were David Killen, John de Beer, Edward O. de Bary, Donald Armentrout, John M. Gessell, Betsy Poist, and Richard Brewer. When Killen left in 1985, Tom Watson became the chairman. Carolyn Kinman Langford, Elizabeth Lang, and Cynthia Sherrill joined the committee in 1986 when it was reconstituted to meet the crisis with Year Two.

of problems to come. The first printing arrived in Sewanee in July 1984. The books were riddled with spelling errors, materials were quoted without having obtained copyright permission, and general quality was lacking. The first run of 5,000 copies was destroyed, and a subsequent run was hastily ordered with most of the errors corrected.

Year One materials were put to use in September 1984. Feedback about spelling and other errors continued to flow into the EfM offices. Two revisions were required over the next three years to put this in order.

In November of 1984, Charles Winters and William Griffin complained vigorously that their names had been left off the Year One material although it was still largely their work. David P. Killen acknowledged this and apologized in a letter, which appeared in the Spring 1985 *EfM News*. As a result, new covers were ordered and sent that stated that Charles Winters and William Griffin were joint authors of the Year One materials.

David Killen resigned effective August 1985, and Year Two appeared in September. The materials were distributed, and de Bary advised Watson, interim director, that there might be problems. Brewer[28] had provided a similar warning when the materials were still in the editing stage, but his comments had been disregarded. Reports from students and mentors started coming to the EfM office almost as soon as the materials were introduced. By January 1986 the criticism was a torrent. It was apparent to nearly everyone that the Christian Testament materials prepared by Pheme Perkins were not acceptable. Tom Watson, interim head of EfM, invited Noel Workman of Delta Design, an advertising agency, to help the EfM staff sort through the possible responses.

In February of 1986, the editorial advisory board was quickly reconstituted. During the course of a daylong meeting at the

---

28. Under the direction of John de Beer, director of education, Richard E. Brewer wrote the study guides that accompany each lesson. His observations were made to John de Beer while David Killen was still executive director. Tom Watson unexpectedly inherited the problem when he began his year as interim director of the center.

Nashville airport, the board advised that the Perkins materials be abandoned and suggested using a book with a study guide as an interim replacement until a complete rewrite could be done. Realizing that a cause of the problems had been lack of time, it was quickly decided to provide the book for two years, so as to allow sufficient time for the writing, editing, and publishing process. To allay discontent, the students were promised that they would receive the revised materials once they were published if they stayed in the EfM program.

In March, *The New Testament and Early Christianity* (New York: Macmillan, 1984) by Joseph B. Tyson was selected as an interim measure. A team assembled in May 1986 to prepare a study guide to accompany the book. This textbook covered the Christian Testament and the history of the early Church, which was needed for the first ten chapters of Year Three that Perkins had also prepared. These chapters were slightly edited, and then dropped altogether. They were never printed in the United States.[29] The interim solution was put in place for September 1986. That same autumn Christopher Bryan[30] agreed to write a new set of Christian Testament materials.

The Year Two problems had a financial impact as well. The EfM budgets of fiscal years 1987 and 1988[31] produced less income toward indirect costs than was budgeted—the only times this occurred during the history of the EfM program. In a decreasing progression, the following three fiscal years were affected negatively by the losses caused by the revision process.

Direct financial losses were only part of the negative impact caused by the Year Two problems. The lack of confidence was reflected in diminishing new enrollments. The problem had been

---

29. EfM granted permission to print EfM materials in New Zealand, and the New Zealand Church liked the Perkins materials. Some of the Year Two materials that would have been otherwise discarded were provided to EfM New Zealand, which edited and printed the ten chapters by Perkins as part of the Year Three materials. EfM New Zealand abandoned the Perkins materials in 1989.

30. Professor of New Testament, The School of Theology, The University of the South.

31. The University of the South begins its fiscal year on July 1. Fiscal year 1987, therefore, refers to July 1, 1986, through June 30, 1987.

handled quite well by the staff, however, and these losses were minimal when considering the possibilities. The damage was real, but by being candid with the EfM public, by acting quickly and decisively, and by providing reassurance to students and mentors, the program was saved from disaster. Year Three was written by Ross Mackenzie. By this time there existed an editorial review board to review the materials while still in the early stages of publication. In addition, better proofreading procedures[32] were in place and there now existed sufficient administration support to handle the process properly.

The production of Year Four would have been a debacle like that of Year Two if the editorial board had not existed. One of the authors produced materials that were nearly useless. To make the deadlines a team was assembled to complete the writing job, and Year Four was published on time in 1987. While this increased the cost slightly, catastrophic problems were thus avoided.

The long-awaited index was completed in 1990 under the leadership of Associate Dean J. Carleton Hayden. It had not been planned in the original revision. In spite of a clamor from EfM students and mentors, and extensive discussions among the trainers and the EfM staff, David Killen had blocked all suggestions to include an index[33] during his tenure as director.

EfM for the Visually Impaired

The production of a version of the Education for Ministry program in a format appropriate for use by the visually impaired was an early request. Today, of course, making materials available in an appropriate format is an obligation. Recording for the Blind,

---

32. Several persons participated in the proofreading. Priscilla Fort began to work with this almost from the start. Later, Phebe Hethcock did much of the work as well as others, including Mary Stuart Turner, who also provided support in some of the computer operations around the revision process, especially the indexing.

33. Killen thought that an index would enable students to use the materials for research rather than for programmed learning. He understood these to be study materials, like classroom notes, and thought it would violate the spirit of the program to make them appear "academic" by inserting research tools.

Inc., of Princeton, New Jersey, prepared some of the first EfM materials. This process stopped before 1982, but the materials were transcribed on tape in certain localities.

Recordings for the blind were specialized because the equipment operated differently from a normal cassette tape recorder. Tapes for the blind used slower speeds and had additional tracks so that the amount of tape needed to record a particular document was significantly reduced when preparing materials. This meant that the tapes were not suitable for use by the general public.

When the revised materials became available in 1984, Recording for the Blind recommended Clearer Vision Ministries, Inc., of Orlando, Florida. This agency agreed to take on the task of recording EfM materials for the blind. The entire program was recorded, including the *Manual for Mentors*, *Common Lessons*, and all four years of the text, and it became available in 1991.

The Spanish Translation

The first two years of the original version of the EfM program was translated into Spanish in Ecuador. It never received widespread distribution. The Ecuador version was used for a time in Nicaragua without license from Sewanee, but this too died out when the political conditions made it too difficult to continue.

In 1982 David Killen initiated the Spanish translation of the revised materials at the behest of the bishop of the Episcopal Diocese of Northern Mexico. At the time, SPCK[34] was just beginning its work in Sewanee, and this became an SPCK project. Money was raised and the translation was begun under the leadership of Harold Lowe, who was then living in Mexico. Richard Kew of SPCK had overall responsibility for the project and

---

34. The Society for Promoting Christian Knowledge has existed since the seventeenth century. A branch was established in the United States in 1983 at Sewanee. SPCK works with churches throughout the world, making possible publishing, education, broadcasting, and worship for the communication of the Christian message.

worked closely with Tom Watson. Edward O. de Bary became the staff contact in September of 1986.

The translation process was difficult and the materials prepared in Mexico were less than satisfactory. Rosa Lindahl, a native of Colombia and a graduate of the seminary, who was thoroughly bilingual, edited and retranslated much of the material. Year Three was completed in 1992.

Theological Reflection:
The Manual for Mentors

From its infancy, EfM developed numerous guides for mentors, which were brought together into a "manual." This *Manual for Mentors* passed through a series of editions until the bound version appeared in 1988. Refining this tool provided significant support to the program. Eventually, many administrative problems were resolved by trial and error, feedback, careful listening, and hard work. The aids to the mentor were also constantly refined. In a 1983 training session for trainers, the essentials of the microscope method were worked out. This method for organizing the seminar became the dominant way to approach the task of theological reflection in the EfM program, supplanting the use of the issue method, which dominated at the beginning. In addition, John de Beer and Patricia Killen produced documentation for the EfM work in a paper devoted to the EfM model.[35]

The manual provided substantial information to help mentors learn how groups work and how to make them function effectively. Eventually, these aids to the life of the group were partially incorporated into the materials provided each student. *Common Lessons* became an important vehicle for the mentor and student to use as tools for beginning, developing group life, practicing theological reflection, developing spirituality, and closing at the end of the year.

---

35. Patricia O'Connell Killen and John de Beer, "'Everyday' Theology: A Model for Religious and Theological Education," *Chicago Studies* 22, no. 2 (August 1983), 2.

Training of Trainers

The EfM program quickly grew beyond the ability of the Sewanee staff to provide training for mentors on a continuing basis. In 1977, Flower Ross and Charles Winters selected five men to begin the training network. These were Vince Eareckson, Henry Lee Hobart Myers, John de Beer, Robert Cook, and William Warren. They worked together in Sewanee for a full week during December of 1977, and were then accredited to train mentors and share responsibility for the training of future trainers.

The trainers agreed to return to Sewanee for a full week each year to maintain their certification. In return they were paid an honoraria of $300 per event plus expenses. Of this first group of five, de Beer later came to Sewanee to fill the position occupied by Flower Ross. By 1982 none of the other persons remained involved with EfM as trainers.

When Charles Winters and Flower Ross left during the summer of 1980, John de Beer came to Sewanee to direct the training program that had become central to the EfM program. John de Beer took the nucleus of trainers that had been formed by Flower Ross and developed it into the EfM training network. He was present for the first training of trainers and was involved with nearly all the others until the spring of 1990. After his departure in 1988, John de Beer continued to supervise the training of trainers and their accreditation during the ensuing year when Gordon Okunsanya served as interim director of education and training.

In 1983 John de Beer's position was renamed as director of education and training, and he introduced "Life Training" to the program. This proved to be a controversial step.[36] The Life Training program was given over a period of four days at a conference of EfM trainers held in April of 1983 at DuBose

---

36. Life Training was inspired by EST (Erhard Seminar Training). This controversial and highly publicized program was at the head of the Human Potential movement during the 1970s. Two Episcopal clergy, Roy Whitten and Brad Brown of San Jose, California, began Life Training, first as a profit-making venture and later reorganized as a nonprofit program. Some EfM trainers found this beneficial and others abhorred it.

Conference Center. Most of the EfM staff in Sewanee rejected it and, subsequently, the dean, John Booty, asked that EfM not continue to work with this program.

Between 1981 and 1988, John de Beer held a continual series of trainings of trainers. New trainers were brought on board, and all trainers were asked to return to Sewanee once a year for recertification. The initial intent under Flower Ross had been to provide each sponsoring diocese with its own trainer, but this would have become too large a network to maintain. A group of about thirty trainers formed by 1982 and slowly expanded to about sixty in 1993.[37] Training of trainers was always done in groups of eight to ten persons, a labor-intensive and demanding process. The training was of extremely high quality, on a par with that offered by the National Training Laboratories and other similar organizations. John de Beer always brought in someone from outside to assist with the event, and participants consistently reported that the training they received was outstanding. Not only did it prepare them to train mentors, but it also provided them with important skills in working with groups, which applied to other areas of their personal and professional lives.

The first national convention for trainers occurred in 1983. It was a way of bringing the entire network together and of reducing the number of weeklong events that were so demanding on the staff, especially John de Beer.

Subsequent conventions were held in 1985 and 1987. In 1990 the first attempt to convene trainers and diocesan coordinators in one large conference occurred.

The Role of the EfM Mentor

The EfM mentor is the key to the program. When this role is filled effectively, the program is well received; when it is not, the

---

37. The word "about" may seem peculiar, but there are always some trainers on leave or in transition, which means that it is difficult to ascertain exactly how many trainers can be said to be active during a particular year. This figure does not include the training network outside the United States. There are twelve trainers in Australia, ten in New Zealand, six in England, three in Canada, three in the Bahamas, and one each in Honduras and Nicaragua.

program falters. Persons who are effective mentors must have the skills to work with people and know how to lead groups effectively so that there is a sense of partnership, quest, shared leadership, ownership, and camaraderie. The best mentors do not need to know all of the answers; they do need to help ask the questions. They are not there to furnish information or to lecture; they are there as guides on a pilgrimage. When Bruce Boston applied for the position of general editor in 1982, his article on the role of mentor was given to the staff. He wrote for another purpose entirely, but his description was germane.

> The concept and role of the mentor come directly to us from ancient Greece. In the *Odyssey*, Mentor was the faithful friend of Odysseus, the King of Ithaca, entrusted by Odysseus with the care of his household during his absence during the Trojan War. Above and beyond this general responsibility, however, Mentor was the guardian and tutor of Telemachus, Odysseus's son.
>
> Mentor exercises his tutorial function within the context of a wider range of responsibility, i.e., the care of Odysseus's household. Mentor functions as a channel for guidance and wisdom which come from beyond him. He is not its source, but its servant. We need not take this to mean that for us the mentor is a religious intermediary but, in a more general sense, functions as a "spiritual guide" and as a kind of gatekeeper to a larger world beyond...
>
> Mentor is presented as the companion in Telemachus's quest for his father, during which he comes into his adulthood. Thus we may think of the mentor as a companion to the pupil as she/he moves toward the responsibility of adulthood. By adulthood we are not specifically referring to chronological age, but to a level of experience and competence which demonstrates that the pupil is ready to "take on" the world at large on his/her own terms rather than simply imitating those of the mentor. The pupil becomes

a subject, capable of speaking his or her own word in the world.[38]

The task of the EfM mentor is threefold: organizing the group, being a mentor or guide for the group, and administering the group by handling enrollments, ordering materials, and providing reports. Groups are expected to meet four times a month over a period of nine months. However, the life of the group is something to be negotiated between the mentor and the group, and there are local variants to this schedule. A mentor for EfM is considered a private contractor who performs a function, but can set their own hours, specific agenda, arrangements, and work plan.

Mentor Training

EfM's program of training trainers provides a corps of able and accredited persons to train the several hundred mentors throughout the United States. Initially, training requirements were minimal. While mentors were asked to return each year, there was no enforcement or follow-up. This changed in 1982 as a result of the survey by Doris Savage and other feedback. Her report had a clear message: it is important to have qualified and able mentors, and training for this is crucial to maintain the quality of the program.

Claudia Porter, who came to Sewanee in 1982, possessed the skills to work with the computer just when that tool was becoming increasingly available to EfM staff. She developed procedures to monitor mentor training. Instead of suggesting that each mentor return for training every twelve months, a window was created to allow some flexibility. Mentors were now required to return for training and recertification between twelve and eighteen months since their previous certification.

By 1982 some mentors had been with the program for six years and were complaining about the repetition of the

---

38. Bruce O. Boston, *The Sorcerer's Apprentice: A Case Study in the Role of the Mentor* (Reston, VA: Council for Exceptional Children, 1976), 1–3.

training. Two innovations were instituted, one in 1983 and the other in 1984. The first innovation allowed mentors who had been trained three times to file a report with the center in lieu of attending mentor training. The second was more complex and continues to be refined. The trainers designed a series of events under the general title of "mentor formation events." These take mentors more deeply into various aspects of the work with the EfM program and provide specialized training in various areas. Experienced mentors who have been trained at least twice through basic mentor training are eligible to attend formation events.

The mentor training network is an unheralded aspect of the EfM program. Without trained mentors there cannot be an EfM program, so the training is an inherent part of the promotion of EfM. But mentor training also provides skills with wider application than the EfM program. Each year the training program of the Extension Center provides training in the skills of theological reflection and the skills for working with groups of up to about 1,000 persons. This alone is a major contribution to the Church. The trainees learn much about how to work with groups and become leaders in the Church community, as well as developing useful skills in theological reflection. Often these skills carry over into other areas of education and ministry.

The Coordinators' Network and Diocesan Contracts

To produce an early infusion of capital, a system of contracts with dioceses of The Episcopal Church developed. The scheme was partially borrowed from the Education Center in St. Louis, which had a history of contracting with parishes and dioceses. In return for certain services, the parish or diocese paid 1 percent of its program budget.

The 1 percent contract was set at $1,200 minimum and $4,500 maximum. The original EfM contracts contained an elaborate plan for returning money to the diocese for each group that was enrolled. During his year with EfM, Tom McElligott saw the problems with this complex contractual arrangement and sought to change the contracting method. These problems were: How do you define the "program" budget of the diocese? How do you explain an elaborate contract to a diocesan committee? How do you reassure the diocesan financial officer that the actual cost to the diocese will not be known until the end of the contract period?

In 1983, Edward O. de Bary developed a new contract schema. He established a three-tiered system—one for parishes, one that provided minimal services to the diocese at a cost of $1,500 per year, and one that provided additional benefits to the diocese for $2,500 per year. The new schema worked effectively, and between 1982 and 1992 the number of supporting dioceses more than tripled. With each contract a coordinator was appointed to act on behalf of the diocese. Along with developing a system of contracting, EfM also developed a system of diocesan coordinators. Initially, the plan called for the trainer and coordinator to be the same person, and in many cases they were. As the program became more complex this approach changed. As of 1992 only four trainers remained among the eighty-seven coordinators.

By 1979 a one-page job description for the coordinator had been compiled and the program had agreed to reimburse the coordinator for administrative expenses. In her 1982 report, Doris Savage suggested that the program might benefit if the coordinators were given more support. By 1985 the coordinators' job description had evolved into a *Manual for Coordinators,* and a system for remunerating coordinators was in place when the diocese elected the more expensive contract.

The role of the coordinator is threefold: promote EfM in the diocese, arrange for mentor training on a regular basis, and provide the focal point for communications between EfM and the diocese. The administration of individual EfM groups remained between the mentor and EfM, but the coordinator may be called to assist should problems develop. Each year there are conferences for coordinators in Sewanee to provide training and support.

Administrative Functions

EfM began as a small operation. After the staff began entering data into a computer database in 1978, occasionally some information would be required, and someone would be sent to the back porch to look in the "shoe box." This was how the original records were kept: cards in boxes.

EfM blossomed just at the time that the computer became a household appliance and the cost of electronic equipment plummeted. Thus, EfM soon had its own toll-free telephone line, and computers became part of the normal equipment. By 1990, the full-time employees all had computers on their own desks. Using the equipment had become a part of the office routine.

The benefits of the electronic media cannot be overstated. It would not be possible to maintain the EfM program at an affordable price without using computers, which are used to track students, keep accounts, maintain inventory, prepare materials for publication, communicate between staff members, and prepare correspondence and other documents. The new telephone system and a university-wide computer network have enhanced this work greatly.

One of John de Beer's gifts was to build a team and to invite others to share their creative gifts. When administrative problems with mentors became an issue, he invited the administrative staff to design the training of the trainers so that EfM could improve communications, decrease annoying errors, improve efficiency, and lower costs. The administrative staff did this with gusto. Using amusing settings, they succeeded in demonstrating the importance of administration, and provided an excellent demonstration of how learning can be fun. Various aspects of their work, in presentations such as "Mr. Mentor" and a radio show, became part of the lore of EfM's memorable moments.

From its shoebox beginnings, the administration of EfM, under Cynthia S. Sherrill, has become an efficient and effective mechanism. This system makes it possible for a staff of eleven and a half persons (plus one hired during the autumn rush) and some students on work-study scholarships to handle the administration of a program that, as of academic year 1992–93, encompassed more than 800 mentors and 7,500 students in a worldwide network.[39]

EfM Promotion

Promotion during the 1980s focused on increasing the number of sponsoring dioceses and providing mentor training. New brochures and a new prospectus were printed. Articles were placed in the *Episcopalian,* and numerous articles appeared in diocesan newspapers. The secular press also took note of EfM, and articles appeared in places as diverse as Honolulu, Hawaii and Roanoke, Virginia.

The 1982 General Convention of The Episcopal Church was held in New Orleans. Because of staff changes in Sewanee, the reservation for an EfM booth was canceled. EfM was represented at the convention of 1985 (Anaheim) with its own booth. This led to a cooperative arrangement with the Office of University Relations. EfM was represented in the University of the South's booth at the conventions of 1988 (Detroit) and 1991 (Phoenix).

Much EfM promotion has been done by the staff through visits to the sponsoring dioceses. These act as catalysts to bring people together. Often much energy and activity is generated as a result of visits in the diocese. These visits provide an opportunity to gather mentors, students, and/or graduates; thus the EfM network grows and nurtures the people in it. Many national and international relationships have grown through the EfM network. These have produced cooperative endeavors, job opportunities, marriages, lifelong friendships, and many opportunities for Christian ministry.

---

39. By 1994 there were 1,000 mentors and almost 7,900 students in the worldwide network.

IV. EfM: 1986–92

During the academic year 1985–86, the seminary had an interim dean, Donald P. Armentrout, and the EfM program had an interim head, Tom Watson, who became the university's vice president for development and university relations in 1986. It was a time of transition.

Two major changes in 1986–87 occurred that greatly affected life in the Extension Center: the computer programs were completely redone; and the EfM offices and storage facilities moved from the old house, Bairnwick, to new facilities especially prepared for the program. There was a great deal of attachment to the house which had provided the program with conference facilities. Many trainers and staff members were saddened when it was remodeled for use as a Women's Center. Initially, the new facilities included conference center facilities, but this did not work well. Soon training sessions were housed in other campus facilities, usually the Sewanee Inn. When the inn closed, St. Mary's Conference Center became the most-used choice for lodging overnight guests. Dining and meeting facilities were available in the EfM building, an extension of Hamilton Hall, and in rooms assigned to EfM by the seminary in Hamilton Hall.

In spring 1986, Robert Giannini accepted the call to serve as dean, and Tom Watson proposed that the job of directing EfM (formerly titled executive director) be given to an associate dean, who would have duties at the seminary and also act on behalf of the dean when out of the office. Since EfM would now have a part-time head, the staff prepared new job descriptions and developed a method of working together that would allow the associate dean time to work at the seminary. Watson and Giannini wrote a memo to Arthur Schaefer, university provost, on July 1, 1986, that described the new arrangement:

> In order properly to administer the full range of programs at the School of Theology, we are proposing that instead of establishing a position of dean of administration as originally proposed by the vice chancellor and the former

dean, that a position of associate dean for the School of Theology be established. The person filling this new position would spend approximately half of his time administering on a day-to-day basis the Education for Ministry and related programs. The experience of the interim director is that an executive director devoting full-time responsibilities to the program is not essential. The other half of the associate dean's time would be devoted to responsibilities assigned or delegated by the dean. (Attached you will find a proposed job description for both portions of the associate dean's responsibilities.) It is the intention of the new dean of the seminary to serve as something more than a figurehead for the Education for Ministry program. The intention is that he be involved in a significant way in administering that program as he does all of the programs of the School of Theology.

This proposal put the day-to-day operation with the professional staff at EfM: John de Beer, Edward O. de Bary, and Cynthia Sherrill. It freed the associate dean to be involved in the life of the seminary and perform support duties for the dean. It was decided that an administrative assistant for the professional staff—but working directly for the associate dean—would help make this plan work. It was also decided that John de Beer be permitted to hire an assistant since he would be taking on a substantial workload from Edward O. de Bary and the work in the office had increased with the growth of the program and the revision process. Edward O. de Bary continued to have an assistant since added to his duties was the contract work, both overseas and with other denominations, that had been part of the director's duties. Job titles changed. John de Beer became the director of education and training, Cindy Sherrill became the director of administration, and Edward O. de Bary became the field director. Carolyn Kinman moved to the new position of assistant director of education and training, and began working for John de Beer. Karen Keele joined the staff to become the assistant field director.

The search for associate dean began in October 1986. J. Carleton Hayden was selected; he did not begin work, however, until July 1987. The dean of the seminary personally headed the Extension Center during the academic and fiscal year 1987. In practice this meant that the staff handled day-to-day operations since the dean was frequently immersed in his new job and the demands of the seminary community—students, faculty, and constituencies. After Carleton Hayden arrived on the scene, contrary to the Watson memo, the dean removed himself almost completely from direct interaction with the EfM staff.

The new arrangement did not always work well. Carleton Hayden soon became immersed in seminary and other activities, and he required more administrative support than had been anticipated. The administrative assistant on whom the staff had relied was not able to meet all the demands of other staff since she was asked to support Hayden in many of the seminary activities, as well as arranging for seminary functions such as receptions for visiting scholars and bishops. The staff picked up some of the publishing responsibilities and maintained the routines of administering the program.

In 1988 John de Beer left the EfM staff for new work in Florida. Gordon Okunsanya was hired as interim director of education and training, and he remained for one year, during which he produced a new *Manual of Trainers*. Gail Jones arrived in Sewanee to fill the position in August 1989. She also assumed responsibility for teaching Christian Education at the seminary.

The DOCC Program

The program now known as DOCC (Disciples of Christ in Community) originated at Trinity Church, New Orleans, in 1975. It was first known as Disciples of Christ (DOC). It was the brainchild of John Stone Jenkins. Started as a parish renewal project, it became popular in a number of parishes, principally in the southeast, and was funded by grants from Trinity Church.

John Jenkins spent the 1984–85 academic year in Sewanee, but he was unable to obtain support for his program. No one in Sewanee seemed very interested at the time. In 1985, just as Booty and Killen were leaving, William Barnwell visited Edward O. de Bary to explore the possibility of DOC being handled through the Extension Center. De Bary asked him to wait a year since matters in Sewanee were in transition. In spring 1986, de Bary called Barnwell to say that matters were now making it possible to explore the possibility of a relationship between the EfM and DOC programs.

Barnwell had been on John Jenkins's staff at Trinity Church, and he had helped to create the DOC program. He was also an EfM mentor. De Bary was familiar with DOC from his Mississippi days and thought that DOC was a good leadoff to EfM. They both saw the programs as complementary, although Barnwell and other DOC leaders were uneasy about the possibility that the university might bureaucratize DOC. Both Barnwell and de Bary thought that the two programs aimed at different educational needs. They were not competitive. While they were different in form, content, impact, and purpose, they shared an understanding of ministry that arises out of the baptismal covenant and extends to everyone. They also both shared a commitment to provide programs of quality to meet the educational needs of the laity.

There were several informal discussions and letters between de Bary and Barnwell during 1985–86. De Bary attended a DOC training in Monteagle in May 1987, just as Carleton Hayden was arriving to begin work in Sewanee. De Bary then urged further exploration, and a full meeting took place in September 1988 of EfM staff and key DOC people, including John Jenkins and the new rector of Trinity, New Orleans, Hill Riddle. Carleton Hayden, John de Beer, and Karen Keele attended a DOC training during spring 1988.

De Bary drew up the initial proposal, contract, and budget for DOC to come to Sewanee. This was circulated among the staff in Sewanee and DOC leadership in New Orleans. In January of 1989, at a lengthy meeting in New Orleans chaired by Carleton Hayden,[40] arrangements were completed to bring DOC to Sewanee, effective July 1, 1989. The name was changed to Disciples of Christ in Community (DOCC) so as not to conflict with the denomination known as the Disciples of Christ. The proposal and budget were revised and an agreement was reached. Initially, DOCC was to be funded by fees from participants and equal amounts of startup support from Trinity Church and the University of the South. Charging a fee for participating in the DOCC program carried the potential for difficulties since the program had been free in the past. DOC users had not known the extent to which Trinity Church had supported the program. This support had limits, and thus the program itself was limited until it could find a more substantial financial and administrative base of its own.

Karen Keele set to work to bring DOCC under the Extension Center and to produce the expansion necessary to make it self-sufficient. The 1,200 students that were thought to be possible for the first year, based on conservative estimates derived from EfM and provided by Trinity Church, proved to be too optimistic. About 800 students enrolled for the 1990–91 academic cycle, somewhat less than anticipated. In 1992, a complete revision of the DOCC syllabus was published under the editorship of Ward Ewing of Buffalo, New York, and enrollment rose slightly.

The 1989–92 Academic Years

In 1989–90 a whole series of changes took place that affected the Extension Center, which now included EfM and DOCC as parallel programs. The seminary appointed two new associate deans, and Carleton Hayden was relieved of most of his

---

40. Giannini was dean at the time, and he was later credited with bringing DOCC to Sewanee. Carleton Hayden's leadership in the negotiation process, however, was crucial. He had the support of Dean Giannini and Samuel Williamson, who became vice chancellor and president of the university during the 1987–88 academic term.

duties with the seminary. Cynthia Sherrill realigned her staff, doing away with a salaried position and hiring two employees as registrars. Sarah Davis moved out of the administrative section and became administrative assistant to the associate dean. Mary Stuart Turner and Patti Huber became registration specialists. Karen Keele moved to become director of DOCC on July 1, 1989, and Jeanne Jansenius became half-time secretary for DOCC and half-time director of training and educational design. Edward O. de Bary, who had shared a secretary with the director of training and educational design, hired James David Jones as secretary/clerical assistant, but did not hire an assistant field director of EfM to replace Karen Keele. Gail Jones (no relation to James) joined the staff on September 1, 1989, as director of training and educational design.

In July 1990, Dean Robert Giannini resigned to take the position of dean of St. Paul's Cathedral, Indianapolis, and Donald Armentrout became interim dean for the second time. In August 1991, Guy F. Lytle became the new dean of the School of Theology. The university administration decided that he should also direct the Extension Center. Carleton Hayden was given other duties, and he left the university in July 1992.

Additional staff changes took place in 1991–92. James David Jones worked for Edward O. de Bary for a year and a half, and then took a position as managing editor of the *St. Luke's Journal of Theology* (renamed *Sewanee Theological Review* in September 1991). Cindy C. Caldwell filled that position during summer 1991. Jeanne Jansenius accepted an offer to manage the university's Office of Telecommunications, and Belinda Powell came on board to assist Karen Keele and Gail Jones. Sarah Davis continued to serve as administrative assistant, first to Carleton Hayden, and then later to Guy Lytle.

The early 1990s were a time of staff changes and consolidation. Contracts were renewed with Australia and New Zealand. Work was launched in a major way in the United Kingdom and an EfM group began in Georgetown, Guyana. During these years the program grew about seven percent each year. Thus, by the end of the fiscal year in June 1992, the program was in sound financial condition and in a position to continue its expansion.

EfM and The Episcopal Church

With fifteen years of experience, EfM has become a significant force in the life of The Episcopal Church. The titles of EfM mentor and EfM trainer are recognized by the Clergy Deployment Office and are categories in the clergy job description. A number of dioceses use EfM to augment their diaconate and nonstipendiary clergy training programs. More important, many people who have been deeply influenced by EfM now serve in positions of leadership in The Episcopal Church. Three trainers were deputies to the 1991 General Convention, and about 25 percent of the laity and clergy at the last General Convention of The Episcopal Church had some affiliation with EfM as student, graduate, mentor, or trainer. For the past few years, about one-third of the students coming to seminary in Sewanee had some EfM experience. A number of bishops were mentors, including the bishops of Massachusetts, New York, Alabama, and Oklahoma. The first woman to serve as bishop in New Zealand was an EfM mentor, and four bishops in Australia were mentors and trainers for the program. At the end of the 1992–93 academic cycle, there were over 8,000 EfM graduates. Many of them feel a tie to the University of the South, and they may truly serve in the future as part of its "never failing succession of benefactors." But more heart-warming than success and statistics are the many personal stories of lives changed, vocations found, and important questions answered. We hear of those who pursued EfM and decided to attend seminary and seek ordination. But there are others less heralded, those who had dreams of seminary but who found through EfM that the ministry of the laity was theirs. There are also countless stories of people who used the skills they learned in EfM to improve their daily work and thus bring Christ to life and work in truly amazing ways—the banker who changed the way he treated his employees, the lawyer who found an adaptation of theological reflection useful when dealing with people in the throes of divorce, the mentors who used theological reflection to channel and learn from conflict in their parish, and the adaptation of EfM methods for use with other programs.

Perhaps imitation or adaptation of our work is the best applause. When Trinity Seminary, Pittsburgh, sought to develop an adult education program, they hired Ray Smith from Australia, who had completed a doctoral dissertation on EfM in Australia. When the Diocese of Massachusetts designed a new program, they asked and received permission to use EfM methods of reflection. At Virginia Theological Seminary EfM methods were deemed one of several approved methods for use in their seminars. Texas A&M adapted EfM methods to their extension programs in rural sociology. Numerous dioceses, charged by the General Convention with presenting discussions on human sexuality, used EfM reflection methods as a way to broach this subject.

In its own unique way, the Education for Ministry program is quite different from traditional educational methods. EfM provides the Anglican Communion with a unique educational resource that contains much of a "basic" seminary education. EfM provides a venue for students to discover the meaning of what they learn and how this impacts their lives. EfM delivers skills to those who lead the groups and offers portability so that someone can begin EfM in New Zealand, continue in San Francisco, and complete the program in Manchester, England. EfM brings the University of the South to the world so that others can also affirm the motto that we often see on the Sewanee campus, *Ecce quam bonum*—"Behold, how good."

The Beginnings of Theological Reflection in EfM

Flower Ross
September 2006

In 1975, I was working in the Diocese of Alabama half-time as the resource person for Christian Education. The other half of my time I worked as administrative assistant for the Association for Creative Change. The latter was an organization that was involved in training and accrediting trainers in human relations, organization development, and conflict management. I had been trained and accredited by this organization in these areas.

I enjoyed both jobs, but I was feeling a great yearning to do something more meaningful. I felt the need for additional theological education even though I knew that ordination was not the right track for me. I had been searching around for the right place to acquire this knowledge and at just that time the Rev. Dr. Charles Winters came to visit in our diocese and told the bishop and some of the staff about a new program he was working on. At that moment it was known unofficially as Theological Education by Extension. Charles had been my bishop's professor in seminary and the professor of my former husband, so he was known and respected by those of us who attended that meeting. As he described the program, he led us to look at the Baptismal Covenant and mentioned that we could envision ministry in three different ways. The ministry *to* the Church, which is primarily the work of the ordained, the ministry *in* the Church, which is the work of the ordained and all the many laypersons who were active in various jobs in the parish, and the ministry *of* the Church, which is the work of all the members out in the world.

It was this last ministry for which his program, officially titled *Education for Ministry*, was designed. He then described a two-rail-fence model of education. The top rail symbolized "content," or the material that would be contained in a lecture, or, in EfM, in the readings. But this alone is not truly education. We have only to think of doctors or airplane pilots to know that simply having read "the material" is not enough. One must have *experience* and put the theoretical information together with it for real education to take place. The bottom rail in the fence model stands for this experience. The fence posts stand for the process that links the two together. In the EfM program, small seminar groups were to be the fence posts, and the process in them was to be theological reflection.

I knew immediately that it sounded like something that I wanted very much to do. As Charles described it, however, the process he wanted people to use for reflection sounded like one that needed development and people trained in doing it.

When Charles had been in Alabama, we were talking in the vestibule of the Diocesan Center waiting for a rain shower to pass over. I said to him, "If you ever need a good assistant, call me." And then I forgot all about having said that, as I worried him about the training during telephone calls. He, of course, was working diligently trying to get the material written.

Imagine my surprise when, in November, I received a telephone call from the dean of the seminary, Dr. Urban T. Holmes. (Better known to all as Terry.) He asked if I would be interested in coming to talk to them about a job working for the EfM program as director of training and programming. At that point Charles had a part-time secretary, and she was the person who had the task of typing the manuscripts and keeping up with all the other office work.

In January I made the trip to Sewanee and talked to Charles and Dean Holmes about this job. It was clear that I knew what I thought was needed and so they believed in me enough to offer me the job as of July 1 of 1976. Obviously, I said yes. I knew that I had some ideas about what the training should be, but no clear step-by-step way to go about it. The experiential model of education had four steps: Experience, Identify, Analyze, and Generalize. This was how I planned to work with the groups.

The instruction I was given was first and foremost Charles's desire that people use the material they were studying to inform their own lives and help them know if they were being faithful in making the decisions that would shape their actions. First, I knew that we must have a way for people to form themselves into a group that was trusting before they would be willing to talk about their own lives and see whether they were being faithful. I had worked with storytelling before and thought that such a process would develop trust among the members. I decided to call the stories "spiritual autobiographies," not because I wanted people to talk only about the churchy parts of their lives, but because I wanted to focus their attention on the fact that *all* parts of our lives were related to our spirit. This would help people realize that reflecting on very ordinary decisions could indeed be fruitful.

I got another important tool that I modified from one by my good friend, the Rev. Harry Pritchett. It was a model, triangular in shape, which named each point of the angles in the following way: (1) our Christian story, (2) my actions, and (3) my professed beliefs. These were all connected. I could check my actions against my professed beliefs to see if they were consistent, and check both against the Christian story to see if they were consistent with it.

The term "critical incident" as a way for people to begin to examine their own lives was taken from Clinical Pastoral Education (CPE). I think it was a poor term to use since most people didn't recognize that "critical" came from the Greek word *krisis*, which means decision, which is what we wanted them to look at—a specific decision they had made that they could reflect on.

It soon became obvious to me after working with only one or two groups that we had to find a way to work that neither allowed people to try to be problem solvers for others, nor to get too heavily into a psychological frame of reference. This was not easy. It was at this point that I realized we needed to make each person's story one that could be identified with by the other members of the group, and then used by each person to learn about their own individual life. For this reason I asked each person who shared a story to identify the feelings and the thoughts about it separately. Thoughts about a particular story were those of the person who experienced it, but feelings could be generalized among the other members of the group too. Therefore, we were going to begin the reflection based on the common feelings. We used a metaphor to move from the feelings we shared to a piece of the tradition that seemed similar.

I started the first trainings using a story from my experience, and then I asked them questions and allowed discussion to follow with no sense of a process (which I was aware of, but had not described to them) except their interest. When we had finished, I led them back through what we had done and showed that we had, in fact, just done a TR. We identified the process by looking at our own experience of it. Most often I had the help of newsprint on which I drew the triangle and explained how it worked. Then we took turns, with each having a chance to work with another story, and also using the questions I had suggested to them.

In doing things this way, I also had lots of comments from them about what might be helpful to them and what might be confusing. We learned an enormous amount together. In fact, had it not been for all the people who participated in the earliest trainings, we would never have come to the place we had by the time I had left Sewanee.

As time went along and I continually added what I was learning to the process, it was modified. Different ways of approaching the way of doing a TR became possible. The issue method began to develop. The triangle, which was a mainstay, needed to have an additional dimension that helped people acknowledge the way in which the culture surrounding them affected their understandings. The importance of this came to light by traveling to places all over the United States and outside the country. The first place that this became so apparent to me was a trip to Nicaragua, where the bishop was an American from South Carolina and thought that this might be just the way to train some of his people for Indigenous ministries. In addition to the difficulties with language, the life there was entirely unlike what many of us were accustomed to. This was the first but not the only time I was faced with a different culture. There was also work in Western Canada, Alaska, and of course, most importantly, Australia.

It did not take long for the program to grow at a most amazing rate. It seemed to be the right thing for the time. After only a year, I was so overbooked that I had a summer when I was in Sewanee for only seven days total. At that point I needed help and Charles suggested that I train some people to assist me in training mentors. I was very careful to invite people who I knew had some training and educational background. Among the first were John de Beer, Rick Brewer, and Betsy Poist. John became almost as busy training as I was before he ever moved his family to Sewanee and became director of training when I left.

To this point in the program's life, there was nothing written for use in training since I spent all my time on the road doing it. In a way I am very glad that was the case. Although it was difficult, it also made great flexibility necessary and there never was a time when people all over were not entering into, modifying, and sharpening the TR process. It was understood that this was a collaborative process to have disciplined conversation among people who became more thoughtful about their lives as ministries in the world around them.

Contributing Authors

Ashley, Bobbie
Bobbie Ashley joined the EfM staff in 1999 and has held several positions, including EfM registration specialist, registrar, and database coordinator. Her job led her to places she never imagined. Ashley has been able to talk with folks from all parts of the world and has seen the profound effect the program has had on the lives of many people. She has made friends that she has never seen by talking to them on the phone or by email.

Ashley resides in Cowan, Tennessee, and has been married to her husband, James, for five years. She loves fall weather and considers the mountains her home, even though she enjoys trips to the beach. She loves making memories with her family and spending time with her work family. She considers herself lucky to work with the EfM staff, which is supportive of each other through life's changes.

Baker, Dawn
Dawn Baker began working for EfM in January 2003. She has been a database specialist and registration coordinator, and is currently the materials coordinator for the program. A lifelong resident of Franklin County, Tennessee, Baker has a Bachelor of Science degree in business administration with a major in accounting. Before beginning her work with EfM at the Beecken Center of the School of Theology, she worked as a manufacturing cost accountant, loan clerk, and church administrative assistant and bookkeeper.

Baker has three wonderful adult children, Mary Catherine, Barry, and Sarah, and nine precious grandchildren. Her favorite pastimes are visiting with her children and grandchildren, reading, being a loyal follower of the Atlanta Braves and baseball in general, and cheering on the Tennessee Volunteers.

Bakkum, Elsa S.
Elsa Bakkum, MDiv, began the EfM program as a mentor when members of her church asked her to mentor a group because she had a Master of Divinity degree. She was accredited as a mentor in 1993 and received her diploma in 1997 after four years of mentoring two groups. Bakkum retired in 2023 after thirty years serving as mentor, coordinator in the Diocese of Southern Virginia, online mentor, trainer of mentors, and associate director for training for twelve years.

She is a concert organist offering music for worship services and musical collaborations in various venues. She maintains a long-term practice as a spiritual director where she is privileged to celebrate the presence of the Divine in ordinary life experience.

Booher, Joshua D.
Joshua Booher, PhD, enrolled in EfM in 2004 and became a mentor in 2006. He completed the four-year program in 2008. In 2009, he became an EfM trainer. Shortly after, he agreed to serve as the EfM coordinator for the Diocese of East Tennessee. He moved to Sewanee, Tennessee, in 2014 to become the associate director of operations for EfM. He now serves as the associate director and mentors two groups online.

Brewer, Richard E.
The Rev. Richard E. Brewer has been involved with EfM since 1975 as a mentor, and as a trainer since 1978. He has served in every capacity except as a participant, hence, he does not claim to be a graduate of the program. Brewer watched as Charlie Winters wrote the content known as the "yellow books" and participated actively in the development of the training network. When the first edition of the content was revised, he was asked to develop the support for learning (the *Common Lessons* and the *Parallel Guides*.)

Brewer states that EfM has shaped his life as a Christian and credits it for how he understands ministry formation, theology, and his life in Christ. He considers it a privilege to have been active in EfM his entire adult life.

Byers, Karen D.
Karen Byers graduated from the EfM program in 2002 and has been a mentor ever since and a trainer since 2009. She is a member of the 2024–25 EfM Curriculum Revision Task Force. With Beth Cavey, she produces the video series, *EfM Week x Week* for the EfM mentor group "Reflections." Byers serves on several nonprofit boards in a finance capacity, including a community newspaper and a regional community foundation. She also sits on the vestry council of her "Lutherpalian" church. For twenty-seven years she was the managing director and chief financial officer of a private foundation in New York City. Her career encompassed work in government, the private sector, the academy, and several nonprofit organizations. She holds a Bachelor of Arts degree and a Master of Arts degree in philosophy, and Master of Business Administration. Byers lives in the northwest corner of Connecticut with her spouse and two dogs.

Campbell, Gaines
Gaines Campbell has been involved in Education for Ministry since 2000, serving as participant, mentor, and trainer. He has been an active member in The Episcopal Church all his life, including stints as a leader of Christian education classes and as a licensed lay preacher (to give his rector an occasional break).

Campbell is a passionate pursuer of retirement activities including, but not limited to, yard care, boating, fishing, golfing, and most importantly, rolling on the floor with his granddaughters. He resides in Umatilla, Florida, with Amy, his wife of forty-seven years. This is his first foray into publishing an essay, which completely took him out of his comfort zone.

Carter, Tricia
The Rev. Tricia Carter, BTheol, MTheol (Hons) ACM, has been an Anglican priest for almost thirty years. Based in Auckland, Aotearoa, New Zealand, she is now semi-retired and works as a ministry enabler

with local ministry teams. Her ministry has included being a parish priest in both rural and urban settings, archdeacon of Parininhi, ministry development officer, and a professional supervisor. Involved in EfM since the early 1980s, Carter has been a group member, mentor, trainer, board member, and chair (national director) of EfM New Zealand. She continues to offer action and reflection skills to new ordinands at the Theological College.

In retirement, Carter is discovering the joy of extra time with her husband of fifty-one years, John, the growing grandchildren, and the freedom to travel more.

Casparian, Marguerite
Growing up with a Methodist Sunday School teacher mother, Marguerite Casparian had ample opportunity to discuss theology and faith. After marrying an Episcopal priest, birthing two daughters, and having a commercial illustration career, the deeper study and theological reflection of EfM became a more than forty-year spiritual journey with groups in Kansas, Kentucky, Italy, New York, and Texas. The Casparian family never gets tired of metaphors.

Cavey, Elizabeth
Before becoming immersed in the Education for Ministry program, Elizabeth (Beth) Cavey lived a secular life in public affairs and energy policy for private firms and the federal government, culminating in a position at Cantor Fitzgerald to grow a climate-change trading business. Since 2001, Cavey has spent most of her time in charitable endeavors while raising two children. She created a theology-based curriculum for children and adults, and is Daring Way certified.

After graduating from EfM in 2014, Cavey inherited an EfM group as its mentor and has continued since that time. She became an EfM trainer during COVID-19, which led to her position as trainer in residence for mentor empowerment for the EfM program. Cavey builds on the work of previous EfM stewards and is involved with the 2024 curriculum revision to determine implications for training and empowering mentors.

Cavey is married to Brian and they have two children, Tina and Michael. They split time between their Arlington, Virginia, home and a farm in Warrenton, Virginia.

Cowan, Annette
Annette Cowan is the current director of EfM Canada and the fourth director in the almost forty years of the program in Canada, having been appointed in January of 2023. Cowan has been involved in EfM since 1991 as a participant, a mentor, a diocesan coordinator, an online coordinator, and a trainer.

Cowan is a retired recreation therapist, having worked with mentally challenged individuals and those with dementia. She currently lives in the North Okanagan district of British Columbia with her husband, James, retired bishop of British Columbia. They have two grown children and two granddaughters.

Davies, Greg
The Rev. Greg Davies's introduction to EfM began when he joined the parish of Christ Church Claremont in Perth, Western Australia, as a curate in 1984. He began as a participant, and since then, has always been involved with EfM, first as a mentor, then trainer, and finally as national director, taking on this role in 2015. EfM has been an essential part of his parish ministry for forty years. He considers it a great privilege to experience, both personally and in others, the difference it has made to the journey of faith and ministry.

In 2017, he retired from full-time parish ministry and continues in the role of national director on a volunteer basis.

De Beer, John
For decades, the Rev. John de Beer, MA, DMin, has been a pioneer of adult faith formation programs, most notably the Education for Ministry program at the University of the South, where he has been training mentors and trainers since 1977. He also trained mentors for the Leadership Development Initiative, which transformed parish teams through spiritual practice, community organizing, and local action. With Patricia Killen, he is the co-author of *The Art of Theological*

Reflection, Crossroad, 1994. He served as director of training for EfM from 1982–88 and has a Master of Arts degree in theology and a Doctor of Ministry degree in congregational development.

De Beer retired from parish ministry in 2016, leaving him more time to integrate body-centered psychology with ancient forms of spirituality. He draws deeply from Philip Shepherd's work on *The Embodied Presence Process* and Resmaa Menakem's writings.

De Beer, Tricia

The Rev. Tricia de Beer, MDiv, DMin, has been an EfM trainer since 1980 and was a part-time adjunct faculty with the School of Theology of the University of the South for two to three years, where she mentored several EfM groups each week for seminarians and one for seminarian spouses. She continued mentoring in Florida and Maryland until 2000. De Beer is an Episcopal priest serving as a rector and chaplain in various settings. For more than forty years, her joy has been in spiritual formation and adult education. She is a spiritual director, a trainer of mentors and trainers, and a certified life coach (triciadebeercoach.com). For the past fifteen years, her focus has expanded to include racial equity, criminal justice reform, and teaching the skills of nonviolent communication.

Fernández, José R.

The Rev. José R. Fernández is a bi-vocational priest serving as the rector of Grace Episcopal Church in the Woodlawn neighborhood of Birmingham, Alabama. After a successful career as a researcher, scientist, and academic professor, he responded to a call to holy orders and was ordained as an Episcopal priest in 2021.

As he transitions the identity of Dr. Fernández to the identity of Father José, he is grateful for the spiritual nurturing and constancy of EfM in his life, where he has served as a mentor and trainer.

Flores, Kay

The Rev. Kay Flores was a member of the EfM Online pilot project that began in 2001 in Wyoming. She was the first person trained as a mentor as someone who had only participated in EfM Online, and it was like learning a new language. Flores subsequently started a face-to-face group in her own church. In 2008, Flores became the first EfM trainer who began in an online group. Flores continues as a mentor and trainer today. She is the rector of St. Timothy Episcopal Church in Chehalis, Washington, in the Diocese of Olympia.

Goodman, Kevin M.
The Rev. Kevin M. Goodman has been involved as a participant, mentor, and trainer for EfM for thirty years and currently serves as executive director. After working as a television producer for eighteen years, he attended the General Seminary in New York City. He was ordained in the Diocese of Chicago and served as a street pastor to homeless youth and a rector for congregations during times of transition.

When not in residence at the University of the South, he lives with his husband, Anton, in the Edgewater neighborhood in Chicago, Illinois.

Graham, Hannah
Hannah Graham is dedicated to providing space for people to know God and deepen their faith. As a lifelong learner and mother of three boys, she balances her personal and professional life with a commitment to nurturing her family and community. With a passion for gardening, she embraces her role as a steward of the Earth. Her experience spans congregational formation ministry and working in a faith-adjacent business, where she continues to inspire others in their spiritual journeys.

Halliday, Christopher
The Rev. Dr. Christopher Halliday has been an EfM mentor since 2000, when he traveled from southern Maryland to Roslyn, Virginia, for mentor training, having never encountered EfM before. Later, he moved to Manchester, United Kingdom, and encountered an EfM group needing a mentor. That group continues to this day. In 2010, he was recommended for trainer training and has been a trainer in the United Kingdom, Europe, and the United States ever since. In 2019,

he was appointed the interim director of EfM United Kingdom and Europe and continues to mentor two groups.

Hargis, Cynthia C.
Cynthia (Cindy) Hargis, BS, MA, serves as diocesan relations liaison for the EfM program by working closely with The Episcopal Church dioceses that sponsor EfM and EfM constituents. She supports and encourages the ministry of EfM diocesan coordinators. Hargis has worked for the University of the South since 1984 in various capacities including the vice-chancellor's office and the University counseling service before joining the EfM staff in 1991. Hargis holds a Bachelor of Science degree in organizational management and a Master of Arts degree in organizational leadership.

Hargis and her husband, Gerald Wayne Hargis, live in Tracy City, Tennessee. They have three children, seven grandchildren, and three great-grandchildren. She is a lifelong member of Tracy City Methodist Church and a 2024 graduate of EfM.

Hicks, Termaine
Termaine Hicks, exoneree, born and raised in Philadelphia, Pennsylvania, was wrongfully convicted while trying to help a woman who had been brutally raped. He was shot three times in the back by a Philadelphia police officer after the officer mistook his hand in his pocket as a threatening gesture. The officers covered it up and Hicks served nineteen years of a wrongful conviction before being exonerated in December 2020, through the advocacy work of the New York Innocence Project.

Hicks is now a national speaker, bringing awareness to wrongful convictions and police misconduct. He is also the founder of STEPUP, a nonprofit established in 2008 and dedicated to helping curb gun violence and bullying within schools and neighborhoods (stepup4youth.org). He completed EfM in 2012 while incarcerated.

Hock, Angela
Angela Hock was raised in The Episcopal Church in Louisville, Kentucky, but after her marriage, converted to Roman Catholicism and remained

with that church for twelve years. Upon returning to The Episcopal Church in 1980, she discovered a new and renewed faith and quickly realized that she hungered for a place to study deeply and talk with others on that path. Someone suggested EfM, which she was able to join in 1982 in Woodward, Oklahoma. After moving to Tulsa in 1984, she transferred to a group mentored by Rick Brewer. And the rest, as they say, is history. Hock and Brewer worked in adult Christian education for the diocese for many years. They co-mentored EfM groups and married in 2013.

Holland, Melford E.
The Rev. Dr. Melford E. (Bud) Holland Jr., completed a Bachelor Degree from Wake Forest University in 1965, a Master of Divinity degree from The General Theological Seminary in 1968, a Master of Theology degree from Princeton Theological Seminary in 1985, and Doctor of Ministry degree in 1993. He began mentoring in EfM in 1983 and was a trainer from 1992 until 2022. Holland was ordained a deacon and a priest in 1968 and served in a variety of parishes from 1968–93. He has served on three bishops' staffs in various capacities: program coordinator in Western North Carolina from 1976–81, deployment officer in Pennsylvania from 1994–98, and coordinator for ministry development in the presiding bishop's office from 1998–2009. He has been a consultant since 2009.

Holland has been married to Martha Ann Henkle since 1967 and has three children: David Craig Holland, Charles Eric Holland, and Amanda Christine Holland.

Lang, Elizabeth H.
Elizabeth Lang, MAT, MA, PhD, became a mentor in 1979 and a trainer in 1982, but has never been a participant of the program. EfM has shaped her life as a Christian, family member, and educator. She retired from the Episcopal School of Dallas, where she was the chair of the religion department, a teacher, and a grade level dean. She has a certificate in spiritual direction and continues to teach adults so that she can grow spiritually and deepen the faith of others.

She is married to John Lang, an EfM graduate, and has a daughter and two grandsons. She enjoys her family, cats, and reading.

Layne, Donna G.
Donna Layne has been with the EfM staff since December 2015. She started as a database assistant and in 2017 became a registration specialist. In 2020, she became the administrative assistant and onsite registrar and, in 2023, her job title changed to operations coordinator.

She resides in Monteagle, Tennessee, with her husband, John, and two children, Jake and Madi. She enjoys spending time with her family, working on DIY projects, and spending time outdoors.

Limbaugh, Sara E.
Sara Limbaugh has worked in a number of positions at the School of Theology for more than forty years, including the Education for Ministry Program for more than thirty years. She currently manages the School of Theology's master calendar and coordinates special events, including conferences, seminars, and visits of special guests such as lecturers, fellows-in-residence, scholars-in-residence, bishops-in-residence, and others.

Limbaugh is married to Charlie Limbaugh, and together they have five grown children, five grandchildren, and two mini schnauzers. They live in Manchester, Tennessee.

McCall, Kay
Kay McCall, MTS, MSLS, enrolled in EfM in 1995 in Charlottesville, Virginia, became a mentor in 2001 in Atlanta, Georgia, and became a trainer in 2013. She continues to be a participant in an online group and a mentor of a West Coast online group. As a trainer, McCall is honored to train mentors to continue this amazing, transformative program.

Meridith, Karen M.
Karen Meridith, MATS, was the executive director of Education for Ministry from 2010 until her retirement in 2023. A graduate of the University of South Carolina and the Episcopal Divinity School, with doctoral studies in practical theology at the Boston University School

of Theology, she has been an educator in The Episcopal Church for more than forty years and has written curricula supporting adult Christian formation at parish, diocesan, and national Church levels. A designer (with Richard Brewer) of the 2012 revision of the EfM curriculum, she served as managing editor of the EfM *Reading and Reflection Guides* series from 2012–24. Meridith is a graduate of EfM; she mentored seminar groups in Virginia and Tennessee for ten years.

Upon her retirement, she returned to Virginia Beach, where she is active in Christian formation in her parish and in the Diocese of Southern Virginia.

Moore, Marcia Houck
Marci Houck Moore was born and raised in the Washington, DC suburbs. As a lifelong Episcopalian, she was nurtured in a spiritual tradition of welcome and inquiry. She is retired from a career as a social worker and agency director. She has been an active member of St. Andrew's Church and the Diocese of North Carolina for more than forty years, and a participant, mentor, co-mentor, and coordinator in the EfM community for twenty years.

Moore and her husband, Rob, have made their home and raised their son, Taylor, in Greensboro, North Carolina.

Nakamura Rengers, Katie
The Rev. Katie Nakamura Rengers serves as the staff officer for Church planting with The Episcopal Church. She lives in Birmingham, Alabama, where she planted an untraditional Episcopal Community called the Abbey. The Abbey ran a coffee shop ministry for four years, before "settling down" to become a worshiping community. Rengers is especially energized to work with church planters who are actively engaged with their neighbors, are imagining new forms of worship, and who are reaching out to people historically underrepresented in The Episcopal Church. She has been associated with EfM for ten years as a mentor and trainer, and she is currently on the executive director's Council of Advice.

Papile, Jim
The Rev. Jim Papile is an Episcopal priest and EfM mentor, trainer, and advocate. He lives in Wilmington, North Carolina, with his wife Kay, and their dog, Moana, and cat, LuLuMay.

Patterson, Mary Ann
Mary Ann Patterson's invitation to EfM was bittersweet. Following the death of her daughter, she asked the priest at her Delaplane, Virginia, church the usual questions about death, faith, God, and heaven. The priest answered with a simple question, but one that changed Patterson's life, "What do you believe?" One month later she enrolled in EfM and graduated in 2009. That led to a position at the School of Theology in Sewanee, Tennessee, in 2010. For the next twelve years, Patterson brought her more than thirty years of experience in the communications field to the School of Theology. In her position as communications director and editor of the *Sewanee Theological Review*, she had the privilege of sharing with the world how the seminary was training lay and ordained leaders.

Now retired, Patterson lives in Nashville, Tennessee, and most recently served as editor for EfM's fiftieth anniversary publication.

Replogle, Jenny
The Rev. Canon Jenny Replogle currently serves as the canon for lay-led parishes and parishes-in-transition in the Diocese of Islands and Inlets in the Anglican Church of Canada. She joined The Episcopal Church while studying at Princeton Theological Seminary and subsequently completed a Diploma in Anglican Studies at Virginia Theological Seminary before being ordained as a deacon and priest in 2011. She served at Trinity Church in Princeton, New Jersey and St. Paul's in Peoria, Illinois, before moving to Victoria, British Columbia, with her husband, the Very Rev. Jonathan Thomas, and their two children.

Replogle is passionate about working with individuals and communities as they discern how God is calling them into their ministries, bringing the processes and work of the Church in line with the faith and values it professes, and keeping the baptismal vows to seek and serve Christ in all persons and respect the dignity of every human being at the center of the work. She was an EfM mentor from 2015–20 and serves on the executive director's Council of Advice.

Roaf, Phoebe A.
The Rt. Rev. Phoebe A. Roaf became the fourth bishop of the Diocese of West Tennessee on May 4, 2019. She is an EfM graduate and served as an EfM mentor for six years when she was rector of a congregation in Richmond, Virginia. During her tenure in West Tennessee, Roaf has focused on supporting small congregations and initiatives for children, youth, and young adults. She has also encouraged the diocesan leadership team to reimagine the function and role of a diocese through participation in the Diocesan Leadership Initiative and the Diocesan Vitality Initiative.

Shrum, Deborah
Deborah (Debbie) Shrum began as a clerk on staff with EfM in 1994. Shrum has valued her time in EfM because of the wonderful people she met from all walks of life and the friendships she has developed.

She retired in May 2020 as administrative assistant/conference coordinator. That date was significant to her because her granddaughter graduated college and her grandson graduated high school in that same month. She enjoys spending time with her husband, Tim, her grandson, and great grandson.

Soughers, Tara K.
The Rev. Tara K. Soughers, PhD, has been a part of the EfM program since 1983 as student, mentor, diocesan coordinator, and trainer. When not doing EfM work, she is a parish priest in Silver City, New Mexico, and is a writer. She is the author of four books, three on spirituality and the fourth exploring a theology for trans allies, which has been used as an EfM Interlude book.

Symmonett, Yvonne
Prior to being an EfM coordinator, Yvonne Symmonett was a registered nurse and midwife with specialty ophthalmic nurse training. Additionally, she taught Sunday school at St. James Episcopal Church, Adelaide, New Providence, Bahamas, for ten years. Symmonett was

an ALATEEN sponsor for three years and completed grief recovery training, which better equipped her to counsel persons struggling with loss of any kind.

Taliaferro, Margaret
Margaret (Maggie) Taliaferro, MEd, was introduced to The Episcopal Church in 1986 when she married her husband, Bob. She has three children and eight grandchildren. She completed EfM in 1997, the same year she began mentoring. She was coordinator for the Diocese of Oklahoma from 2004 to 2008. She became a trainer in 2009 and coordinator for the Diocese of Texas in 2021. She has mentored/co-mentored face-to-face and online groups and is currently co-mentoring an online group that first formed in 2010.

Turner, Mary Stuart
Mary Turner began working with EfM in 1981 at the tender age of nineteen while her mother, Barbara Stuart, was on staff with EfM. She was known as the joke teller with the EfM trainers and enjoyed many wonderful relationships. She served EfM and the seminary for twenty-five years, with time split between the two, and she finished as seminary registrar before retiring early.

Turner is now a volunteer with Court Appointed Special Advocates (CASA) in Franklin County, Tennessee. Her work involves working with abused and neglected children in the court system.

Turrell, James F.
The Very Rev. James F. Turrell, PhD, is dean and professor of liturgy at the School of Theology at the University of the South, where he has taught since 2002. He is the author of *Celebrating the Rites of Initiation* (Church Publishing), and his articles have appeared in *Studia Liturgica*, *Anglican Theological Review*, *The Seventeenth Century*, and *Anglican and Episcopal History*.

Wile, Sissie
Sissie Wile, BA, MEd, lives in Meridian, Mississippi, where she started EfM as a participant in her local parish in 1981. After taking a break

for a few years to tend to family life, she graduated in 1989 and became a mentor soon after. In 2003, she became a trainer and was made assistant director of training in 2005, interim director in 2008, and assistant director of training again in 2010. Wile began her work life as a systems engineer with IBM, then a teacher in a local community college.

Wile and her husband started a steel foundry, for which she served as bookkeeper and continues to be secretary/treasurer of the board.

Williams, Anne Moats
The Rev. Anne Moats Williams is a cradle Episcopalian. She grew up attending Trinity Episcopal Church in Morgantown, West Virginia. For most of her time in Iowa, she attended St. Mark's Episcopal Church in Anamosa, where she served as lay leader for years before being ordained to the diaconate and then the priesthood in 2002. She graduated from Education for Ministry in 1994 and served as the diocesan coordinator for Iowa for twenty-five years and as a trainer for more than twenty years. Williams began her volunteer prison ministry at Anamosa State Penitentiary in Anamosa, Iowa, and became the staff chaplain in 2016.